10 RIGHTS OF ASSET MANAGEMENT:

Achieve Reliability, Asset Performance and Operational Excellence

Ramesh Gulati and Terrence O'Hanlon

10 RIGHTS OF ASSET MANAGEMENT

Achieve Reliability, Asset Performance and Operational Excellence

Ramesh Gulati and Terrence O'Hanlon

ISBN 978-1-941872-65-9
HF052018

© 2017 NetexpressUSA dba Reliabilityweb.com
(Reliabilityweb.com) and its affiliates.
Printed in the United States of America.
All rights reserved.

This book, or any parts thereof, may not be reproduced, stored in a retrieval system, or transmitted in any form without the permission of the Publisher.
Opinions expressed in this book are solely the authors' and do not necessarily reflect the views of the Publisher.

Publisher: Reliabilityweb.com
Design and Layout: Jocelyn Brown

For information: Reliabilityweb.com
www.reliabilityweb.com
8991 Daniels Center Drive, Suite 105, Ft. Myers, FL 33912
Toll Free: 888-575-1245 | Phone: 239-333-2500
E-mail: crm@reliabilityweb.com

10 9 8 7 6

Dedicated to all performers, gurus, managers and leaders of asset management for your commitment to ensuring assets are delivering the best value.

TABLE OF CONTENTS

ACKNOWLEDGMENTS

This book is the result of continued persuasion from many of my professional friends, including my dear friend and coauthor, Terrence O'Hanlon. They have influenced my thoughts and ideas to write it so others in the maintenance/reliability/asset management tribe can benefit.

In this journey of learning, writing and sharing knowledge, we were blessed with many colleagues and friends who supported us greatly by reviewing and critiquing the work and providing their constructive feedback.

I would like to thank my colleagues and friends: Lynn Moran, Scott Bartlett, Christopher Mears, Debbie Bayer, Sherry Stovall, Vijay Narain, Sheila Sullivan, Tori Pope, and many more at AEDC-Jacobs for their continued support and for reviewing the manuscript in a controlled rush while ensuring high quality of content. There were a lot of intense, but constructive, discussions and learnings, especially with Scott Bartlett, Lynn Moran and a few others, including my coauthor, Terrence O'Hanlon. Those learnings are included in the book and made very valuable additions. Terrence's input and his quest for high quality content were noticeable during the entire project's life. I also want to thank Bart Jones and Jacobs Management for their encouragement and continued support.

I'm also thankful to the entire publishing team at Reliabilityweb® for their support and patience with my constantly changing schedule. They have been a wonderful support team.

Lastly and most importantly, I can't express enough gratitude to my wife, Prabha, and my daughter, Sona. Their support and understanding of my writing challenges and their sacrifices during the creation of this book are very appreciated, especially from Prabha. Without her continued support, I would not have finished this valuable work.

Ramesh Gulati

PUBLISHER'S NOTES

As someone who travels outside of the United States often, I am always open to discovering new perspectives and new ways of doing things. Over the past few years, I have learned how to advance reliability and asset management from friends in the Netherlands, United Kingdom, Ireland, India, Saudi Arabia, Qatar, Australia, Canada, Mexico, Peru and many other countries.

As wonderful and powerful as those lessons are, I notice two things about most of them.

1. They are based on foundational thinking that originated in the United States (for the most part).
2. They have aspects that might work better in their own countries, where the economic systems are more centrally controlled, where the public systems and politics are more socialistic and where the scale is minuscule compared to the United States.

The United States has led the world in asset management since World War II. We are home to the top four asset owners in terms of value. Forty-two percent of the world's physical assets are in the United States. The next nearest countries are Japan with 11 percent of the world's physical assets and China with 9 percent. The United States government is the second largest asset owner in the world. The Metropolitan Transportation Authority (MTA) calculates over a trillion dollars in transportation assets alone.

How you feel about how effective the U.S. government is at asset management probably has a lot more to do with your political persuasion than the "facts on the ground."

I have the honor of working with the National Ignition Facility, Lawrence Livermore National Laboratory, NASA, U.S. Air Force, National Reconnaissance Office, U.S. Department of State, MTA and many other state and local agencies. The people I meet work in alignment with the aim and organizational objectives of their agency. They work cross-functionally and have robust processes to understand risk and deliver value. They practice asset management on a scale unknown outside the United States.

When I got the chance to publish and work with the guy who guided the U.S. Air Force's Arnold Engineering Development Center, I jumped at it. I understood that to work with a leader on the team that earned the first ISO9001 certification for an asset management process anywhere in the world would provide great opportunities for me to learn and deepen my journey to understand asset management.

Ramesh Gulati is a friend, mentor, guide and leader in my life. As you read this book, I want you to know that he did most of the heavy lifting. Not that I was simply along for the ride, but those of you who know Ramesh understand that he is mission driven – and communicating his knowledge and experience about asset management was no different. I did my best to hang on and pitch in with ideas, edits and suggestions as we sailed down the highway at NASCAR® speed.

I am very proud to publish this book because it is also important to bring the United States' subject matter experts' work to the front of the line where they belong. I am pleased that Ramesh has stepped up in that role.

I would also like to extend a special thanks to the Reliabilityweb.com publishing team who rose to the challenge of the unique process this book took as it was being created. Nothing worthwhile is ever easy and you all continue to amaze me as you raise the bar with each new project.

Let's work together to make American Asset Management Great Again.

Enjoy the book!

Best regards,
Terrence O'Hanlon

PREFACE

What Is Asset Management?

According to ISO55000, published by the International Organization for Standardization (ISO), asset management is a coordinated set of activities designed to realize value from assets.

That means people working together toward the same goal.

While that might seem obvious, most organizations have a natural segmentation of roles and responsibilities, both vertically and horizontally.

Although there is a standard, international consensus definition, asset management still means different things to different people depending on where they are on that vertical and horizontal axis.

At the C-level, the main concern for asset management is ensuring that stakeholder concerns are being met.

At the Portfolio level, asset management is about assuring smart capital investment and assured capabilities.

At the Systems level, asset management is about creating the end flow of systems needed to create the value outcomes and manage the risk.

At the Asset level, asset management is about lifecycle activities to ensure short- and long-term reliable operations to deliver value (outcome).

There is a fair bit of confusion around the term asset management, and for good reason. Although there is an International Standard that includes a definition, a quick read of the standard will likely not clear things up for you.

Basically, "managing assets" are activities you do to an asset to assure asset performance. These activities include design for reliability, precision commissioning, preventive maintenance, precision lubrication, RCM, vibration analysis, and other techniques and activities.

"Asset management" is about delivering or assuring the "aim" of your organization. It determines what assets you need to deliver the aim, and how to ensure that everyone in the organization is working collaboratively and cross-functionally toward that aim.

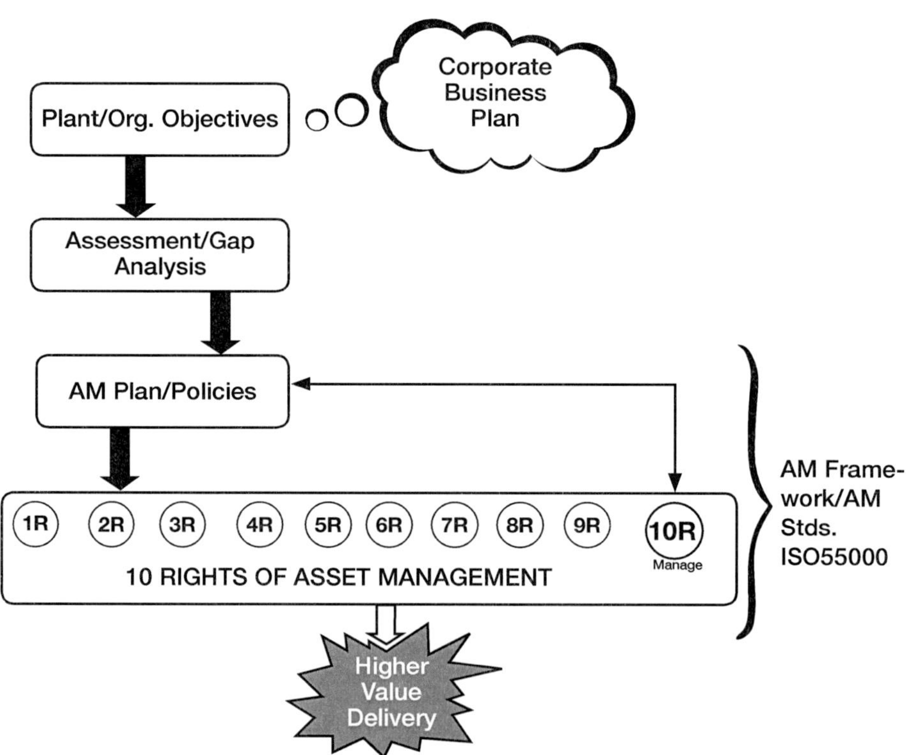

Figure 1: Linkage of corporate objectives to value delivery with "The 10 Rights of Asset Management"

Managing assets are about the asset. Asset management is about the business. They go together like hand and glove, but they are two different things.

The 10 Rights of Asset Management is about doing the right things at a system asset level in order to create greater value from the assets during their lifecycle. However, it's very important to ensure open communication and leadership support in creating the right policies and plans, as indicated in Figure 1.

Linkage of Corporate Business Plan to Value Delivery

Figure 1 shows a relationship between the corporate plan/objectives and value delivery.

Plant or organization-wide objectives are developed based on the corporate business plan. The next step is to develop asset management plans (AMPs). Policies are formulated after an assessment and gap analysis.

The next step in the process is implementing *The 10 Rights of Asset Management* in a **right** manner that supports higher value realization from assets.

The asset management standard ISO55000, which is discussed in more detail in Chapter 10, can be utilized to set up an asset management process. A healthy, robust asset management process will maximize the return from an organization's assets, thus creating more value for the stakeholders. In addition, asset management processes can easily achieve compliance with applicable standards, such as ISO55000.

Each of the 10 Rights (Specify It Right, Design It Right, Source It Right, Build/Fabricate It Right, Install/Commission It Right, Operate It Right, Maintain It Right, Improve/Modify It Right, Dispose/Decommission It Right, and Manage It Right) are elaborated in ten separate chapters in the book.

Types of Assets

Organizations deal with different types of assets that are necessary to achieve their objectives. Assets in organizations can be classified into four major categories:

- **Tangible Assets:** Assets that you can touch, see and feel, such as the building, infrastructure, equipment, inventories, controls, devices, etc.
- **Intangible Assets:** Assets you can't see or feel, such as goodwill, agreements, patents, etc.
- **Financial Assets:** Bonds, bank deposits, securities, etc.
- **Human Assets:** Employees, managers, suppliers, etc.

Tangible assets are used primarily to produce products and services. They deliver value with the support of people (i.e., human assets). The focus of this book is the tangible assets, such as buildings, infrastructure, and machines and equipment, including controls and software, along with the human assets or people.

By implementing *The 10 Rights of Asset Management* discussed in this book, you will enable your organization to get more value from its assets and be in compliant with ISO55000.

PROLOGUE: SETTING THE STAGE

What Is This Book of "Rights" and Why Is It Needed?

Do we do everything right the first time? Do we? Many of us actually don't because we're always in a hurry. It could be our habits, part of our culture, or at times, dictated by our system. Our management systems may force us to make mistakes the first time. These systems may focus on quantity, but not necessarily on quality.

We have also observed that many times, we blindly follow protocols and forget (or ignore) to do the right things. This results in spending more time trying to correct the problem or treating it as a completely new problem to mask the real issues.

We don't achieve excellence with these habits and systems.

Excellence is achieved when we do the right things the right way all the time, every time, not just *one* time.

> *People of excellence go the extra mile to do what's right.*
> *~ Joel Osteen*

The objective of this book is to provide readers with a simple, easy to understand "road map" on how to manage assets more efficiently and effectively during their life span, with a goal of reducing their total cost of ownership.

In order to help readers manage assets effectively, this book includes 10 "Rights" to achieve excellence and add value. Each "Right" may involve many people in the process, or just one. However, we *all* need to do our part correctly, wherever we may be in the asset's lifecycle or process, to improve asset performance. If we do the right things at every stage, we will improve asset performance and reduce the total cost of asset ownership during its life.

These principles, the "Rights," can be applied to new assets or currently used assets. Each chapter of this book includes a checklist that can be used to ensure you are following a proven path to achieving excellence in asset management.

We have used the term "Rights" in the book's title, as well as many times throughout the book. "Right" is defined as *doing the right things* and *doing things right.* Generally speaking, leaders do the right things and managers do things right. However, we have to do both in order to achieve excellence.

The time is always right to do what is right.

~ Martin Luther King, Jr.

Defining Excellence and Operational Excellence

What Is Excellence?

Excellence means greatness. The very best. Excellence is the quality of excelling, of being truly the best at something. We love Picasso's paintings and Shakespeare's writings for their excellence. Michael Jordan's basketball career reflected excellence. When we see excellence, we should appreciate the work that went into it. So much in the world falls short of excellence because achieving excellence is never easy to do.

What Is Operational Excellence?

Operational excellence (OE) is a term now commonly used in the business world. But what exactly *is* OE? The BusinessDictionary defines operational excellence as, "a philosophy of the workplace where problem-solving, teamwork and leadership results in the ongoing improvement in an organization."

The process involves focusing on customers' needs, keeping employees positive and empowered, and continually improving current activities in the workplace.

The Institute for Operational Excellence (IOE), along with Kevin Duggan, President of Duggan Associates, defines OE as, "when each and every employee can see the flow of value to the customer and fixes that flow when it breaks down."

In the Uptime® Elements™ A Reliability Framework and Asset Management System™, a similar definition is used. However, the concept of flow is not included. Operational excellence is described as, "everyone in the organization possessing an understanding of value (as defined by senior leadership) and recognizing when that value breaks down and what they need to do to restore it." It also differs from the concept of value being delivered to a *customer* and expands it into value being delivered to all *stakeholders*, both internal and external. This specific concept requires that all work is to be aligned to value through the line of sight.

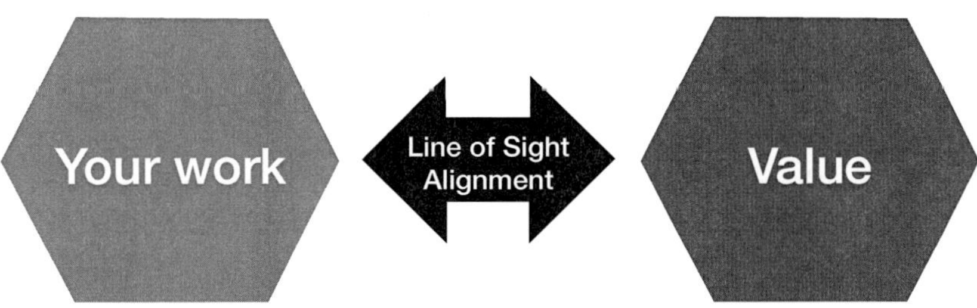

Source: Certified Reliability Leader Workshop by www.Reliabilityweb.com

Simply stated, OE requires everyone in the organization to work together to provide value.

Value is a key word. In many instances, the value is created and delivered by the people with the help of assets, such as equipment, machines and facilities, through effective and efficient processes. Other times, value is created and delivered through information management, data processes, brand, reputation, history, supply chain management, relationships and intellectual property.

While we explore most of the sources of value, this book focuses on people deriving value from effective physical asset lifecycle management.

The clichéd phrase often quoted by company executives is, "People are our number one asset!" However, this is far from the truth. More accurately, the quote would be, "People with the right skills applied at the right time are our number one asset!"

We need people with the right knowledge, skills and attitude, as well as reliable assets that perform as expected when needed. Assets are the key to delivering value, and when those assets do not perform as expected, a breakdown in value delivery is created. In reality, most of the time, one or both of these contributors (i.e., assets or people) fail to create and deliver value.

This book focuses on doing the "10 Right Things" to manage assets from the concept stage to creation and on to disposal, over the whole asset's lifecycle so that assets keep delivering value to their customers and organizations remain financially healthy. Or, as Mr. O'Hanlon says, "We must manage assets for value from lust to dust."

We all need to be doing the *right things* in a *right way* with quality in *all our activities, all the time* to achieve excellence.

I do the very best I know how, the very best I can, and I mean to keep on doing so until the end.

~ Abraham Lincoln

Understanding Asset Management and Lifecycle

Asset management is a very popular term today, but is very poorly understood by many. The terms "maintenance" and "reliability" are being replaced by *asset management* in many organizations. For example, the titles of some conference papers and workshops are listed as "Asset Management," when, in fact, most of the topics of these conferences and workshops are still centered on maintenance and reliability. This should not be the case. Is "asset management" a glorified word for "maintenance" or "reliability"? Not necessarily.

Instead, asset management is actually a process used to maximize the value from an asset during its life. The ISO55000 standard defines asset management as, "coordinated activity of an organization to realize value from assets." Realization of value typically involves balancing costs, risks, opportunities and performance benefits.

An asset's lifecycle starts when a need is conceived. A person, group, or an organization considers how they can provide a product or service. This initial step in the process results in the development of a concept or a preliminary design for an asset, also called a "system." This concept goes through several phases, such as detailed design, build construction and installation of the asset. We can then start using this asset for its intended purpose to make products or provide services. This is the phase we are all familiar with. This operations and maintenance (O&M) or usage phase is the most critical phase of the asset's life. This is the phase where we begin to reap value from the asset. It may last for five years, ten years, thirty years, seventy years, or more. During the O&M phase, assets may undergo several improvements and modifications. Finally, if and when its need is over, or it doesn't provide economic value, the asset is disposed of or retired.

Asset phases can be categorized as follows:

- Concept (start of life);
- Design (includes development);
- Build, construct, or procure;

- Install and commission;
- Operate and maintain;
- Dispose/decommission (end of life).

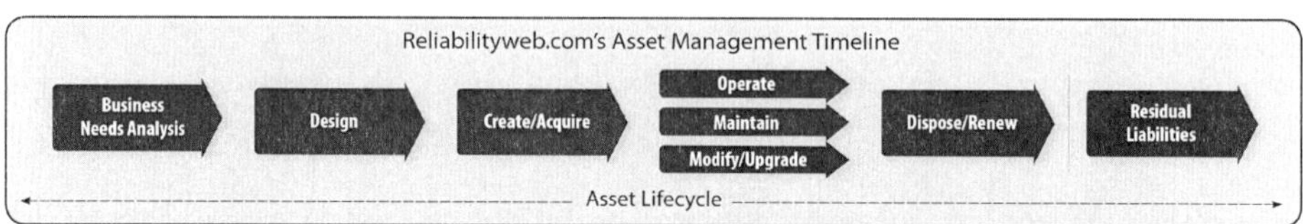

Unfortunately, the phases of the asset's lifecycle are usually managed in silos. Generally, the focus is on an individual phase without concern for the impact this phase might have on other phases. We don't think about total cost of ownership for an asset's entire lifecycle in current practices.

An Organization's Mission and Objectives

Why do organizations or companies exist? The most common answer to this question is to make money. Despite this common belief, making money is not the mission of an organization. Money is an outcome of *pursuing* a mission, but it is *not* the mission. Companies exist to satisfy the needs of their interest groups or stakeholders, with the objective of providing them value. Monetary gains are just a consequence.

In his article, "Why Does Your New Company Exist?," Dick Barnett writes, "A company's mission is the single most important reason for its existence, and every organization should best express it as clearly and concisely as possible in the fewest words as possible. The mission is what the organization '*is.*' The very '*being*' of the company. *The mission is the 'core' of the organization.* If this distinction is not made absolutely clear to everyone concerned, then nothing else will really hold the organization together."

The Uptime Elements uses the term "aim" to describe why a company exists. In ISO terminology, you'll find the term "organizational objectives" to describe the *what* and *why* of most organizations.

Numerous studies and our personal experience have shown that when assets and their components (e.g., motors, pumps, or entire plants) are acquired, renovated, or modified as part of capital projects, they invariably don't meet expectations. These projects are always late and over budget. This value leakage from capital expenditure (Capex) to operational expenditure (Opex) has become a major issue for most asset owners. Schedule delays and cost overruns significantly reduce the return on investment (ROI), thus curtailing the value to the stakeholders.

Not specifying the asset requirements appropriately, or "rightly," and allowing scope creep are two major causes of this problem. Specifying the right requirements are discussed in more detail in a later chapter.

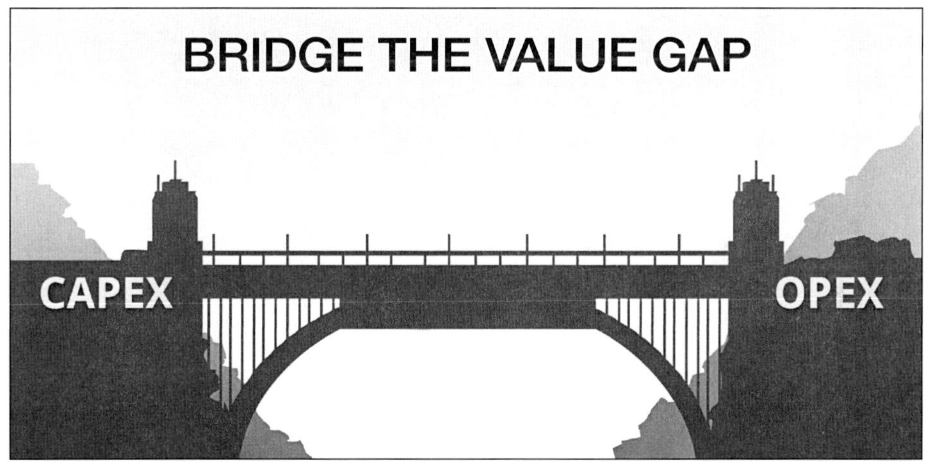

Applying some of the "Rights" principles described in this book will reduce the value leakage from Capex to Opex.

To make an organization's mission and objectives a reality and a success, you need two types of assets: *people* and *physical*. Both are important and both have to be reliable, robust and available when you need them to produce or provide a service. Managing these assets — specifically physical assets, such as equipment and machines — efficiently and effectively to get more value by doing the 10 Rights is the essence of this book.

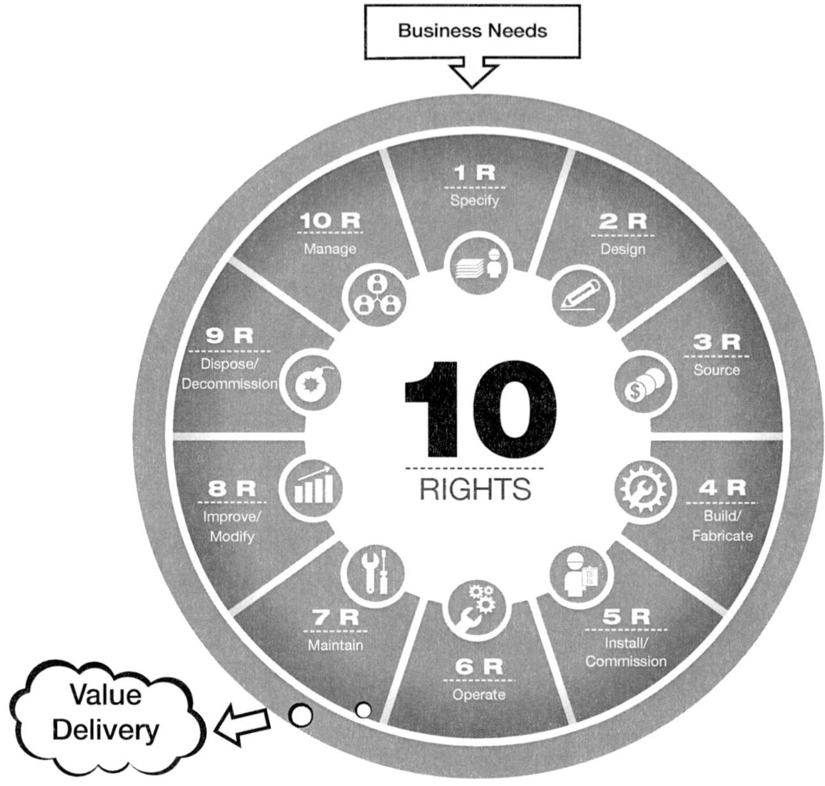

10 RIGHTS of Asset (Lifecycle) Management

The 10 Rights of Asset Management

The 10 Rights for asset management are:

1. **Specify It Right;**
2. **Design It Right;**
3. **Source It Right;**
4. **Build/Fabricate It Right;**
5. **Install/Commission It Right;**
6. **Operate It Right;**
7. **Maintain It Right;**
8. **Improve/Modify It Right;**
9. **Dispose/Decommission It Right;**
10. **Manage It Right.**

Doing all the right things for asset management creates a culture of excellence — reliability and operational excellence — which leads to business excellence. Each Right is discussed in more detail in separate chapters of this book.

Many of us do great things in our organizations. The questions are: Do we do the 10 Rights all the time and are they being carried out by everyone in the organization, by all the stakeholders? Does everyone do their part correctly to create a culture of excellence?

Some questions to consider:

- Is buying components, such as oil seals, bearings, motors, etc., being done according to general principles and per the organization's policy at the lowest cost, or should you buy "best value," considering the component's life and available failure data?
- Are the designers designing assets for lowest cost because their performance is evaluated by the lowest cost design factor, or do they design for lowest lifecycle cost for the asset to minimize total cost of ownership for the organization?
- Are operators misusing assets by operating them to their limits and trying to exceed production numbers or a quota, or are they operating assets with care as if they are the owners of these assets?
- Do your operators and maintainers have the right skills to operate or maintain? Do you have plans to update their skill sets on a regular basis?
- Do you provide the right tools so your people can work efficiently and effectively?
- Do you have the right metrics to change behavior and make lasting improvements, or are they there just as a "feel good?"
- Do you dispose of assets rightly considering the environment, sustainability and data security impacts?

It is very difficult to have everyone do the right things all the time, but it *is* achievable. We need to make a habit of doing the right things to achieve excellence.

> *We are what we repeatedly do. Excellence, then, is not an act, but a habit.*
>
> *~ Aristotle*

References and Suggested Reading

1. *Why Does Your New Company Exist?* by Dick Barnett, http://www.reigniteyourbusiness.com/article-yexist.html
2. *Sustainable Asset Management* by Roopchan Lutchman
3. *Maintenance and Reliability Best Practices* by Ramesh Gulati
4. *The (New) Asset Management Handbook* by Industry Experts, Reliabilityweb.com Press
5. Uptime Elements CRL Body of Knowledge
6. *Certified Reliability Leader Pocket Dictionary* by Ramesh Gulati
7. ISO55000, ISO55001, ISO55002, Asset Management Standards, https://www.iso.org/standard/55088.html
8. BSI PAS:1192-2 and 1192-3, Specification for Information Management
9. *Megaprojects* by Independent Project Analysis, http://www.ipaglobal.com/84-megaprojects
10. Fiatech, www.fiatech.org

CHAPTER 1
SPECIFY IT RIGHT

Learning Objectives to Understand

- Needs, requirements and specifications
- The importance of well-defined and accurate requirements
- Needs vs. wants
- The importance of testing and acceptance criteria

1.1 The Importance of Specifications and Requirements

This is NOT what we wanted!

How many times have you heard (or said) this criticism when an asset owner/operator gets a new or revamped asset or system? It's a universal problem, especially in large capital projects.

Most asset-related projects end up above their estimated cost, are late in completion and invariably do not meet the owner's original expectations or intent. Many studies by consulting and management companies, such as Booz Allen Hamilton, McKinsey & Company and Bentley, as well as our personal experience in many industries, substantiate this problem. More recently, the problem has become an important topic of discussion at trade conferences and Internet forums. Some of the reasons for not meeting the owner's original expectations are:

- Vague and unclear requirements;
- Changing and unspecified requirements;
- Work scope creep;
- Budget constraints;
- Unanticipated technical issues;
- Poor cost estimates.

A lack of a clear understanding of what is needed or required is one of the key reasons for not meeting expectations. Also, as more of the owner's needs are understood, requirements are typically increased, resulting in scope creep. Budget limitations or funding cuts and unanticipated or new technical challenges to meet pre-established requirements also lead to schedule delays and create dissatisfaction with the project's progress.

Requirements can be classified into two broad categories:

1. Production or operational needs of the customers. For example, a number of gadgets, tons of production or servings at a certain quality level per hour, day, week, month, etc.
2. Operations' and maintenance's needs of the assets producing the gadgets or service being provided.

These requirements specify how assets will be sustained over time to minimize their lifecycle costs, ensure reliable and cost-effective performance, and eliminate major sources of concerns within the asset's lifecycle. These are the requirements. Many times, one does not do a good job in specifying, or the requirements get cut due to budget constraints. Also, maintenance reliability and asset management professionals don't do a good job in justifying and making a good case for it.

Asset requirements and specification for a new or modified asset need to be based on an organization's asset management plan (sometimes called an organization's long-range plan) to meet organizational objectives. It should include reliability, availability, maintainability, and safety and sustainability (RAMS[2]) goals, as well as total lifecycle cost objectives.

There is nothing so useless as doing efficiently that which should not be done at all.

~ Peter Drucker

1.2 Defining Requirements

1.2.1 Needs vs. Wants

Needs can be defined as goods or services that are required to meet defined objectives. These include essentials, such as food, clothing, shelter and health care for human survival.

Wants are goods or services that are not necessary for survival, but are desired or wished for. For example, you need clothes, but one may not need *designer* clothes to meet his or her basic needs. Some may call designer clothes as "gold plating" your needs.

Similarly, you need assets to make products or provide services. These assets need to have the right functions and those functions need to work reliably and safely at all times.

Although needs are finite, wants, which spring from desires or wishes, are boundless. You must be careful and very specific to assemble your requirements so they meet the asset's needs instead of your wants or desires.

1.3 Guidelines for Developing Asset Needs

Every organization has (or should have) an organization-wide plan that identifies primary product or service requirements. Based on these requirements, an asset management plan (AMP) should be developed that identifies which assets are needed at what performance level and in what time frame. This plan should help you specify your needs. Also, it should have its RAMS[2] needs specified. Acquiring new assets or improving existing assets should be guided by this information.

The next step in this process is to develop a set of specifications to modify existing assets or acquire new assets.

1.4 Specification Development

1.4.1 Key Issues by Roles/Functions

We've all heard horror stories about new assets: Purchasing complaints that the vendors don't have enough information to quote the asset or system. Bids are received, but management buy-in is not forthcoming. As soon as the contract is awarded, the vendor asks for more money to make the asset meet minimal requirements. The equipment is installed, but it doesn't work. Operators complain that it's too difficult to run. Maintenance grumbles that it's too difficult to maintain. Quality protests that the equipment doesn't make good product consistently.

Writing equipment specifications is a critical, but often overlooked, facet of every capital project. Engineers hate this task, finding it tedious and difficult. They believe it has little to do with engineering. As a result, they often do a poor job or don't write a specification at all. In reality, writing a specification is the best opportunity to do the most critical part of engineering—the part that anticipates and avoids problems.

Engineers who take the time to plan, look at the big picture and communicate expectations will lay the groundwork for a successful installation of an asset that meets the needs of everyone in their organization.

The first step in writing a specification is to understand who your customers are and what their needs are. This process will enable you to incorporate solutions to their concerns in your specification. Table 1.1 is an

Table 1.1: Key Issues by Roles and Functions

Management	Will this asset be good for the organization? Is it the right approach? Have we considered all risks?
Purchasing	Do these specifications tell the vendor what it needs to know? Will it allow all bidders to compete on equal footing?
Asset/Project Manager	Will this asset or system meet the project's goals and requirements? Do the specifications contain enough information to control the scope and budget of the project? How will we know if the asset is designed and built correctly?
Asset Builder	What does this asset need to do? What are the performance requirements? Do I have all the information I need to determine if I can meet them? Do I have the information I need to develop a good quote?
Product/Process Engineer	Will the product or service provided by this asset meet all the process requirements?
Support Functions: O&M, Quality, Etc.	Can we support, operate and maintain this asset appropriately within the budgeted amount? How will we know if the asset is producing good quality products? How will this affect the organization?

example of roles and their key issues. It lists roles/functions and their issues and expectations.

Your customers are all the stakeholders who have an interest in the asset: upper management, sourcing (purchasing) managers, project managers, project engineers, machine builders, process and asset design engineers, and support staff, including operations, quality, facilities and maintenance. These people will have disparate concerns because of their particular niches in the organization.

Upper management will want assurance that they're making a good investment. The project manager will want to know if the equipment will do what it's supposed to do and whether the specification contains adequate detail to control the project's scope and budget. Operations will want to know how the new equipment will affect them. How many operators will they need? What training will be required? Maintenance wants to know if they can maintain the asset within allocated resources and what specialized tools and training they'll need to get. Will the asset be designed with standard components meeting their plant's standard?

1.4.2 Specifying Ergonomics and Safety

Safety, including ergonomics, can be another big concern. Under U.S. Occupational Safety and Health Administration (OSHA) regulations and other regulatory requirements, organizations must provide a workplace free from recognized hazards. Poor asset specification decisions can result in expensive litigation.

Ergonomics is also an accident avoidance issue. Poor ergonomics reduces operator comfort, increasing fatigue, which is a key contributor to preventable accidents. Resolving ergonomic issues during the design of an asset can have a significant impact on reducing workers' compensation costs, improving user productivity and reducing fatigue-induced operator errors. A corollary to an ergonomically designed asset is the importance of all users being thoroughly trained in the safe use of this asset. Also, asset/user managers should regularly inspect assets to ensure their safe working condition and that the equipment is used only for its intended purpose.

When developing specifications, your goal is to avoid problems previously mentioned in this chapter. Of course, even a perfect specification will not solve all the problems. However, the one factor that is responsible for more of these problems than any other is a lack of up-front engineering, which includes the right specifications.

1.4.3 Key Principles for Writing Good Specifications

The following are some general guidelines for developing good specifications:

- **The specifications should be clear and easy to understand:** It's very important to develop adequate specifications since they form the basis for competitive bidding. Unclear, unnecessarily detailed and biased specifications will reduce the number of vendors participating and the overall quality of the acquisition. Unclear specifications also will confuse vendors, which may result in more expensive bids or incomplete proposals.
- **Units of measurement:** Specify what units of measurements should be used (e.g., metric, pounds or feet).
- **Avoid unnecessary details:** Only the key characteristics should be specified. Each characteristic listed should be required for evaluation.
- **Using technical literature or references:** Usually, it's not possible and, in some cases, even risky to write specifications without using technical literature from manufacturers or an industry standard. Therefore, it is acceptable to use technical literature, but keep the following in mind:
    - Use literature only as a reference. When using literature, avoid preparing locked specifications that favor one supplier over others. Ensure the written specifications are general enough to be met by a typical supplier dealing with such products.
    - Do not include every specification listed in the literature. Only list the important key characteristics.
- **Subjective statements:** Do not use subjective statements, such as "high quality," "easy to use," etc. The equipment specifications must

be objective and definitive. Subjective statements are open to interpretation and are impossible to evaluate.

- **Specifications should be definitive, not very restrictive:** The objective of writing technical specifications is to explain to the suppliers what is required. Even a simple item, such as a chair, requires technical specifications. Bidders need to know the material of the chair, such as plastic, wood, metal, or leather. Whether it will have adjustable height arrangement, rotating wheels, etc. If you don't give enough detail, the vendor may be confused and probably offer a bare bones chair.
- **Space and weight:** In some cases, the space available and the weight in pounds/square feet, loading) should be part of the specifications.
- **Operations and Service Manual:** Be specific that X copies of the operating and service manual should be provided. Also be specific as to what the manual should contain. Each manual should contain installation, operations and maintenance procedures, detailed flow schematics and complete electrical drawings. Each manual also should contain a complete list of spare parts and recommended spare parts storage levels based on a failure mode and effects analysis (FMEA). It is also important to request a digital version of the manual in an acceptable format.

1.4.4 Project Needs

Sometimes, if an asset is a large system and part of a capital project, it may have additional requirements, including:

- **Taxonomy and Hierarchy:** Specify which standard should be used for naming components and in creating the asset register.
- **Operator and Maintainer Training:** Provide the number of days of training to X number of operators and maintainers for understanding the operation and maintenance aspect of the asset.
- **Acceptance Tests (Test Plans):** The acceptance test should consist of checking the asset for compliance with the requirements listed in the test plan. Specify that the duration of the acceptance test shall be no

less than X days and no longer than Y days. If the asset does not meet the specifications listed, the supplier has one opportunity to repair or replace the asset or asset's component to correct all defects. The vendor is responsible for the repair of all defects, whether or not the purchaser initially declared the defects. After the vendor corrects the defects, specify that the acceptance test should be completed in less than X number of days after the receipt of the repaired asset.

- **Warranty:** The vendor shall provide a written warranty covering the asset, including components, parts and field service. The warranty period should be for specified year(s) and begin on the date of acceptance. A payment plan and shipment details also could be added to the warranty. In the warranty, the vendor should agree to the following conditions:

    1. The asset shall comply with all the specifications.
    2. In the event the asset develops a malfunction during the warranty period that cannot be solved by the application of routine troubleshooting procedures described in the operating and service manual or by component or part replacement, the vendor shall send trained service personnel to repair the asset at the original delivery point. The purchaser shall have the option of returning the asset, at the vendor's expense.
    3. The vendor shall agree to supply spare parts for the asset for at least X years following the date of acceptance. The vendor shall agree to ship replacement parts to the purchaser within 30 days after receiving a parts order. Also, the warranty should guarantee that all replacement parts are of equal or superior quality to parts in the original unit.

In summary, the specifications must have enough details to leave no question in the vendor's mind as to what is required, but should be generic enough to allow multiple manufacturers' equipment to be offered.

1.5 The "V" Model

On large projects, a good practice is to follow the "V" model process. The V-shape of this method represents the various stages an asset goes through, including its software development lifecycle. Beginning at the top left stage and working, over time, toward the top right tip, the stages represent a linear progression of development.

The "V" describes a structured approach, the process of requirements development, preliminary design, detail design and then the closure of all requirements after design via analysis, testing and verification.

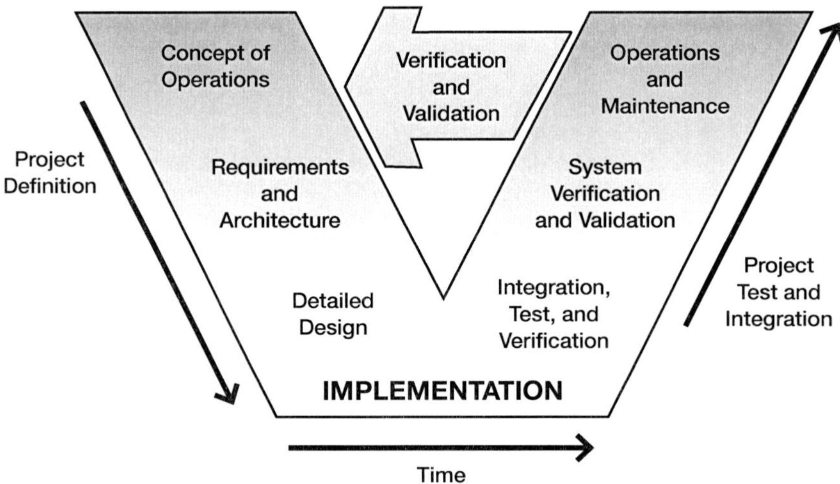

Figure 1.1: The "V" model method

1.6 Specify It Right Summary and Checklist

1.6.1 Summary

Writing asset specifications is a critical, but often overlooked, facet of every project. A specification is an engineering, sales and communications tool. Besides describing the asset to be purchased, it must identify the needs of the organization as they relate to that asset.

No doubt you've heard your share of horror stories where vendors don't have sufficient information to bid, vendors want more money due to scope creep, or operations, production, or maintenance is not happy with the asset's performance after it's built. All blame may lead back to bad or poor specifications.

Good specifications require a team effort of stakeholders that includes the participation of operations or production, maintenance, quality, engineering and others, as needed. It involves:

- Identifying and validating the problem;
- Determining the requirements to solve the problem;
- Developing a possible solution or design;
- Documenting the solution so somebody can build it;
- Ensuring the built or procured asset performs as specified.

Sometimes, the vendor may need to come up with a possible solution to solve a problem based on requirements/specifications in a design-build project.

Specifications should be clear and easy to understand. There shouldn't be any vagueness.

You must keep in mind that a specification is a functional description of an asset. It should describe what you want the asset to do while leaving as much latitude as possible for how to do it. The best way to accomplish this task is to think of the asset as a black box and describe its inputs and outputs.

Specifications also should include:

a. The purpose of the asset;
b. An acceptance testing plan;
c. Asset-related standards, such as types of programmable logic controllers to meet NFPA 70: National Electrical Code of the National Fire Protection Association (NFPA) or the Institute of Electrical and Electronics Engineers (IEEE) standards, etc.;
d. Documentation and training;
e. Delivery schedule and other project needs.

1.6.2 Checklist

Specify It Right Assurance Checklist		Check - √
1.	**Do the specifications reflect the right production/ operational needs based on past history plus XX% or to meet corporate objective (20xx)? Examples:**	
	a. Gadget "z" 60 pieces/min at 4 sigma (6,210 defects/million) or 5 sigma (230 defects/million) level quality for 100 hours/week or 5,000 hours/year of operation basis	
	b. 10,000 CFM of air at xx temp, xx dryness, etc.	
	c. Other examples	
2.	**Are reliability, availability, maintainability, and safety and sustainability (RAMS[2]) requirements specified in the design of the assets? Examples:**	
	a. Achieve a goal of 90% reliability (and/or 98% of availability) for 22 hours/day or 100 hours/week of operation, or no more than 5 failures in 5,000 hours of operation. These failures should not exceed mean time to repair (MTTR) of 4 hours.	
	b. Design of asset will incorporate minimum usage of energy and hazardous material. Use of energy efficient devices and green energy is highly encouraged. A noncompliance in this area needs to be justified.	
	c. Design should incorporate safety of people and the asset itself by incorporating fail-safe and double safety features when needed. Exposure to hazardous material, including noise levels, should be contained as practical as possible. Use of ergonomic design to minimize operator's fatigue is highly recommended.	
	d. Do the specifications include appropriate industry standards, regulatory requirements, etc.?	

3.	**Do the specifications include how the performance of the asset will be measured at the build site and after installation at the plant/facility? Examples:**	
	a. Specify what test will be performed when/where to measure performance. What action will be taken if it does not meet expectations?	
	b. All drives will be balanced and aligned to exhibit and not to exceed vibration level of xx mils and alignment of xxx. Results of these tests will be submitted with other documentation. Presence of owner's representative at these tests is required.	
4.	**Have you specified how the design will be evaluated to ensure it meets the intent of RAMS[2] principles? Examples:**	
	a. Are you requiring to perform FMEA and reliability-centered maintenance (RCM) to optimize design?	
	b. Are you requiring to deliver maintenance plan needs, including spares, based on FMEA/RCM analysis?	
	c. Are you requiring to have standardized taxonomy and asset hierarchy to comply with your organization's standards?	
5.	**Have you specified how the workforce (e.g., operator, maintainer, etc.) will be trained and when and where?**	
6.	**Have you specified what the deliverables will be at what stage or schedule? For the:**	
	a. Asset	
	b. Documentation, manuals, drawings, including updated redlines, test results, etc.	
	c. Training for operators, maintainers, etc.	
	d. Warranties and other support	

7.	**Have you specified shipping requirements or information needed? Examples:**	
	a. Preferred way to ship, such as by rail, truck, or other	
	b. Provided size and weight, and marking for lifting or any other instructions	

1.7 References and Suggested Reading

1. *Making Common Sense Common Practice* by Ron Moore
2. *Assurance Technologies Principles and Practices* by Dev Raheja and Michael Allocco
3. *Uptime,* Second Edition, by John D. Campbell and James V. Reyes-Picknell
4. "Writing Capital Equipment Specifications," by Assembly Magazine http://www.assemblymag.com/articles/83258-writing-capital-equipment-specifications
5. *Guide to Specification Writing* and related acquisition material at http://www.navair.navy.mil/nawctsd/Resources/Library/Acqguide/Acqguide.htm
6. *Overview of the System Engineering Process* by Ed Ryen, North Dakota Department of Transportation, https://www.dot.nd.gov/divisions/maintenance/docs/OverviewOfSEA.pdf

CHAPTER 2
DESIGN IT RIGHT

Learning Objectives to Understand

- Failure and failure mechanism
- Total cost of ownership (TCO)
- Attributes of a good design
- The importance of involving key stakeholders in the design process

2.1 The Importance of Design It Right

Here are just a few examples of asset design related issues reported in the media.

East Rutherford, New Jersey, January 15, 2015: "The flash fire that burned seven workers, one seriously, at a U.S. ink plant in New Jersey in 2012 resulted from the accumulation of combustible dust inside of a poorly-designed dust collection system that had been put into operation only four days before the accident, an investigation by the U.S. Chemical Safety Board (CSB) has found. In a report released today, the investigation team concludes that the system design was so flawed that it only took a day to accumulate enough combustible dust and hydrocarbons in the duct work to overheat, ignite spontaneously, cause an explosion in the rooftop dust collector, and send back a fiery flash that enveloped seven workers." (Source: U.S. Chemical Safety Board, http://www.csb.gov)

Baikonur, Kazakhstan, May 16, 2015: "Russian authorities investigating the Proton-M rocket failure have determined that the cause was a design flaw in the turbopump for the third stage steering engine and concluded it was the same cause of a prior crash in 1988. Human error was initially suspected in the May 2015 crash, and although the specific cause turned out to be a design flaw, the investigation also identified quality management and manufacturing process inconsistencies." (Source: SpacePolicyOnline.com, http://www.spacepolicyonline.com)

Boston, Massachusetts, January 7, 2013: "The battery fire that led to the grounding of Boeing Co.'s 787 Dreamliner jets for more than three months last year was caused by inadequate design and testing, investigators concluded." (Source: Bloomberg, https://www.bloomberg.com)

Cape Canaveral, Florida, January 28, 1986: According to a review board analysis, the 1986 explosion of the space shuttle *Challenger* was the result of the failure of rubber O-rings that were used to seal four sections of booster rockets, an application for which the O-rings had not been designed. They were supposed to operate at warmer temperatures. There was a fundamental design flaw in the joint design. On the morning of the launch, the cold weather hardened the O-rings, stopping them from being able to form a proper seal. This allowed hot gases to escape, which caused the external tanks to explode.

In a recent reliability assessment of a consumer products company's manufacturing plant, inadequate and poorly designed equipment and tooling were found to be major causes of equipment failures. They also were causing product quality problems due to tooling and fixtures instability. The plant was not able to meet its production needs due to frequent failure interruptions and quality issues.

These are just a few examples of the consequences of poor design. Research conducted for this chapter found many more incidents of buildings, walls, roofs, dams, bridges and other structure failures due to poor design practices. These poor design practices could be a result of limited design budgets, meeting schedules, or a simple lack of knowledge.

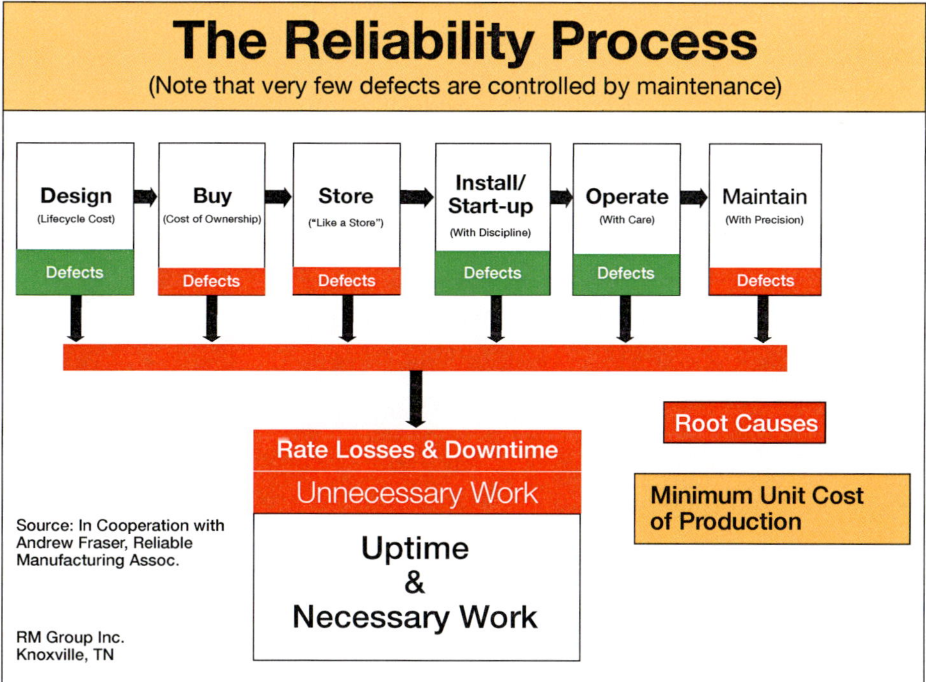

Figure 2.1: Major contributors of defects during stages of an asset's lifecycle (Source: Ron Moore)

According to Ron Moore, a well-known reliability expert and author, poor design is one of the major contributors of failures in assets.

As shown in Figure 2.1, his study indicates that Design, Install/Start-up and Operate are three major contributors of failures during an asset's operational phase.

My own experience working in various industries for many years brings out a similar conclusion. Many asset failures can be avoided by designing it right or paying attention to design with the right stakeholders' input.

In fact, in the last few years, I had the opportunity to spend considerable time with designers and capital project managers when I was assigned to the Capital Projects Group to improve reliability and maintainability of new or modified assets. It was a very challenging task, as most of the capital project managers and designers were driven to meet budgeted or allocated costs and schedules. Their major concerns and focus were to have good technical and production requirements, but these were always changing. They worked under ever increasing pressure due to limited project budgets, time schedules and a lack of consideration about reliability and total cost of ownership. Often, requirements were vague, unclear and almost always fluid, even during the asset build phase.

Designing right or designing for reliability, availability, maintainability, safety and sustainability (RAMS[2]) is not a new concept, but it has begun to receive a great deal of attention in recent years. Why should an organization commit resources for deploying a "Design It Right" process? The answer to this question is quite simple: Delivering products or services on time and at reasonable costs keep customers happy.

Field failures are very costly. Clearly, in order to be profitable, an organization's products must be reliable, and reliable products require robust, safe and sustainable assets to produce them. Assets designed right with the right processes will be reliable, robust and safe to operate with lower total cost of ownership.

You can't improve the reliability of an asset during the operations and maintenance phase unless you change the design. Maintenance just sustains the reliability that has been designed in the asset.

> *If you don't have time to do it right, you must have time to do it over.*
>
> ~ John Wooden

2.2 Design It Right Practices

As discussed earlier, poor design is one of the major contributors of failures in assets, causing an increase in total cost of ownership.

Often, the fact that designers misunderstand or have a different understanding of requirements based on their knowledge of the area can be a problem.

Major causes of asset failure are rooted in defective design or in its improper usage. A human error involving the skill set of the user in operating and maintaining the asset also plays a key part. Many of the failures caused by human error can be minimized by a better design.

The life of an asset starts when you conceive the concept, design it, build it, acquire the asset and install it. During installation, the potential for future failures gets magnified due to incorrect installation, incorrect site assembly, incorrect mounting practices, inadequate environmental protection and deficient foundations or supports issues.

Many of these errors, along with commissioning, operations and maintenance errors, cause failures early in the asset's operating life, characterized by infant mortality failures. Other defects and errors that do not appear during asset infancy will eventually surface and cause failures later, during its operating life.

The preferred terminology is to call the errors *defects* because that's what you see as a consequence of a mistake. But the truth is, an early inaction or wrong action results in a defect that is really a consequence. Another truth is that most of the time, most things go right. Failure is not a normal occurrence. The problem with failures isn't the failure itself, it's the consequences *resulting* from these failures.

When these consequences are bad, you want to do everything possible to never let them happen again, or to find ways to mitigate a consequence to alleviate its possibility of occurrence. The best way to eliminate or minimize these defects is to design them out at the source itself. Designing them right!

During design, you should be thinking about all aspects of RAMS[2]. There is a good possibility that a right design or a design done well will cost you a little more, but it will reduce the total cost of ownership during the lifecycle of the asset.

System interactions, interfaces, complex usage and stress profiles need to be addressed and accounted for in a design done right. With increasing complexity in all aspects of asset development, it becomes a necessity to have a well-defined process for incorporating reliability tools into the design cycle. Without such an orderly process, using various reliability tools for asset development can become very chaotic. When different reliability tools are deployed too late, randomly, or not at all, it results in a waste of time and resources and leads to frequent occurrences of problems in the field.

Design is not just what it looks like and feels like. Design is how it works.

~ Steve Jobs

2.3 Understanding Total Cost of Ownership

In Chapter 1, you learned that an asset's lifecycle starts when a need is conceived. Some entity, person, group, or organization starts thinking about producing a product or providing a service and that starts a process of conceptualizing how that product will be made or how the service will be provided. A concept or preliminary design is developed for an asset or system. This process goes through several phases, such as detailed design, build/construction, installation, etc. Finally, you start using the asset to make products or provide services.

This usage phase or operations and maintenance (O&M) of the asset's lifecycle is a key phase. It may continue for many years. This is the phase when you derive value from this asset. During this phase, the asset may undergo several improvements or modifications. And finally, if and when its need or life is over, the asset will be retired or disposed of.

Asset phases can be categorized as:

- Concept (start of lifecycle);
- Design (includes development);
- Build, construct, or procure;
- Install and commission;
- Operate and maintain;
- Dispose of/decommission (end of lifecycle).

The costs incurred during the whole life span of the asset (i.e., each of these phases) is called the total cost of ownership (TCO).

TCO is an analysis meant to uncover all lifetime costs from owning certain kinds of assets. For this reason, TCO is sometimes called lifecycle cost analysis.

Ownership brings purchase costs, of course, but it can also bring substantial costs for installing, deploying, operating, upgrading and maintaining the same assets. For many kinds of acquisitions, a TCO analysis finds a very large difference between purchase price and total lifecycle costs, especially when viewed across a long ownership period. The example in Table 2.1 illustrates how this is done.

As shown in Table 2.1, Asset A, with installation costing $1 million, has a total TCO of about $6 million during its 20-year life span. Asset B, with

Table 2.1: Example of Asset Total Cost of Ownership		
	Asset A – Capital ~$ 1,000K ($ '000)	**Asset B – Capital ~$ 10,000 K ($ '000)**
Design	100	700
Build/Fabricate	750	8,000
Install/Commission	80	800
Project Mgmt., plus	70	500
Installed Cost or Acquisition (capital) Cost	**1,000**	**10,000**
Operations	4,200	20,000
Maintenance	900	9,000
Disposal	100	700
Total Life - TCO	**6,200**	**39,700**
Design Cost as % of TCO	**1.6%**	**1.8%**
Installed Cost (acquisition cost) as % of TCO	**16.1%**	**25.2%**

* Data in Table 2.1 is based on the following assumptions: One operator for Asset A, two operators for Asset B at estimated cost of $80K per year plus operations cost, including energy and consumables ~10% of estimated replacement value (ERV); maintenance cost ~4% of ERV; annual inflation cost increase ~2% per year; 20-year asset life span

an installed cost of $10 million, has a TCO of almost $40 million during its life span.

It should be noted that design costs are less than two percent of TCO. Later on, the analysis will show that by investing additional funds to improve the design and asset reliability during the build/fabricate and install phases, TCO will be reduced and additional gains in capacity realized by a reduction in downtime.

Today, a TCO analysis is used to support acquisition and planning decisions for a wide range of assets that bring significant maintenance or operating costs across ownership life. The TCO analysis is center stage when management is faced with acquisition decisions for data and monitoring systems, vehicles, buildings, laboratory and medical equipment, factory equipment or machines, aircraft, etc.

2.4 Tools and Practices for Designing It Right

Simplicity is about subtracting the obvious and adding the meaningful.

~John Maeda, The Laws of Simplicity

(Simplicity: Design, Technology, Business, Life)

2.4.1 The Voice of the Customer

The voice of the customer (VOC), also called the house of quality, is a management approach for basic design based on quality function deployment (QFD). This approach was originated in 1972 at Mitsubishi's Kobe shipyard site. The house of quality tool has been used successfully by Japanese manufacturers and other global manufacturers of consumer electronics, home appliances, clothing, integrated circuits, rubber, construction equipment and automobiles to improve product quality and reliability. This design approach has been used successfully in consumer products, but can be used for the design of industrial products and assets.

With a set of planning and communication routines, QFD focuses and coordinates skills within an organization to first design, then manufacture and market goods that customers will want to purchase and continue purchasing.

The foundation of the house of quality is the belief that products should be designed to reflect customers' desires and tastes. Therefore, marketing people, design engineers and manufacturing staff must work closely together from the time a product is conceived.

The house of quality is a diagram resembling a house. It's used for defining the relationship between customers' desires and product/asset capabilities. It utilizes a planning matrix to relate what the customer needs and how the product is going to meet those needs. It looks like a house with a correlation matrix as its roof, customer wants versus product features as the main part, competitor evaluation as the porch, etc.

The house of quality is a very powerful tool as it incorporates customers' needs into design parameters so the final product or asset is better designed to meet customers' or owners' expectations.

More details about the house of quality are discussed in Appendix A.

2.4.2 Design FMEA to Mitigate Failures

Design failure mode and effects analysis (DFMEA) is a method for evaluating a design for reliability (DFR) and robustness against potential failures. It's a specific failure mode and effects analysis (FMEA) method for identifying possible failures during the design phase of a product, whether it's an asset or a service.

Failure mode means the ways or modes in which something might fail. Failures, which can be potential or actual, are any errors or defects, especially ones that affect the asset performance.

Effects analysis refers to studying the consequences of those failures.

Failures are prioritized according to the seriousness of their consequences, how frequently they occur and how easily they can be detected. The purpose of the FMEA is to take actions to eliminate or reduce failures, starting with the highest priority ones.

FMEA also documents current knowledge and actions about the risks of failures for use in continuous improvement. It is used during the design phase to prevent failures. It's a proactive approach at this time, but later it's used for control before and during the ongoing operation of the asset or process. Ideally, FMEA is applied during the earliest conceptual stages of design and continues throughout the life of an asset or service.

Started in the 1940s by the U.S. military, FMEA was further developed by the aerospace and automotive industries. Several industries maintain formal FMEA standards.

The application of the DFMEA process is normally employed:

- When an asset, service, or process is being designed or redesigned (may be after QFD);
- When an existing asset, service, or process is being applied in a new way;
- Before developing control plans for a new or modified asset or process;
- When improvement goals are planned for an existing asset or service;
- When analyzing failures of an existing asset or service;
- Periodically throughout the life of an asset or service.

Details for conducting the 10-step DFMEA process is provided in Appendix B.

2.4.3 Design for Manufacturability and Assembly

Design for manufacturing (DFM) and design for assembly (DFA) have some common attributes. Nowadays, DFM and DFA are commonly referred to as a single process called design for manufacturing and assembly (DFMA).

The goal is to design an asset so it's easily and economically manufactured and assembled. The importance of designing for manufacturing is underlined by the fact that about seventy percent of manufacturing costs of an asset (i.e., cost of materials, processing and assembly) are determined by design decisions, with production decisions, such as process planning or machine tool selection, responsible for only twenty percent, as reported in the book, *Computer-Aided Manufacturing* by Tien-Chien Chang, Richard A. Wysk and Hsu-Pin Wang.

Key guidelines for a good DFMA are:

1. Minimize the number of components;
2. Use standard, commercially available components;
3. Use modular design;

4. Design parts with tolerances that are within the current process capability;
5. Design for ease of part fabrication;
6. Design for ease of assembly;
7. Minimize the use of flexible components;
8. Eliminate or reduce the amount of adjustment required;
9. Ensure ease of handling and shipping.

These guidelines to implement DFMA are discussed in more detail in Appendix C.

2.4.4 Design for Reliability/Reliability Allocation Methodology

The reliability allocation methodology establishes a hierarchy of design requirements about reliability goals. The purpose is to distribute the operational reliability goals from the top system level to the subsystem, subassemblies and all the way down to component levels, and then design or select components accordingly.

Allocation starts with the asset system goal. For example, Figure 2.2 shows a hierarchical reliability diagram of an assembly machine. The requirements are to design and build a machine with these reliability requirements:

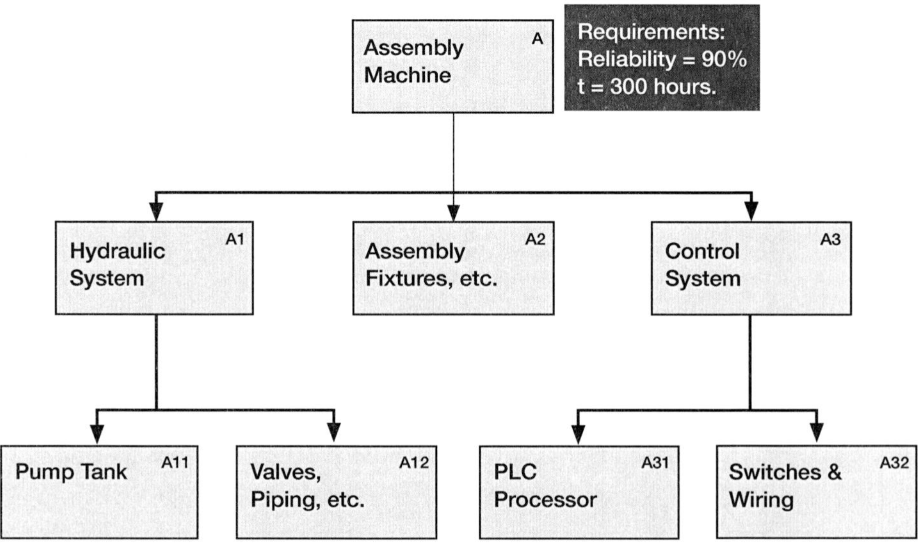

Figure 2.2: Hierarchical diagram of an assembly machine

- Operating hours = 300 hours per month;
- Reliability = minimum 90%.

In Figure 2.3, the reliability requirements, failure rate and mean time between failures (MTBF) are allocated and then calculated to subsystem and component level. This helps the designer to then find or design components to meet those requirements. For example, in this case, the pump tank and valves are subsystems of a hydraulic system, which is a subassembly or subsystem of the assembly machine. If, for example, forty percent reliability was allocated to the hydraulic system, which equates to a failure rate of 0.000133 failures per hour or an MTBF of 7,500 hours, and the pump tank and valves are allocated fifty percent reliability, equating to a failure rate of 0.000067 or MTBF of 15,000 hours, the designer should design a pump tank system to match the MTBF of 15,000 hours.

All the components and the subsystem have been designed with their estimated failure rates and MTBF, so the system reliability can be calculated to confirm that the required reliability has been designed to meet the requirements. At the top of each block, the calculated reliability (R) is shown in the oval figures.

The failure rate (i.e., MTBF) is calculated from these formulas:

$$\text{Failure rate} = 1/\text{MTBF}$$

$$\text{Reliability (R)} = e^{-t/\text{MTBF}}$$

$$t = \text{operating/mission time}$$

Also, note that in order to get a reliability of ninety percent at the machine assembly level, the component needs to have very high reliability, in the range of ninety-eight percent or better or MTBF of 15,000 hours or more.

Many times, you may not have the reliability data available on components, so you may have to do some accelerated product testing to determine failure rates or use estimates based on your best knowledge of similar types of components and equipment.

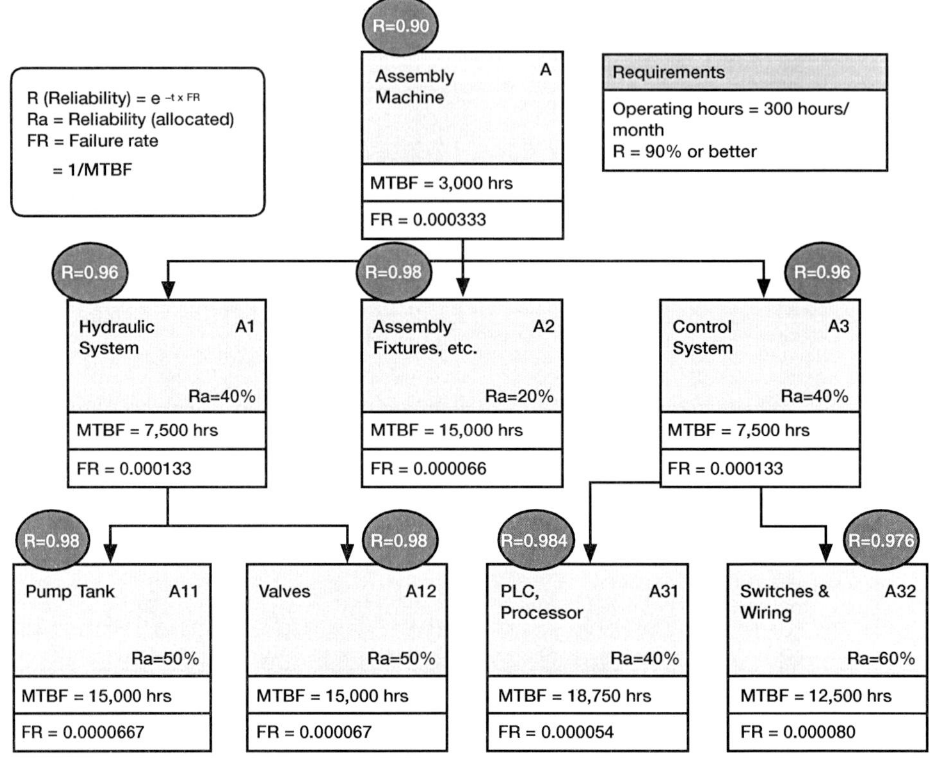

Figure 2.3: Reliability allocation diagram of an assembly machine

2.4.5 Design for RAMS[2]

Designing for reliability, availability, maintainability, safety and sustainability (RAMS[2]) should be the major focus of your design effort. Your design should incorporate the following:

- Use of highly reliable components and parts (i.e., with higher MTBF):
    - Use redundancy where needed to achieve desired reliability;
- Ease of operations to minimize repair time:
    - Design in condition monitoring and diagnostic to facilitate repairs;
    - Minimize use of special tools;
    - Use total productive maintenance (TPM) and 5S principles to optimize design:

    - Ease of adjustment to belts, chains, oil filling and lubrication;
    - Labeling of piping, hoses, devices, etc., for efficient operation;
- Achieve required availability by balancing reliability and maintainability requirements;
- Safe and ergonomically designed features to eliminate or minimize accidents and enhance safety of personnel and the asset itself;
- Use of environmentally clean and energy efficient components and material;
- Extensive use of standard components, including control devices, such as programmable logic controllers (PLCs);
- Establish what data will be needed to measure asset performance and design the process on how it will be collected:
    - Use a standardized methodology for asset and component hierarchy and taxonomy (i.e., naming structure).

Another area in RAMS^2 to be considered is mechanical integrity. Mechanical integrity (MI), also known as asset integrity management (AIM), refers to the management of all the processing equipment of an organization to ensure it's sound and operating within the realms of safety.

Equipment, such as tanks, pressure vessels, piping, etc., are the key assets in the process industry and they need to be fit for service all the time since they operate continuously. Any failure, such as leaks, over pressure, or corrosion, in these systems can be very dangerous and costly. They need to be designed and maintained with special care, meeting all the applicable standards of OSHA (OSHA1910.119) and American Petroleum Institute (API) codes, such as API580, API581, etc.

2.4.6 Design for Total Cost of Ownership

Previous sections discussed designing for RAMS^2 and other methodologies to Design It Right. However, this is likely to cost you more, perhaps ten to thirty percent extra in design just one time, but it will reduce the operations and maintenance (O&M) cost by ten to twenty percent every year for the life of the asset. Plus, you will reduce asset downtime while providing additional production capacity. Also, despite the added cost of the right design and build, the total cost of ownership will reduce. This is based on my own personal experience and has been confirmed by many experts in the industry. We are certain these findings will be validated soon.

In Table 2.2 for Asset A (as previously identified in Table 2.1) is a notional example of total cost of ownership (TCO). It shows that if you spend twenty percent more during the design and build phases, this design can reduce the O&M cost by ten percent. Even then, the TCO still will be lower than the original for the total life span of the asset, which is 20 years in

Table 2.2: System/Asset A TCO

	Asset A – Capital ~$1,000K ($ '000)	**Asset A with Reliability plus Capital ~$1,200K (+ 20%) ($ '000)**
Design	100	120
Build/Fabricate	750	900
Install/Commission	80	100
Project Mgmt., plus	70	80
Installed Cost or Acquisition (capital) Cost	**1,000**	**1,200**
Operations	4,200	3,800
Maintenance	900	800
Disposal	100	100
Total Lifecycle Cost – TCO (Est. 20-year life)	**6,200**	**5,900**

Table. 2.2 assumptions: One operator for Asset A at an estimated cost of $80K a year, plus operations cost, including energy/consumables ~10% of estimated replacement value (ERV); maintenance cost ~4% of ERV; annual inflation cost increase ~2% a year; 20-year asset life span

this example. In this example, the cost ignores the interest rate to simplify the calculations. In real applications, you should or could use interest tables to calculate net present value (NPV) based on a standard interest rate.

Reliability plus design may cost twenty percent more, but it reduces O&M by ten percent for the asset's life span, as shown in Table 2.3.

Table 2.3 shows the impact on key operational and reliability parameters with a design for reliability (DFR) design. This table is based on Asset A, as shown in Table 2.2, and the notion that by investing in improved design and build while implementing tools and practices discussed in Section 2.3, you can reduce the TCO and also improve reliability, reduce failures and add capacity. These estimates are very conservative based on my experience. Actual savings could be higher.

This chapter discussed just a few of the tools and practices available to improve and/or optimize design. There are many other tools available, such as fault tree analysis (FTA), reliability block diagram (RBD), event tree analysis, barrier analysis and physics of failure. You should use a combina-

Table 2.3: DFR Impact Plus Reduction in Failures and Increase in Availability Factors

	Asset A	Asset A + DFR	% Change
Operating Hours/Year	4,000	4,000	0%
Number of Failures/Year	20	16	20%
Total Downtime Hours	300	140	53%
Repair Time Hours	400	220	45%
Net Hours Available	3,700	3,860	4%
MTBF	200	250	25%
MTTR	20	14	30%
Availability	0.91	0.95	4%
Est. Prod. Rate/Hour	120	120	0%
Est. Prod./Year	444,000	463,200	4%

tion of any number of tools to make your design RIGHT and to weed out any failure modes. This will help in reducing the total cost of ownership.

> *A common mistake that people make when trying to design something completely foolproof is to underestimate the ingenuity of complete fools.*
>
> *~ Douglas Adams, Mostly Harmless*

2.5 Design It Right Summary and Checklist

2.5.1 Summary

Things, products, or assets fail in service. All of us have witnessed the various failure of products in our daily life. It might have been a water heater leak, a dead car battery, a failing washing machine, a corrupted computer hard drive, the TV remote control stops functioning, or a car fails to start.

Similarly, you have likely experienced equipment and machine failures in industrial plants and factories. Most of these failures could be eliminated or reduced by focusing on designing failure modes out during the design phase.

To be reliable, assets must be robust and adequately designed to avoid failure modes, even in the presence of a broad range of conditions, including harsh environments, changing operational demands and internal deterioration due to wear and fatigue.

Many industry experts have indicated that as much as sixty percent of failures can be prevented by making changes in design. Designers and engineers should use a combination of tools and practices discussed in this chapter and summarized again here:

- Voice of customers:
  - Involving stakeholders, specifically operators, maintainers, etc., to understand the requirements and issues;
- Eliminating or minimizing failure modes:
  - Applying DFMEA/FMEA types of tools to identify failure modes and mitigate their consequences;
- Design based on RAMS[2] principles:
  - Use of reliable components based on reliability analysis, etc.;
  - Use of energy efficient and environmentally safe components;
  - Use of modular and standardized components;
  - Making design ergonomically safe and easy to operate and maintain;
  - Considering the use of condition monitoring, diagnostic devices and display data/dashboard to support O&M in design;
- Manufacturability and assembly of design:
  - Ensuring design is easy, economical and safe to manufacture, assemble and ship.

Finally, the design should be based not on the lowest cost of design, but an optimum cost to reduce total cost of ownership.

2.5.2 Checklist

Design It Right Assurance Checklist		Check - √
1.	**General Review – Preliminary Design**	
	a. Have similar designs been used before?	
	i. Can it be visited to witness its operation and to help us make necessary improvements in new design?	
	b. Have alternative concepts been considered to reduce operations and maintenance costs?	

	c. If this asset is to be integrated into an existing system, has the existing system been evaluated to ensure it will accept the new asset without affecting the operation or reliability of the new system as a whole?	
	d. Have problems encountered in its past usage been adequately addressed in the new design?	
	e. Is RAMS-related data, such as MTBF, MTTR, etc., available to optimize the new design?	
	f. Has DFMEA been performed to identify failure modes and has needed action been taken to mitigate them?	
	g. If redundancy has been provided in the new design, can both main and redundant equipment be monitored for performance?	
2.	**Reliability/Availability/Dependability Review**	
	a. Are the designed stresses and loads commensurate with the predicted operating environment?	
	b. Have the effects of stresses induced by assembly and operation (e.g., vibrations, etc.) been considered in the design?	
	c. Does the safety factor used in the design of components conform to the applicable standard practices or industry standards?	
	d. Are highly reliable (e.g., high MTBF and best value) components being used in the design?	
	e. Are the number of components in the new design reasonable from a reliability standpoint?	
	f. Are redundancies incorporated in the design at the asset and component levels adequate to meet required reliability requirements?	
3.	**Maintainability and Maintenance Review**	
	a. Have critical spare parts been identified and provisions made to make them readily available at start-up?	

	b. Has the design been reviewed for ease of troubleshooting/diagnostic, parts or components replacement and material handling?	
	i. Can components be monitored for progression of wear, if applicable?	
	ii. Can component deterioration be detected and predicted?	
	iii. Are continuous asset health monitoring provisions incorporated where appropriate, including the use of the Internet of Things (IoT) and Industrial IoT?	
	iv. Have inspection windows (e.g., wire mesh windows in v-belt safety covers, IR windows on electrical control panels, etc.) been provided appropriately to allow easy viewing of components during operation?	
	c. Are lubrication points, oil fill and test ports easily accessible?	
	d. Can components be opened for maintenance without disturbing auxiliaries, such as piping and cables?	
	e. Has the possibility for injury or damage from abrasion, pinching and cutting for all components been considered and minimized?	
	f. Have components been designed to allow for easy and quick maintenance (e.g., fewer fasteners, quick disconnects, easy assembly, simple adjustments, replaceable modules, etc.)?	
	g. Have adjustments during operation and alignment requirements been minimized or made easier without using special tools?	
	h. Are key components easily accessible for the performance of both operator and maintenance tasks? Are ladders, platforms, walkways, etc., provided for easy reach or access?	
	i. Has interchangeability and standardization of components been maximized?	

	j. Are components, such as piping, wiring, subassemblies, etc., labeled for ease of identification? Examples include:	
	i. Color marking of permissible operating ranges on dials and gauges;	
	ii. Marking of oil level gauges to ensure the presence of the correct quantity of oil and type of lubricant required.	
	k. Have the possibilities of predictive maintenance been evaluated and the necessary devices installed (e.g., ports for oil sampling, location for vibration sensors, etc.)?	
	l. Does the control maintenance software provide adequate diagnostic information?	
	m. Do all controls, readings and assets get set up in a logical and ergonomic pattern (e.g., height, size, location, orientation, etc.)?	
	n. Have the levels of maintenance requirements been identified and defined for each level of operations? This includes equipment servicing and lubrication plans.	
4.	**Simplicity and Ergonomics Review**	
	a. Are features to reduce the chance of failures caused by human errors incorporated? Has the poka-yoke principle (easy to do it right and difficult to do it wrong) been applied?	
	b. Are operators able to maintain a comfortable working posture?	
	c. Is adequate illumination provided for all processes performed?	
	d. Have floors, platforms and other walkways been designed to promote stability and reduce slippage?	
5.	**Safety and Sustainability Review**	
	a. Are any fail-safe mechanisms incorporated into the design, (i.e., protection against secondary failures resulting from primary failures)?	

	b. Can protective devices be tested without causing a shutdown or an outage?	
	c. Are warning mechanisms (e.g., wear indicators, vibration switches, gauges with limits indicated) incorporated to give advance indication of potential failures?	
	d. Are mechanical overload protection devices provided, including a mechanism to monitor working stresses, such as slip clutches, shear pins, etc.?	
	e. Are alarms incorporated in the design if a process approaches unsafe operating conditions? Consider:	
	i. Are all alarms and warnings necessary?	
	f. Has the design maximized use of energy efficient parts/components and minimized the use of hazardous materials?	
	g. Has barrier analysis been performed and appropriate action taken to minimize the impact of high energy sources? Example:	
	i. Have spill pans, dikes, drains, etc., been provided and made accessible to control spills to minimize the environmental impact?	
	h. Have personal protective equipment (PPE) needs for operations and maintenance personnel been considered and minimized?	
	i. Can important performance indicators be easily observed by the operator and maintainer?	
	j. Have handles, grips, etc., been incorporated for all heavy or difficult to carry components and are they located properly to prevent swinging or other movements?	
	k. Have corrosion controls, deterioration and environmental requirements been incorporated?	

6.	**Documentation and Shipping Review**	
	a. Have measures been taken to facilitate trouble free shipping, assembly, installation and start-up (e.g., templates for anchor bolts, modular design to allow for equipment to be shipped easily, match marks for reassembly, etc.)? For example:	
	i. Have hoist lugs or base lifting provisions or other movement aids been provided for components that are too heavy to lift?	
	b. Have measures been taken to prevent equipment damage, if any, during shipping and installation? Have special provisions and instructions been provided for asset storage before installation?	
	c. Have the appropriate assembly, operations and maintenance instructions, including results of FMEA/DFMEA analyses, been included with the design documentation?	

2.6 References and Suggested Reading

1. *Computer-Aided Manufacturing,* Second Edition, by Tien-Chien Chang, Richard A. Wysk, and Hsu-Pin Wang
2. *Assurance Technologies Principles and Practices* by Dev G. Raheja and Michael Allocco
3. *Maintenance and Reliability Best Practices* by Ramesh Gulati
4. *Design for Reliability Handbook* by the U.S. Army Material Systems Analysis Activity (AMSAA) organization
5. *Reliability-Based Design* by S. S. Rao
6. *Quality Function Deployment: How to Make QFD Work for You* by Louis Cohen
7. *Design to Cost* by Jack V. Michaels and Williams P. Wood
8. Papers presented at various International Maintenance Conferences (IMCs) and published in *Uptime* Magazine

CHAPTER 3
SOURCE IT RIGHT

Learning Objectives to Understand

- The importance of sourcing in asset management
- Insourcing vs. Outsourcing
- "Best value" sourcing or procuring
- Best practices for sourcing

3.1 The Importance of Right Sourcing or Procuring

Many times, when you buy a cheap, low-cost appliance or tool, it starts breaking or doesn't provide the service you had expected. You get very upset and start questioning the value of that purchase.

Similar instances occur at the workplace. Due to cost cutting mandates, employees purchase parts, such as bearings and oil seals, from the lowest cost supplier. Perhaps it is twenty percent cheaper, but what about the quality and reliability of the product? Your maintenance repair crew might have some problems with the item. It could take longer to install because it has some tolerance discrepancies, or it doesn't last very long. It fails to provide its purpose in less than half of its anticipated life.

Was it a counterfeit part? Yes or maybe. You saved some money on procuring it, but then you paid the exceedingly high price in repair costs.

Materials or services that your company is not good at making need to be sourced or procured. Your organization can't be good at *everything* it makes or *every* service it provides. It needs to focus on the things that it does the best—its core competencies. You can outsource things that others are better at and provide those products or services at a lower cost with high quality. Outsourcing is important to those in asset management.

Rightsourcing enhances quality, ensures reliability, meets sustainability goals of the organization and helps in reducing the whole lifecycle cost. However, outsourcing to the right people and to the right company is important.

The asset management standard ISO55001, published by the International Organization for Standardization (ISO), identifies the importance of outsourcing in Section 8.3, stating that: "When an organization outsources any activities that can have an impact on the achievement of its asset management objectives, it shall assess the associated risks. The organization shall ensure that outsourced processes and activities are controlled. The organization shall determine and document how these activities will be controlled and integrated into the asset management system."

It's your responsibility to ensure that the outsourced company you work with has the appropriate skill set and process to do the right things in the right manner.

Outsourcing, including offshoring and insourcing, has been talked about a lot in the last few years. The real question is how do you source or procure your material or design/modify an asset? Should you design and build in-house or outsource it?

If doing it in-house, do you have competent people with the expertise to do it right? Is it more economical to outsource it from an organization who designs, builds, or provides these services as part of its core business?

If you don't do the "right" sourcing, ensuring that the sourcing organization has the right capabilities, people and processes, you may not be happy with its services.

This chapter discuss these concerns.

INSANITY:

doing the same thing over and over again and expecting different results.

~Albert Einstein

3.2 Insourcing vs. Outsourcing

Insourcing and outsourcing are methods of dispersing work among different departments within an organization or outside companies for strategic reasons. Insourcing is typically done solely from within an organization's own operational infrastructure, while outsourcing uses outside companies to perform tasks, such as provide assets, components, or services.

There are cost and resource differences between outsourcing and insourcing that influence an organization's decision on which method to use.

Outsourcing is a well-known concept and has been accepted and implemented by organizations across the globe. Often seen as a cost saving tactic, outsourcing allows a business to focus on its core competencies while off-loading its non-core functions to outsourcing providers.

Before deciding whether insourcing or outsourcing is the best option, it's important to first define business goals. A poorly defined objective may result in neither insourcing nor outsourcing being successful. Outsourcing can provide access to specialized skill sets of resources and processes that insourcing simply cannot match without significant costs. This is perhaps one of the most important factors when it comes to businesses choosing to outsource.

Though there are many outsourcing vendors, it's important to assess potential vendors before shaking hands on a partnership. Doing a little homework before choosing an outsourcing partner can lead to long-term gains and help build a long-term competitive advantage for the business.

Specifically for those in the maintenance, reliability and asset management area, outsourcing some services, such as ground maintenance, building maintenance, HVAC, or design/build of tooling or specialized equipment and production systems, is due to a constraint on resources. However, you need to be very careful in selecting the right vendors to perform the required tasks.

3.3 Best Value Approach in Sourcing

In a best value system, a vendor or supplier is selected through a process in which vendors are researched prior to procurement. Typically, values are assigned to factors, such as price, past performance, product reliability, schedule, warranty support, etc. These values are tabulated for each potential vendor and the one with the highest score wins the procurement contract. This system is widely adopted because it minimizes bias and risk, and supports a reduction in total cost of ownership. This system has even been used by governments, specifically U.S. government agencies and the U.S. Department of Defense.

One of the most important aspects of the best value procurement approach is looking at past performance. If an organization is considering building an expensive structure or designing an expensive, new and complex production system, it's important to see how potential vendors have handled similar projects in the past. Do these vendors have the right skill sets and experience to build such systems? Have they supplied or built reliable and quality products in the past? Can they provide evidence of their capabilities? Knowing this information enables organizations to select capable vendors based on best value and not necessarily a lower bid.

Best value procurement is allowed for U.S. federal government projects under the Federal Acquisition Regulation (FAR). The FAR system is codified at Title 48, Chapter 1 of the Code of Federal Regulations. The requirements can be found in the Code of Federal Regulations at 48 C.F.R. 31.

When determining best value, a procurement may take advantage of the full spectrum of best value techniques as defined in FAR 2.101, from lowest priced, technically acceptable bids through a full trade-off process. When determining which non-price evaluation factors to include in the request for quotation (RFQ), the selection criteria should indicate how these factors will be weighted in their relative importance to other non-price factors.

Procurement activities should consider:

- **Past performance:**
  - Does available information indicate that the vendor has significantly different past performance records or has specialized performance experience that will significantly improve its chance of success in meeting the requirements?
  - If warranties are offered, does the organization have the administrative tracking and logistics capabilities necessary to take advantage of them?
- **Ownership costs:**
  - What installation costs are associated with the various components and the total asset or system?

- What are the historical or estimated operating costs for the various components and the total asset or system?
- What are the reliability (i.e., mean time between failures) and maintainability (i.e., mean time to repair) of the various components and the total asset or system that meet the functional requirements?
- What are the historical or estimated repair costs for the various components and the total asset or system?
- What are the historical or estimated preventive maintenance (PM) and predictive maintenance (PdM) costs for the various components and total asset or system?
- What are the historical or estimated disposal costs for the various components and the total asset or system?

- **Maintenance and availability:**
  - Does the vendor provide maintenance for the identified item at the plant?
  - If the vendor is not the original equipment manufacturer (OEM), is there an agreement in place that ensures services provided by the vendor will not void the warranty?

- **Useful life:**
  - How long are components or the asset expected to remain useful?
  - Are there any significant differences in useful life between components?

- **Environmental and energy conservation and efficiency:**
  - Do the assets to be supplied use green products?
  - Do the parts and components meet the sustainability performance goals of the organization and its toxic/hazardous chemical management plan?
  - Do the parts and components generate hazardous waste or can they be disposed as solid waste or recycled at the end of their useful life?
  - Do the parts and components meet applicable energy efficiency standards or the organization's specific requirements, water efficiency

standards, recycled or biobased content, or other energy or environmental requirements?
  - Does the vendor offer opportunities for waste prevention, such as reduced packaging or packaging take back programs?

- **Technical processes or qualifications:**
  - Are there significant differences in vendor or supplier technical qualifications?
  - If for services, is the proposed labor mix likely to result in successful performance?
  - If the requirement is performance-based services, has the vendor proposed appropriate performance standards and a quality assurance plan that measures the right things to ensure success?
  - Are there unique or specialized qualifications required to meet the activity requirement?
  - Training and customer support issues:
    - Is training or other customer support important?
    - Do vendors offer significantly enhanced levels of training or other customer support?

- **Transportation costs:**
  - If items are priced other than free on board (FOB) destination, will the transportation cost be significantly different for shipments from different vendors and suppliers?

- **Administrative costs:**
  - Will the administrative costs of contracting with one prospective vendor likely be different from other suppliers?

- **Delivery and performance terms:**
  - Can the vendor meet delivery or performance requirements?
  - Is the delivery or performance provided by one vendor significantly different from the delivery or performance available from other sources?

- **Warranty:**
  - Do the vendors offer warranties?
  - Do available warranties protect the organization from significant risk?

10 Guiding Principles to Achieve Best Value for Sourcing:

1. **Competition:** Suppliers should be encouraged in the most efficient and effective way.
2. **Efficiency and effectiveness:** Should be sought in the procurement process to secure value for money.
3. **Fairness/non-discrimination:** Should be fairly followed during the procurement process without imposing unnecessary burdens or constraints on suppliers or potential suppliers. Avoid any favorable treatment to a specific or potential supplier.
4. **Objectivity/integrity/honesty:** Declare any conflict of interest that affects or appears to affect vendors' judgment. Reject gifts, hospitality and benefits of any kind from suppliers or potential suppliers that might be reasonably seen to compromise their objectivity or integrity.
5. **Transparency:** Ensure equal conditions and accessibility to all economic operators by informing them in an open and transparent way.
6. **Accountability:** Be accountable for the responsibilities assigned to suppliers, as well as for the decisions made by them. Keep the appropriate records.
7. **Confidentiality, the accuracy of information and protection of intellectual property:** Respect the confidentiality of information acquired over the course of performing duties and do not disclose any such information without having the proper and legitimate authority to do so.
8. **Conformity to the laws serving the public interest/responsiveness:** Conform to national and international legislation, as well as other requirements and commitments regarding public procurement. Serve the public's interest and act with responsiveness in using taxpayers' money.

9. **Professionalism:** Work to a high standard of professionalism by complying with legislation in force and applying best practices.
10. **Green purchasing:** Exploit opportunities to incorporate environmental considerations and issues in each stage of the procurement lifecycle.

The benefit of making a best value selection decision can result in improved mission performance and lower lifecycle costs and ownership cost.

> *Strive not to be a success,*
> *but rather to be of value.*
>
> *~Albert Einstein*

3.4 Practices for Right Sourcing

In today's economic environment, doing what you've always done—even if you do it very well—is no longer acceptable. Under pressure to contain costs and produce results despite challenging circumstances, you must *transform* rather than simply improve your operations. That means adopting the philosophies, methods and processes that will make your organization best in class or world-class.

You don't want everyone grabbing their phone and calling suppliers for procurement. You need to manage acquisitions systematically, either through a purchasing department or by assigning this responsibility to a specific employee. It's also important to have a clear process that outlines the rules of sourcing or buying.

Some of the purchasing practices that will make you best in class are:

a. Conduct an overall cost analysis

Creating a detailed overview of how much will be spent over the next few years on a significant item is crucial to its effective procurement. You need to have a closer look at exactly how spending affects the bottom line. Review costs, such as:

- Cost of materials, both raw and finished;
- Inventory costs, such as interest, space requirement, heating, extra handling, additional workforce and insurance;
- Taxes and tariffs;
- Inbound and outbound transportation expenses, including freight forwarder fees;
- Payment terms;
- Third-party warehousing and handling costs.

b. Conduct a functional analysis

You need to focus on the essential functional needs of the component, system, or services you are trying to source or purchase. This may require you to overhaul your internal policies to include criteria that determines what is essential when it comes to purchasing. For instance, do you need to buy a new asset or do you use refurbished equipment to meet your functional requirements? A functional analysis also enables you to focus not only on cost, but on related quality and quantity. Such an analysis allows you to question why you have items in inventory that you aren't going to use for a few months or several years.

c. Buying from best value suppliers

As discussed earlier, you shouldn't buy for the lowest price, but rather for the *best value*. Quality and reliability of materials and components are critical. You need to go beyond price with a total cost of ownership (TCO) concept. TCO includes the cost of hardware and software acquisition, management support, communications, end user expenses and the opportunity costs of downtime, training and related productivity losses.

By considering direct costs, indirect costs, transaction costs and disposal costs, TCO gives procurement professionals a complete picture about a specific financial decision. It also helps them compare and contrast different variables associated with a purchase and to bring concepts, such as sustainability, into the procurement process.

You also need to be vigilant about counterfeit parts, especially if you're sourcing cheaper goods and services from abroad. Procuring from foreign suppliers triggers additional costs, such as shipping, logistics, or expenses associated with customs and duties. Fluctuating currency rates also have an impact on the cost of such procuring.

d. Reduce supply complexity

Your strategy should be to buy more standard parts, goods, or services from established suppliers. Customized items are invariably more costly. Ensure that purchases fit the basic needs of the organization and that you are not overspending due to unnecessary customization.

e. Establish strategic partnerships with key suppliers

Dealing with fewer suppliers saves time and resources. Also, you will be more likely to have better bargaining power when it comes to negotiating contracts. Your supply partners will appreciate and value your business and be more flexible when it comes to adapting to your needs. Make sure your suppliers work with you closely, for example, to improve the procurement process or the supply chain, or to conduct research and development when needed. Partnerships should be mutually beneficial.

When you negotiate with your suppliers, you need to remember that if the relationship is to thrive long-term, a win-win situation is important for both parties. Trust is essential to generate a continuous stream of value-added activities from suppliers. Collaboration with suppliers will have a positive effect on your bottom line due to a reduced inventory, lower warehousing costs and fewer stockouts.

f. Invest in technology

You need to evaluate and invest in technological tools that can streamline your procurement process. These investments will generally give you long-term benefits. However, with business cycles becoming increasingly fast, a good and accurate information system becomes very beneficial.

Integrated software, such as enterprise resource planning (ERP), enterprise asset management (EAM), computerized maintenance management system (CMMS), supply chain management (SCM), warehouse management system (WMS) and supplier relationship management (SRM), as well as Web 2.0, Internet of Things (IoT) and Industrial Internet of Things (IIoT) applications, enable suppliers to access material/product specifications and transmit invoices seamlessly. Investment in building auction sites where suppliers can bid for best prices can be very useful and are examples of cost-saving systems.

g. Train employees on procurement process

Establish a procurement training program that includes such aspects as negotiating contracts and following organizational policies. Negotiation skills are particularly important to ensure you are getting the most value from your suppliers. Training also ensures that your procurement personnel understands underlying expectations, specifically the best value concepts and total cost of ownership, and that in the process, they are accountable for their actions.

h. Evaluate suppliers on a regular basis

Establish a system to assess the performance of suppliers on a regular basis. Organizations often use standard forms that help them review factors, such as flexibility, just-in-time delivery, consignment inventory, costs and quality of service. A written document also gives suppliers a means to improve their weak areas.

i Review the purchasing process regularly

Establish a system to assess the purchasing policy and organizational strategy on a regular basis. Factors, such as best value procurement, supplier's support and flexibility adherence to the organization's policies, inventory cost, management, quality of service, etc., can be evaluated during such reviews.

Price is what you pay.
Value is what you get.
~Warren Buffett

3.5 Source It Right Summary and Checklist

3.5.1 Summary

Are you buying the right materials—parts, components, assets, or services—from the right sources? Consider these questions when purchasing your materials, parts, components, assets, or services:

- Do they meet quality and reliability requirements?
- Are they robust enough to stand production or operational needs?
  - Are they made of the right material?
  - Can they meet tolerances (i.e., dimensions) for proper form and fit?
  - Are they designed from an RAMS[2] perspective?
- Is the vendor or supplier reliable based on its past performance?
- If the vendor or supplier is located in a foreign country, is it reliable and able to provide the parts or service on a long-term basis?
- Are you buying parts and services based on best value or assets with the least lifecycle cost?
- Are you ensuring that the parts or components being supplied are not counterfeit?
- Are they being shipped or stored appropriately, with the right maintenance plan?

These are some of the sourcing issues discussed in this chapter. You need to be purchasing material, parts, or services based on best value, not necessarily on the lowest cost. The best value concept is based on the premise that it will reduce the total cost of ownership during the life of the asset, but may not be the lowest cost when it is purchased and installed.

3.5.2 Checklist

Source It Right Assurance Checklist		Check - √
1.	**Are assets, components, parts, etc., being procured, fabricated and assembled in-house?** **If yes:**	
	a. Are these being procured for the lowest price or the best value?	
	b. Do procurement/purchasing agents understand the concept of best value?	
	c. Is a policy established to procure the best value?	
2.	**Is procurement of asset (i.e., fabrication/assembly) being outsourced based on an approved design?** **If yes:**	
	a. Are these being procured for the lowest price or the best value? Do procurement/purchasing agents understand the concept of best value?	
	b. Is a policy established to procure the best value?	
	c. Is something being done differently to ensure vendors will use reliable and best value components available to reduce the total cost of ownership?	
	d. Are there measures in place to ensure the vendor will deliver a high quality and reliable asset?	
3.	**Is the procurement of the entire asset being outsourced? If yes, is it being procured for the best value?**	
	a. Do procurement/purchasing agents understand the concept of best value?	

	b. Is a policy established to procure the best value?	
	c. Is something being done differently to ensure vendors will use reliable and best value components available to reduce the total cost of ownership?	
	d. Are there measures in place to ensure the vendor will deliver a high quality and reliable asset?	
4.	**Have material handling and special needs been identified for shipping and transportation of the asset from the factory to the installation site?**	
	a. Is an appropriate lifting plan included?	
	b. Is an appropriate maintenance plan included if it's being shipped from overseas?	
	c. Are there any special safety precautions or safety permits needed for installation? If yes:	
	i. Has this been arranged or communicated to the right people?	

3.6 References and Suggested Reading

1. *Best Value Procurement*, Defense Acquisition University document, *https://dap.dau.mil/policy/Documents/Policy/BestValue4.rtf*
2. Federal Acquisition Regulation (FAR), https://www.acquisition.gov/?q=browsefar

CHAPTER 4
BUILD/FABRICATE IT RIGHT

Learning Objectives to Understand

- What are you building?
- The importance of planning in building an asset
- Manufacturability and assembly process
- Quality concerns in the asset building process

4.1 The Importance of Build It Right

Those of us who have worked in operations, production and maintenance are aware that new or modified assets don't always perform as expected. Either they weren't built per specifications or inferior quality parts/components were used, or there was poor workmanship during the asset build up phase. Most of these issues, including improper installations, result in high failure rates during start-up of the assets. Such failures are known as infant mortality, as shown in the bathtub curve in Figure 4.1.

The bathtub curve concept is widely used in reliability engineering. It describes a particular form of failure rate that comprises three parts:

a. A decreasing failure rate, known as early failures or infant mortality;
b. A constant failure rate, known as random failures;
c. An increasing failure rate, known as wear out failures.

The name of the curve is derived from the cross-sectional shape of a bathtub: steep sides and a flat bottom. The first part of the curve, also known as early mortality, has a decreasing failure rate. More about this later in this chapter.

Quality Guru Dr. Joseph Juran had pointed out that infant mortality is a major reason for determining the complaints rate. Although the initial

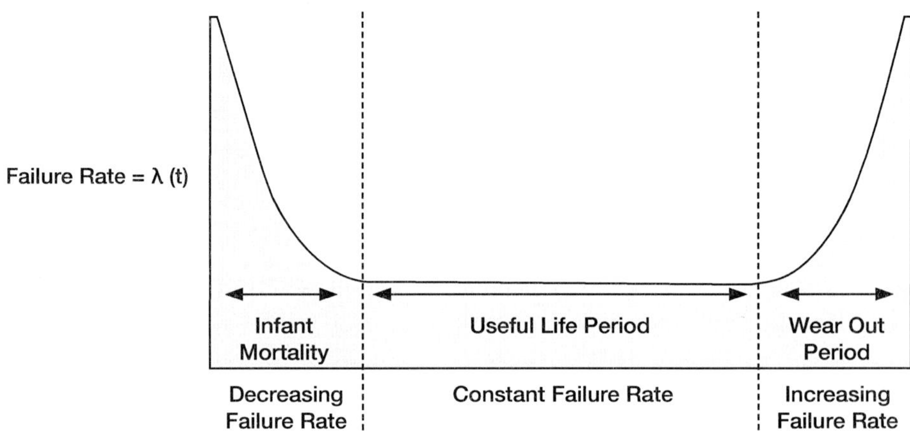

Figure 4.1: Bathtub curve and infant mortality

failure period is generally short, there are some exceptions. This period normally ranges from a few minutes to several hundred hours. So, to achieve high asset reliability, it is necessary to reduce this initial failure rate.

The high failure rate during early stages (i.e., infant mortality) of asset operations could be due to:

- Inadequate design;
- Use of inferior parts/components:
    - Poor quality of components;
    - Use of counterfeit parts;
- Poor shop practices in fabricating parts and assembly:
    - Poor welds or solder joints;
    - Seals leaking;
    - Incorrect positioning of parts;
    - Surface contamination;
- Lack of standards/practices;
- Poor quality control;
- Poor workmanship due to lack of qualified people to build the asset;
- Transportation damage:
    - Parts loosened in transit;
    - Physical damage to parts;
    - Parts becoming overstressed.

Each of these issues is a reason for high failure rates during start-up of an asset and can result in high operating costs, dissatisfaction and an eventual increase in total cost of ownership.

As an owner, operator, or user, you need to ensure that the asset being built, whether in-house or by outsourcing, is robust, reliable and meets specifications. The asset as built should experience minimal infant mortality failures. It needs to be built by properly skilled people using the right materials and with quality workmanship. To attain these goals, you need to get involved in the early build up stages, the assembly process, testing and collecting baseline performance data for the asset.

Such involvement enables you to correct the design or specification omissions early, communicate with the appropriate stakeholders to improve quality and workmanship, and reduce costly downstream fixes.

As a builder of the asset, you need to ensure that the asset is built in accordance with the specifications, using the right components and the right skills. Design or specification improvements based on your manufacturability and assembly experience need to be communicated to the owner or user to improve the quality of the asset build and to minimize failures during operation.

> *Success is a journey, not a destination. The doing is often more important than the outcome.*
>
> *~ Arthur Ashe*

4.2 The Build/Fabricate/Assemble Process

4.2.1 Planning

Planning for building a new asset or modifying an existing one is a very important activity. It is the first step when a build request or build package arrives at the site. The planning process remains similar whether you build the asset inside the organization or outsource it.

Activities that are part of the planning process include:

- Review of build design:
  - What will be built in-house?
    - Machined parts: Where, how and what tolerances to be achieved;
    - Fabricated parts: Where, how and what tolerances to be achieved;

            - Any specialized operations, such as welding or heat treatment, required?
        - Where and how the parts will be assembled?
        - Will any testing, such as leak testing, be performed by components or assembly?
    - What parts or components will be outsourced/procured?
        - Standard, off-the-shelf components:
            - Any specific brand name requirements?
        - Non-standard components:
            - Are there any quality checks required? If so, where from?
    - How and where will assembly be shipped?
        - Is baseline performance data required before getting ready for shipping?
        - Any specific color to be painted?
        - Any specific shipping instructions?
    - Any schedule timeline to adhere to?

All this information becomes part of the shop's routing to ensure a timely build of the asset. If there are any issues, they should be clarified with the customer or user and the designer as early as possible.

4.2.2 Building Parts/Components

In this phase, parts and components will be machined and/or fabricated in accordance with the drawings supplied. Some precautions that should be taken during this phase to ensure quality include:

- Machining
    - Use the right processes to:
        - Achieve the right tolerances, surfaces, finishes, etc.;
        - Identify practical or design omissions:
            - If improvements can be made, communicate with the designer, owner, or user to initiate changes.

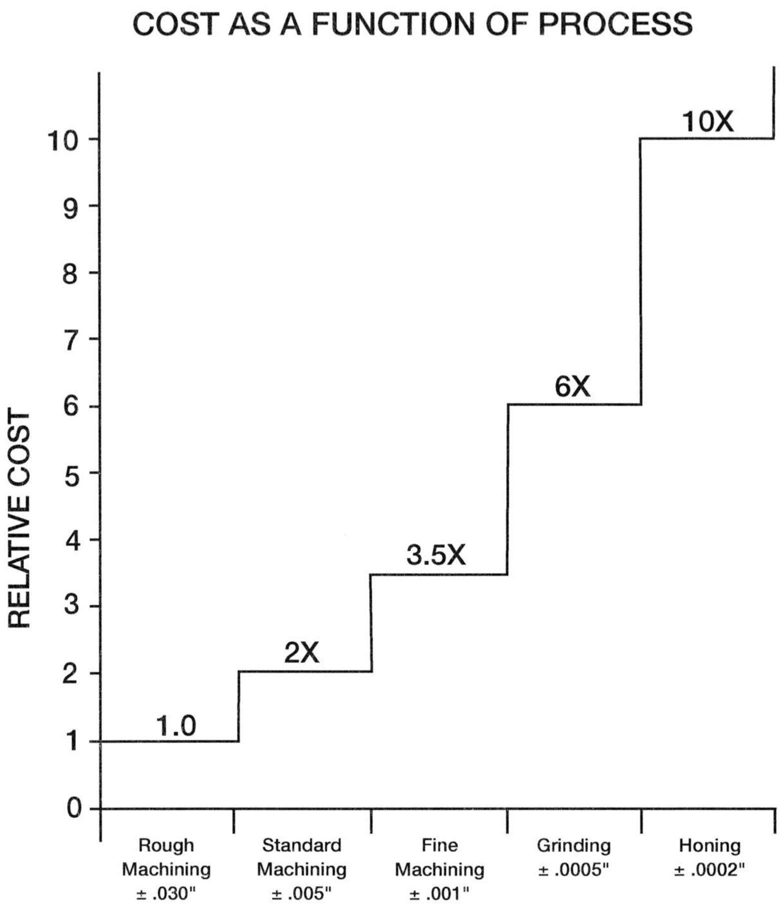

Figure 4.2: Manufacturing cost as a function of the process

As a precaution, be aware that the cost of achieving a specific tolerance varies depending on what process is used. You need to ask what is really essential.

Figure 4.2 shows the cost of machining as a function of the process. If a designer has missed providing the right tolerance, you need to work with the designer and the owner or user to get it changed.

- Use the right material:
  - Ensure you are using the right material;

        - An X-ray fluorescence (XRF) analyzer tester can be very helpful.
    - Does it require heat treat to relieve stresses or increase strength or toughness?
        - Use the right process to achieve proper material properties. If unattainable with available or current processes, use outsourcing.
- Fabricating/Welding
  - Use the right processes, such as arc, gas, resistance, solid-state, laser, etc., to achieve the right joint strength.
    - Use the right material;
    - Are there any special joints or welds that may have specific requirements? Some parts, such as pressure vessels and tanks, may require the use of certified welders.

More detailed lists of welding processes are provided in ISO4063 and are referenced as "N" numbers. The reference codes of the American Welding Society (AWS) are commonly used in North America. For example, the plasma arc welding (PAW) process carries an N15 code in ISO4063 and the equivalent number in the AWS reference code is "PAW."

- Special Process
  - Some parts can be easily made with a 3-D printing process. 3-D printing, also called additive manufacturing, is a process of making three-dimensional solid objects from a digital file. When this type of printing is used, successive layers of material are laid down under computer control.

4.2.3 Assembly Process

An assembly process is when parts or components are added in a sequential manner to create an end product (i.e., the asset). In most cases, an assembly line or area is defined as a semiautomated system in which the assembly takes place.

A consumer product, such as an automobile or a washing machine, goes through a much more automated assembly line process in which the machinery and workers are stationary along the line and the product moves through the cycle from start to finish.

For equipment or system building, it's much simpler and many times, much more manual.

Use precautions during the assembly process to:

a. Prevent damage to parts:
    1. Use proper tools, such as the right type of hammer, rubber mallet for soft material, etc.;
    2. Use special care for bearing installations, specifically for the tapered roller;
    3. Use care in the installation of oil seals, O-rings, etc.;
b. Use the right oil and lubricant for bearings, gearboxes, etc.
c. Ensure proper alignment and balancing of components, such as belts, chains, couplings, etc., within the range specified or to meet a standard. Also, if using multiple belts, ensure they are a matched set.
d. Ensure proper guarding of open moving parts to reduce safety issues.
e. Ensue proper labeling of electrical wiring, piping, switches, etc.
f. Make certain of proper use of fasteners with spring washers. Tighten with a torque wrench to ensure required torque value.

Poka-yoke is a proven, mistake proofing technique to prevent mistakes in operations and manufacturing. It's a design methodology to mistake proof the design so parts cannot be assembled or manufactured incorrectly. Simply stated, you cannot put a square peg into a round hole. Poka-yoke principles can be applied to make an asset simpler and eliminate possibilities of some defects.

If there are any changes being made to improve system design, specifically to the electrical control system, they should be documented and reflected on drawings. This documentation and revised drawings should be part of the asset documentation that becomes the service manual and documentation package that gets shipped with the asset.

These represent just a few examples of the precautions to be taken to ensure assembly is done appropriately.

4.2.4 Testing and Quality Check

Testing and final checks should be performed before the asset is ready to be shipped to the installation site. They ensure the asset meets performance and quality requirements.

The following are typical tests or quality checks that are performed. Some should be part of the customer-user requirements and others are very specific test requirements depending on the type of asset being built.

- Dimensional checks
- Leak tests, vacuum tests, etc.
- Electrical motors and systems tests
- Alignment, balancing checks
- Functional tests

The functional tests may be carried out in limited form, as some inputs and utilities may not be available at the site.

Test results should be documented and may become part of the asset data that goes along with the asset to the user.

It is highly recommended to invite the customer, specifically the user/operator and maintainer, to be part of this testing if it is not already part of the specifications and requirements.

If there are any testing requirements, such as hydrostatic, vacuum check, or other tests to be performed, you need to have the right lab equipment to conduct them. If there are tolerances or dimensional requirements to be met, you need to have a formal testing plan.

If you are using the V-model methodology discussed in Chapter 1, you must ensure that testing and verification/validation are done per plan.

4.3 Asset Packaging and Documentation

4.3.1 Packaging and Shipping

After functional tests and quality checks have been performed, the asset is prepared for shipping. The asset shipping preparation changes based on how far the asset will be traveling and whether it's within the plant, a few hundred miles away, or overseas. This may also require different surface protection treatment and shipping packaging.

Here are some helpful guidelines to follow when preparing the asset for shipping:

- Can it be shipped in one assembly, or does it need to be dismantled into two, three, or more subassemblies? Determine the best place to break down the asset and support the delicate parts appropriately in order to reduce the likelihood of parts damage.
- Do you have lifting points or hooks for safe lifting? If yes, mark them appropriately.
- Drain oil and other liquid and gases to eliminate leak potential during transit.
- Apply a protective coating or lubricants where needed to reduce damage.

4.3.2 Documentation/Manuals and Quality Test Data

Documentation that goes with the asset may include:

- Operations manual;
- Maintenance plan, preferably based on FMEA/RCM methodology;
- Recommended spares, preferably based on FMEA/RCM methodology;
- Identification of any special skills required for operator and maintainer;
- Updated or marked drawings/sketches;
- Functional test and quality check data;
- Installation preparation and installation guide.

4.4 Build/Fabricate It Right Summary and Checklist

4.4.1 Summary

As an owner or user of the asset, you need to ensure that the asset you build, whether in-house or by outsourcing, is built robust, reliable and meets specifications. The asset as built should experience minimal infant mortality failures. It needs to be built by properly skilled people using the right materials and with quality workmanship. To attain these goals, you need to get involved in the early build up stages, the assembly process, testing and collecting baseline performance data for the asset. This involvement will enable you to find design or specification omissions early and communicate with the appropriate stakeholders to improve the quality and reduce costly errors.

As a builder of the asset, you need to ensure the asset is built per specifications using the right components and built by people with the right skills. Design or specification improvements based on your manufacturability and assembly experience need to be communicated to the owner/user to improve the quality of the built asset, which will lead to reduced failures and total cost of ownership.

Some things you can do in this phase of asset build are:

- Ensure the use of the right material;
- Build or buy the right quality components;
- Fabricate and assemble components with skilled people;
- Make or suggest improvements during the build process;
- Test or check to ensure quality and reliability;
- Ensure appropriate packaging and shipping to eliminate potential damage during transit;
- Ensure proper documentation, including operations, maintenance instructions, and performance and test data, is part of the shipment.

4.4.2 Checklist

Build/Fabricate It Right Assurance Checklist		Check - √
1.	**Have you bought/used quality parts and components?**	
	a. Have you checked for counterfeit parts?	
2.	**Have you used the right material for parts and components?**	
	a. Have you checked/verified?	
3.	**Have you used good shop practices in fabricating parts and assembly?**	
	a. Have you checked for bad welds or solder joints?	
	b. Have you checked for seals or other leaks?	
	c. Have you verified that all parts are correctly positioned or placed?	
	d. Have you checked for surface contamination?	
	e. Have you checked for the right oil and lubricant for bearings, gearboxes, etc.?	
	f. Have you checked to ensure proper alignment and balancing of components, such as belts, chains, couplings, etc., within the range specified or to meet a standard? If multiple belts are used, have you ensured that they are matched sets?	
	g. Have you checked to ensure proper guarding of open and moving parts to eliminate safety issues?	
	h. Have you checked labeling of electrical wiring, piping, switches, gauges, etc.? Are they properly labeled?	
	i. Have you checked for proper use of fasteners with spring washers? Have you tightened with a torque wrench to ensure required torque value? Have you used standardized fastener sizes?	

4.	**Have you ensured that qualified people are involved in building the asset to maintain high quality?**	
5.	**Have you performed testing or checks for reliability as specified or required to ensure quality?**	
6.	**Have you ensured an appropriate packaging and shipping plan to eliminate potential damage during transit?**	
	a. Have you ensured that parts will not loosen in transit?	
	b. Have you eliminated the possibility of physical damage to the parts due to rubbing?	
	c. Have you reduced vibration in transit so parts don't get overstressed?	
7.	**Have you drained the oil and other liquid/gases, etc., to eliminate leak potential during transit?**	
8.	**Have you applied a protective coating or lubricants where needed to reduce damage during shipment?**	
9.	**Have you marked lifting points to lift the package/asset appropriately?**	
10.	**Have you included documentation and manuals as required, along with installation instructions?**	

4.5 References and Suggested Reading

1. *Design for Manufacturability & Concurrent Engineering* by Dr. David M. Anderson
2. *Production and Operations Management* by Richard B. Chase, Nicholas J. Aquilano and F. Robert Jacobs
3. *Manufacturing Processes for Design Professionals* by Rob Thompson
4. *Technical papers published and presented* by SME, www.sme.org

CHAPTER 5

INSTALL/COMMISSION IT RIGHT

Learning Objectives to Understand

- The importance of the **right** installation practices
- Why stakeholders and their involvement are important
- The value of the commissioning process
- Pre-start-up activities
- The importance of a safety culture during construction

5.1 The Importance of Installing and Commissioning It Right

Improper installation is a chronic source of asset downtime, reduced capacity, high operating costs and poor quality products. For example, if the foundation of an asset is not properly designed or built, it can "settle" where it sits, bolts can corrode or become loose, and shim packs can deteriorate, causing changes in alignment. Similarly, if the structure is not robust enough to withstand vibration where all the piping or hoses are hung or tied, it can cause damage to the asset.

Likewise, if the asset's component is a rotating type, such as a motor, gearbox, or coupling, and isn't appropriately aligned or is sitting improperly, this can cause undue vibrations from misalignment or soft foot issues, resulting in bearing failures, among others.

While installation requirements vary depending on the type of asset and its function, the right installation process, including commissioning, must be followed to ensure trouble-free asset operations.

Commissioning ensures that assets can perform to meet designed objectives and are ready for operations.

Proper asset installation and commissioning are critical in maximizing reliability and minimizing total cost of ownership during an asset's lifecycle.

Although the focus of this chapter is on equipment and machinery type assets, the best practices principles discussed here to install it right apply to all types of assets, such as buildings or infrastructures, including software and control systems. The control system, including software, should be checked and installed properly so it functions correctly and safely from the start.

The way to get started is to ***quit talking and begin doing.***

~ Walt Disney

5.2 Install It Right Process and Best Practices

Installing an asset requires careful planning prior to installation and commissioning. Proper planning assures the asset can be delivered, rigged to the location, oriented, leveled, plumbed, piped and wired without delays from existing structural restrictions. Though it's tempting to think that an asset, once installed, is effective and correctly situated, this would be premature.

The decision on whether the original equipment manufacturer (OEM), asset vendor/supplier, system integrator, or your own people will be performing the installation should already have been made earlier in the cycle during sourcing or the design phase.

Some of the planning factors to install it right are:

a. Space requirements
   - Is there sufficient space available to install the asset and its associated services and utilities, and guarantee a smooth asset operation?
   - Is there easy access for adjustments and servicing?

b. Floor and Foundation
   - Is the floor properly prepared?
   - Is the foundation for the asset appropriately designed?
   - Are utilities properly routed to the asset without causing any safety hazards?

c. Leveling and alignment
   - Can leveling and alignment of the asset be achieved without any hindrance from other sources?

d. Installation documentation
   - Are appropriate installation drawings, including for utilities, available?

e. Commissioning
   - Who will be doing the commissioning? Will it be the plant owner's personnel or an outsourced vendor?

- Does the commissioning team have a planning checklist?
- Will they provide a final punch list (i.e., issues list)? If yes, who will be responsible for fixing the issues?

f. Fixing issues
- Is there a plan available, including a timetable, for fixing issues?

g. Acceptance plan
- Is there a test plan or an acceptance plan available?
- What test will be performed to accept the asset for operation?

Before the installation process can start, ensure that all materials related to installation, the asset and its components, and other associated materials are at the site, have been inspected and are free of any damage that may have happened during shipment.

5.2.1 Install It Right Best Practices Examples

a. Foundation and grouting

The foundation must be capable of carrying the applied load without settlement, flexing, or crushing. The foundation for heavy assets and machinery is usually concrete or structural steel structures. For these installations, an independent concrete pad is poured that has sufficient mass and stiffness to support the asset and its supporting equipment. It is able to absorb the forces generated by the asset's normal operations. The total foundation mass and its related support structures should be robust to withstand the total rotating or moving mass of the asset and its associated equipment. A lack of mass and stiffness can cause normal operating forces to generate abnormal vibration levels that reduce the asset's useful life.

Rotating-type assets and heavy machinery cannot simply be installed on a concrete foundation because irregularities in the machine base and concrete surface will create load bearing issues and alignment difficulties. A concrete foundation may not be tough enough to withstand compressive and dynamic loading to support the heavy asset and machinery. For this reason, the machinery's bases are aligned and leveled with shims or jack bolts above the mechanically prepared concrete foundation and the resulting space between the machine's bases. This space is filled with a machinery grout for load and energy transfer from the asset into the foundation.

Some assets may require mounting on upper floors. In general, these assets do not have an adequate support structure. Also, direct mounting on concrete or deck plate floors introduces a resonance problem. Normal operating forces are transmitted directly into the floor, which acts as a soundboard and amplifies these energies. In many cases, these amplified energies result in higher than normal noise levels and can coincide with one or more natural frequencies of the asset or foundation, resulting in serious chronic problems.

b. Anchoring

Anchor bolts secure the asset and its supporting equipment to its foundation. The use of proper methods ensures a rigid, permanent mating of parts. When machines are anchored to a concrete foundation, J-bolts are fixed into the concrete as it's poured. Size bolts help ensure adequate holding torque and prevent them from loosening over time. Special care must be taken when selecting grades of anchor bolts and the correct determination of the mounting pattern's ability to be rigid enough to lock mounting plates to the foundation.

For assets mounted on upper floors, anchor bolt selection and configuration are even more critical. In this case, the anchor bolts must perform two critical functions: they must fix the asset in place so it cannot flex, bend, or deflect; and they must isolate the machine from the foundation to prevent transmission of generated energies into the foundation.

c. Isolation

Assets generate energy and vibration that must be either absorbed by the foundation or trapped within the machine. The energy generated by one asset is transmitted into another asset or supporting structure. It is a chronic source of reliability problems. This is especially true in plants with multiple continuous process lines, such as forging/forming presses, high-speed printing, paper machines, metal processing, slitting lines, etc.

When an asset is mounted on a concrete pad, the pad should be independent of the surrounding floor. Normally, the pad is formed and poured directly on bedrock and has a separation between it and the surrounding floor to ensure isolation. This allows energies generated by the machine to be absorbed and prevents outside sources of vibration from entering the machine. When an asset must be mounted directly on the floor, isolation must be accomplished by using springs or elastomeric pads specifically designed to absorb or stop transmission of generated energy.

Many times, isolation pads, also known as machinery mounts, can be used to isolate or minimize vibration issues.

d. Leveling

Normally, a liquid level is sufficient to level a machine properly, but it depends on the type of asset. Some assets may require laser alignment devices to properly align within specified tolerances.

The most common failure is the method used to shim mounting feet. Too many plants fail to use shim packs that provide full footprint support. Shim packs provide a rigid connection between the mounting feet and the foundation. The surfaces must be flat and parallel to ensure there are no voids or flexing in the final bolted joints.

e. Assembly

Many times, the asset may arrive in subassemblies, requiring assembly onsite. The OEM should supply all the necessary construction drawings to support assembly of the asset.

f. Alignment

Proper alignment of the asset's components, such as motors, pumps, pulleys, driven units, etc., is critical. Whereas leveling ensures the entire asset is leveled, alignment ensures the common shaft between the outboard driver bearing and the driven unit are in the same vertical and horizontal planes. Reverse dial indicators or laser alignment instruments are used to provide the required alignment adjustments.

Alignment specifications may vary depending on the asset type. But normally, the shafts must be parallel and in the same plane within a maximum of a 0.001 to 0.002 inch range.

g. Cables, hoses and other moving devices

With many assets and systems, such as hydraulic systems, robots may have moving cables, hoses and switches. Having the sufficient length of hoses, cables, or looseness will prevent failures due to rubbing or tightness.

h. Powering and utility connections

Assets and their systems require electrical and other types of utilities to operate. All utilities need to be routed to ensure the safety of all personnel who will be operating or maintaining the assets and to meet all regulatory requirements.

i. Ready to test/commission

Commissioning becomes necessary to ensure assets, their systems, facility, or plant are installed and functioning properly, and are successfully turned over to the end user.

5.3 Commission It Right Process and Best Practices

Have you ever had something that doesn't work, but discovered it long after start-up? Have you ever had an uneasy feeling that something might not be installed correctly, but don't know how to verify your suspicion?

The commissioning process can help. This process is not a new concept; it has been around for a long time, but most organizations don't do a good job in implementing it effectively.

Commissioning is a quality-focused process by which an asset and associated equipment/system, facility, or plant, which is complete or near completion, are tested to verify and document if the asset functions according to design objectives and specifications.

Commissioning is a planned, documented and managed engineering approach to the start-up and turnover of assets, systems, facilities and total plant to the end user that also meets stakeholders' expectations. It verifies what was specified, what was installed, that it functions properly and was successfully turned over to the user.

The commissioning process consists of:

a. **Planning: Pre-commissioning activities** – This phase covers activities to set up the commissioning, gather information, select the commissioning team, develop the schedule and create documentation. Key activities in this phase are:

   - Identifying/appointing the commissioning project lead/manager;
   - Defining the commissioning scope and schedule;
   - Identifying team members and getting them ready for appropriate training;
   - Collecting data, such as engineering drawings, operating procedures, etc.;
   - Developing a commissioning plan;
   - Preparing commissioning procedures, such as the standard operating procedure (SOP), test plans, checklists, etc.;
   - Identifying hazards and operability, including pre-start-up issues and possible remedies.

It is also a best practice to let the commissioning team get involved in:

1. Attending/witnessing factory acceptance tests;
2. Checking construction and build quality;
3. Cleaning and drying procedures if piping and vessels are involved.

b. **Inspections: Commissioning activities** – This phase, which traditionally has been perceived as commissioning, involves examining the facets that address the installation, inspecting, dry and wet commissioning, and start-up of the new equipment at the job site. Key activities in this phase are:

- Working with the installation team and starting to implement a commissioning plan per schedule;
- Assigning team members to assets/components to check their operation:
  - Check dry (without energy source) if possible;
  - Check wet with safe chemicals and energized;
  - Document all the results.

One of the best practices is to hire a few key operators and maintainers several months before the asset arrives at the site and make them a part of the installation and commissioning team. This way, they can participate and support the installation and commissioning process and learn how the asset and all associated equipment work. Also, they are responsible for developing operating and maintenance procedures. They document details of the installation by taking photos or video using a mobile device or other technology for future reference.

Some of these operators and mechanics may be good candidates to become area supervisors.

c. **Post Inspection: Documentation/report** - This is the final phase of the commissioning process and the one most often neglected. It entails ensuring that all paperwork for the asset and its trials are complete and updated to "as commissioned" status and that the asset and the plant have met the performance and acceptance criteria, allowing the asset or plant to be handed over to the ongoing operations group.

For optimum success in a commissioning process, the members of the project team responsible for the commissioning phase should be involved at an early stage. This ensures that all considerations related to the start-up of the asset or plant are considered.

5.4 Post Commissioning and Pre-Start-Up

As part of the planning pre-commissioning process, there should be a clear understanding of who will be fixing the issues found during the commissioning (sometimes called a punch list) and in what time frame. All issues identified need to be repaired, tested, verified and documented during the post commissioning and pre-start-up phase before the assets are ready to be operated.

It is also important that operators have been trained and certified to operate the asset, if required, before the asset is handed over for production.

The key activities in the post commissioning and pre-start-up phase are to ensure that:

- All items on the commissioning punch list have been corrected and verified. The asset should be completely checked out in a ready state to operate and produce.
- 5S or 6S principles have been applied to make the asset's work area safe and efficient. The area in which the asset will be operated should be safe, appropriately guarded and labeled.
- Operators and maintainers have been appropriately trained to perform their tasks. Total productive maintenance (TPM) concepts, if applicable, should be used in assigning the tasks.
- Standard operating procedures for operations and maintenance have been finalized and loaded into the organization's computerized maintenance management system (CMMS) or enterprise asset management (EAM) system.
- The data/information needed to evaluate asset performance has been finalized. What data, by whom and when it will be collected should be assigned, as well as how it will be displayed.

If asset performance does not meet the requirements, an agreement must be made and documented as to what level of performance is acceptable. Asset performance has three key factors:

a. Throughput level;
b. Quality level;
c. Reliability/availability.

5.5 Safety and Data Management

5.5.1 Safety

Despite risk control improvements, construction and installation remain dangerous phases, specifically in the building construction business. Construction has the second most fatal work injuries in any sector, after transportation.

In a high hazard industry like construction, safety is an investment that provides real benefits. A safe work environment helps keep skilled employees on the job and projects on track by reducing accidents that result in injuries and work schedule delays, while also reducing the risks of litigation and regulatory action. A strong safety record enhances an organization's reputation, makes it more competitive and helps to manage insurance costs over time.

Culturally, construction remains an industry where workers may feel that taking risks is part of the job and may worry about what their peers think of those who take extra precautions. Inherently, construction workers are more involved in working with large machinery and power tools, often many floors above the ground, making them more exposed to workplace injuries. But by focusing on eliminating dangers at the construction site through an approach that personalizes safety and health, companies can embrace and promote a safety philosophy throughout their organization.

This approach modifies the traditional enforcement mentality that immediately threatens employees who violate standard safety rules with disciplinary action. Shifting from a strictly compliance-driven safety program to one that emphasizes the human side of safety and stresses the health and welfare of workers is key. This personal-based safety ideology follows the premise that if employees are reminded on a daily basis of the impact an injury can have on their home life and personal relationships, they will be more likely to work safely and avoid risks that could result in accidents.

A proactive safety culture helps to save lives, retain workers, reduce claims and delays, and enhance productivity and profitability while strengthening the organization's reputation. Fostering a successful safety culture, however, is an organization-wide effort that requires commitment and participation from top management to project managers, area managers, foremen and individual workers on the job site. That commitment should extend to the selection of outsourced subcontractors who should embrace a strong safety culture as well.

Safety should be part of the process from the very beginning. In working toward establishing a safer workplace even before asset installation or building, construction begins. Once a project starts, working safely should be every employee's responsibility, every day, whatever tasks they do and wherever they do them.

Safety is not an industry-specific initiative. Before a job task is undertaken, such as installing a component, drilling a hole, or building a wall, it should be reviewed for hazards and appropriate actions taken to mitigate the risks.

5.5.2 Data Management

All the data created during the asset design, build and installation phases are very valuable and should transition into useful and usable information in the asset usage (i.e., operations and maintenance) phase through a CMMS integration. Although CMMS integration details vary depending on the owner's requirements, the project team needs to ensure that integration occurs more efficiently.

Projects typically feature building information management (BIM) software or another three-dimensional modeling software. Ideally, the software stores valuable asset or facility data that then migrates to the CMMS and an engineering database.

Any member of the project team can be responsible for taking the lead on collecting and entering asset and system data into the CMMS, but many organizations now use the commissioning phase to champion this process. As a result, the commissioning agent serves as the leader because he or she may be present in all the design and construction processes, which overlap with many of the data management steps. Due to the nature of the commissioning agent's roles and responsibilities within the project, his or her ability to help with CMMS integration should be cost-effective.

5.6 Install/Commission It Right Summary and Checklist

5.6.1 Summary

Installation and commissioning are our last opportunities to find and resolve any asset issues that might exist before the asset becomes operational. The asset's safety features will be tested soon by your operators, often inadvertently. If there's a sudden interruption of power, air, cooling water, etc., will you be able to easily and safely recover the asset? Will it stop in safe mode?

You want to be certain that all safety features operate properly now, rather than later in the operational phase. Will the asset and system meet designed performance level?

Improper installation and the lack of a commissioning process for an asset can become major contributors of downtime, reduced capacity, high operating costs and poor quality products produced. Installation and commissioning practices will not correct the inadequate or poor design, but it may identify design deficiencies.

A correct installation process ensures that you have taken care of these key elements when installing an asset, facility, or total plant:

- **Foundation:** Having the right foundation is the cornerstone of a good installation for any type of asset. It provides support for the asset for the entire lifecycle. Mass, quality, material and workmanship all should be carefully monitored as the foundation's plans are executed.

- **The prime mover (driver):** This can be an electric motor, gearbox, an engine, or a steam turbine. There are different aspects to address concerning the different types of drivers.

- **The driven components:** This can be any kind of rotating, reciprocating machinery, such as pumps, blowers, fans, etc. The maintenance and operation of the driven unit will be specific to that type of component.

- **The power transmission system:** This includes gearboxes, variable speed drives, couplings, belts, chains, etc. Many times, they do not receive the attention that they should. Speed, required torque, material and design are all factors to consider carefully during the installation process. Precision alignment is highly desired for all these components.

- **Ducting, piping and valves:** All of these are very important parts of the overall system. They all need to be properly installed with robust hangers to minimize stress and strains. Piping strain is often overlooked as a constant source of hidden equipment failures. Ensure that valves are properly sized because oversized or undersized valves can be difficult to control.

- **Electrical power and control systems:** The electrical wiring and control systems are an important part of the asset. They need to be properly and neatly laid out, without causing any obstruction to mechanical components.

- **Component naming and labeling:** All components, pipes, hoses, cables, switches, etc., should be properly labeled per engineering drawings. If there are changes in a component's configuration or cabling/wiring routes, the drawing should be redlined and properly documented.

After the asset has been installed, the commissioning process is carried out before the asset is released to operations/production. Commissioning is a quality-focused process by which an asset and its equipment/system, facility, or plant, which is complete or near completion, are tested to verify and document if the asset functions according to design objectives and specifications.

Commissioning is a planned, documented and managed engineering approach to the start-up and turnover of assets, systems, facilities and total plant to the end user that also meets stakeholders' expectations.

Commissioning verifies what was specified, what was installed, that it functions properly and was successfully turned over to the user.

Finally, the commissioning process is carried out in order to:

- Ensure what was installed was what you specified (or what you didn't get);
- Get traceable documentation of what you got (baseline data);
- Give a green light that the asset, facility, or plant is ready to operate.

Proper asset installation and commissioning are critical in reducing failures, maximizing reliability and reducing total cost of ownership.

5.6.2 Checklist

Install/Commission It Right Assurance Checklist		Check - √
1.	**Are the asset and its components easily accessible to operate and maintain?**	
	a. Are filters, reservoirs, belts and chains accessible for changeouts?	
	b. Are control panels accessible after the asset is set?	
	c. Does guarding for rotating components meet OSHA safety requirements?	
2.	**Are cables and hoses properly routed so they can't be snagged, pinched, or pulled?**	
3.	**Are all components appropriately leveled, balanced and aligned within allowable limits?**	
4.	**Has an operating envelop been identified and bounded (guarded)?**	

	a. Does the asset system have a robot or automatic extending arm that may need an additional protected area identified and fenced in for safety?	
	b. Did you ensure that the robot or automatic arm can't move outside the designated area.	
5.	**Have all lubrication points or reservoirs been provided with the right lubricant?**	
	a. Have all lubrication points been properly marked to receive the right type of lubricant?	
6.	**Do all safety features operate properly?**	
	a.Does the asset stop in safe mode if there is a sudden interruption of power, air, cooling water, etc.?	
	b. Are the asset and its system easily recoverable after a sudden interruption in utility supply?	
7.	**Are lockout/tagout instructions posted at the asset to ensure safe entry and access by operators or maintainers?**	
8.	**Are operator and maintenance manuals, including the TPM/ODR checklist, easily available? Are they available nearby or attached to the asset?**	
9.	**Have 5S principles been employed for the asset and its system?**	
	a. If not, is an implementation plan available?	
10.	**Does the asset meet its designed cycle time and product quality requirements?**	
	a. If not, is there a timetable available to achieve this?	
11.	**Have operators and maintainers been trained appropriately?**	
12.	**Is the asset ready for operations/production?**	
	a. If not, have issues been documented and is there a resolution plan available?	

5.7 References and Suggested Reading

1. *Building Commissioning* by the WBDG Project Management Committee and Commissioning Industry Leaders Council, www.wbdg.org/building-commissioning
2. *Leading the Commissioning Process,* short courses from the University of Wisconsin-Madison, Department of Engineering Professional Development, https://epd.wisc.edu/course/leading-the-commissioning-process-step-by-step-strategies-for-new-construction-projects/
3. *Chemical and Process Plant Commissioning Handbook: A Practical Guide to Plant System and Equipment Installation and Commissioning* by Martin Killcross
4. *Commissioning Fundamentals and a Practical Approach* by Timothy D. Blackburn, http://www.pdhonline.com/courses/p146/p146_new.htm
5. *Making Common Sense Common Practice, Fourth Edition* by Ron Moore, http://reliabilityweb.com/bookstore/book/making-common-sense-common-practice

CHAPTER 6

OPERATE IT RIGHT

Learning Objectives to Understand

- The role of operators in sustaining and improving reliability
- Total productive maintenance (TPM)
- Overall equipment effectiveness (OEE)
- Workplace design challenges
- Implementing 5S program

6.1 The Importance of Operate It Right

Do your operators operate their assets in the right manner? Do they have the right skill sets and use the right procedures and tools to operate those assets? Do they understand how the asset functions? The data indicates that very often, they do not.

Several studies have shown that more than forty percent of asset failures are the direct result of operational errors or unsuitable operating conditions. Some examples of these operational problems are:

- A lack of understanding on how the asset functions;
- Operators not equipped with proper tools or procedures;
- Asset abuse or misuse to meet the production quota.

These things happen because operators don't think of the asset or equipment as being "theirs." Truly speaking, they often lack the mind-set of an ownership concept.

Asset failures can be minimized or eliminated completely if operators have a good understanding of the asset and the manner in which it's operated. Operators must feel responsible for the proper operation of the assets under their control. They live and breathe with them. They need to be able to sense if something is wrong or abnormal about that asset's operation.

When you operate your own vehicle, you take ownership and operate it safely and within its operating parameters. If something doesn't feel right, you fix it or take it to a service shop to get it repaired. You take care of it by changing the oil on time or making necessary adjustments to keep it in the right operating condition. This is what an ownership concept is all about.

But if you rent a car or an appliance, you probably treat it a little differently. You may not care for it as much as the things you own. The lack of ownership creates a different mind-set altogether.

An operator of an asset is in a position to sense if there is something abnormal or out of the ordinary with it. Often, these incipient problems can be corrected cost-effectively by the operators themselves, or with timely help from the maintainers. However, if incipient problems are not corrected in time, they may result in bigger failures, costing a lot more to fix. In fact, operators should be the first line of defense in watching for abnormal conditions of an asset and initiating corrective actions. However, many organizations haven't been able to involve them successfully in maintenance because of their work culture.

There are two primary reasons for this type of work culture:

1. Division of work and organizational silos, such as:
    - Operations (production) function;
    - Maintenance function;
    - Engineering function.
2. Reward system based on:
    - Operators exceeding a certain quota (target number);
    - Maintenance fixing broken assets quickly;
    - Designers designing for the lowest cost design instead of the lowest operations and maintenance costs or total cost of ownership.

A clear division of labor exists in the workforce today. The production department operates the assets and the maintenance department fixes them when they break. Maintenance is about restoring assets to an operational state. For a maintenance team that has historically defined itself as the "fix it" guys, a paradigm shift to a culture of reliability challenges their self-preservation. They think if assets aren't failing, the value of their contribution goes unnoticed and they wonder who will value their presence.

Likewise, operators just want to operate the assets without any regard to their maintenance needs and proper operating conditions. They sometimes have trouble seeing the overall picture. They can help in reducing the number of failures by getting involved, taking proactive actions, catching failures in the early stages and working with maintenance to get failures attended to in a timely fashion. Thus, there is a need for responsible ownership from both sides.

For decades, organizations have used a reward system that has created a misaligned culture. Design teams are rewarded for achieving functional capability at the lowest cost and aren't really concerned about the downstream problems for operations and maintenance and the true lifecycle cost of ownership of the asset.

Production teams are rewarded when they exceed a production number, regardless of any real demand for the product and without any concern for the effect their actions have on asset health.

Maintenance teams typically have been rewarded for fixing asset failures and not improving reliability or availability. They get extra pay for coming in at inconvenient times when the asset is broken and get "attaboys" from management when they fix it.

If you are rewarded for failures, why would you want reliability? Who would step up and volunteer for a fifteen to twenty percent pay cut for reduced overtime?

People don't pay as much attention to what their managers say with words compared to what they actually do. If management says they want reliability—no failures or minimum failures—but keep *paying* for failures, they will continue to get failures. This culture needs to be changed and improved.

Are your operators engaged? Are they just operating the asset to produce or do they take responsibility as an asset owner? Do operators become involved and operate the asset appropriately and understand how it functions? When operators make small adjustments or repairs and call their maintenance teammates for major maintenance work, assets have very low failure rates and high uptime. Also, when operators understand how the asset and its components function, they try to do things right and not damage the asset.

Asset operators and staff spend a lot of time every day with their assets. They need to be empowered to take care of them correctly and truly take ownership of them.

When operators are involved in not only the operation of an asset to produce, but in taking care of it, it is known as total productive maintenance (TPM) or operator-driven reliability (ODR) and sometimes, operator-based maintenance (OBM). All three practices have the same outcome: the operator's involvement in operations and in supporting maintenance. The operators and maintainers become equal partners in taking care of the assets. These practices identify incipient failures early on so they can be corrected by operators and/or maintainers as a team effort with minimum impact to production.

Start by doing what's necessary; then do what's possible, and suddenly you are doing the impossible.

~ Francis of Assisi

6.2 The Role of Operations (Operators) in Asset Care

The concept of operator-driven reliability (ODR) is an integral part of an overall proactive maintenance strategy.

The objective of ODR is to help keep plants running better, longer, cost-effectively and competitively by reducing unplanned downtime and increasing uptime of production processes and associated assets.

By proactively identifying problems, operators can eliminate or reduce failures, thereby increasing reliability. Owning and operating assets constitute one of the biggest factors in the total cost of a plant. Reducing that cost by increasing asset uptime can generate additional profits without any additional expenditures.

Under the ODR concept, operators perform basic maintenance activities beyond their traditional operator duties. They take responsibility for observing and recording the asset's overall health by checking for leaks and noises, and monitoring temperature, vibration and any abnormal asset/

system conditions. In some cases, operators correct the minor deficiencies they find. They perform tasks, such as cleaning, small adjustments, lubrication and simple preventive maintenance (PM) and corrective tasks traditionally handled by the maintenance technician. These tasks represent a departure from their traditional role as just an equipment operator. ODR encourages production to interact with maintenance and other departments as a team to reduce the number of failures, thus improving plant-wide asset reliability.

In most cases, original equipment manufacturers (OEMs) recommend how equipment should be operated. OEM recommendations are sometimes made without any understanding or appreciation for the process or environment in which the asset is actually operated. OEMs also have very little (if any) knowledge of the operator's skill sets. Usually, they also require operators and maintainers to do a lot more than what is actually needed to preserve the asset's functions. This may result in too many PM tasks and unnecessary inspections, as well as time wasted collecting irrelevant information.

With operators taking responsibility for identifying problems, the probability of detecting early asset failures rises exponentially. This improvement contributes to increased asset reliability at a much lower cost due to earlier fault detection.

In many organizations, maintenance and operations departments function virtually independently of each other, effectively divorced with separate agendas. Such situations do not turn out well for organizations striving to improve productivity and profitability. ODR can serve as a bridge to those achievements by fostering and promoting internal dialogue and offering a cost-effective way to improve asset reliability. ODR encourages a culture that does not tolerate failures. It maximizes cross-functional teamwork and identifies many previously hidden opportunities for continuous improvements.

The ODR concept is similar to another maintenance strategy known as total productive maintenance (TPM), which was developed in Japan in the 1960s. The next section covers TPM in greater detail.

6.3 Building Reliability with TPM/ODR

Total productive maintenance (TPM) is a team-based asset management strategy that emphasizes cooperation between the operations and maintenance departments with a goal of zero defects, zero breakdowns, zero accidents and an effective workplace design.

TPM seeks to engage all levels of an organization and their different functions in an effort that maximizes the overall effectiveness of production assets. This helps bring improvements in existing processes and asset availability by reducing mistakes and accidents. Traditionally, the maintenance department manages the plant's maintenance programs, but TPM seeks to involve employees in all departments—including production and maintenance at all levels from the plant floor to senior executives—to ensure effective asset operation.

TPM is based on the following principles:

- Improving asset and equipment effectiveness;
- Autonomous maintenance by operators:
    - Servicing, adjustments and minor repairs;
- Planned maintenance by the maintenance department;
- Training to improve operations and maintenance skills;
- Better workplace design, including standardization of procedures and cleanliness.

A TPM program closely resembles the popular total quality management (TQM) program. Many of the tools used in TQM, such as employee empowerment, benchmarking and documentation, are also used to implement and optimize TPM. The following shows the similarities between the two programs:

a. Total commitment to the program by upper level management;
b. Employees must be empowered to initiate corrective action;

c. Required long-term strategy as it may take a long time to implement programs and make them part of the routine, ongoing process;
d. Cultural change requiring new mind-sets.

Right from the start, TPM requires effective leadership and involvement of *all* employees, from a craftsperson to senior managers. That is part of the meaning of "total" in total productive maintenance. TPM holds people accountable for performing highly specified or specialized work and improved equipment performance.

Without management support, TPM will become a program of the month and die. Many of today's business leaders have risen through the ranks when maintenance was only responsible for fixing things and not for preventing failures. Viewing maintenance as a non-value-added support function often leads to severe cost-cutting measures. This, in turn, results in higher costs due to decreased equipment effectiveness.

6.3.1 TPM Objectives and Benefits

The objectives of TPM is to:

- Achieve zero defects, zero breakdowns and zero accidents in all functional areas of the organization;
- Involve people at all levels of the organization.

These goals are accomplished by involving all employees in small group activities that identify both the causes of failures and opportunities for plant and equipment modifications. They are also accomplished by adopting the lifecycle approach for improving the overall performance of production equipment.

Benefits of TPM include:

1. Increased productivity;
2. Reduced manufacturing costs;
3. Reduction in customer complaints;

4. Customer needs are satisfied to one hundred percent:
    - Delivering the right quantity at the right time with the best required quality;
5. Reduced safety incidents and environmental concerns.

In addition, TPM creates a positive work culture and environment to:

- Build a higher level of confidence among employees;
- Keep the workplace clean, neat and attractive;
- Foster a favorable and positive attitude from operators and maintainers;
- Deploy a new concept in all areas of the organization;
- Share knowledge and experience.

Employees are empowered and gain a real sense of owning the assets they operate.

6.3.2 Implementing TPM

Many successful organizations usually follow an implementation plan that includes these ten steps:

Step 1: Announcement of TPM

Top management creates an environment that will support the introduction of TPM. Without management support, skepticism and resistance will kill the initiative.

Step 2: Launch a formal education program

This program informs and educates everyone in the organization about TPM activities, benefits and the importance of everyone's contribution.

Step 3: Create an organizational support structure

This group promotes, coordinates and sustains team-based TPM activities. It includes members from every level of the organization, from management to the shop floor. This structure promotes communication and guarantees everyone is working toward the same goals.

Step 4: Establish basic TPM policies and quantifiable goals

Analyze existing conditions, then establish TPM policies and set attainable, realistic goals.

Step 5: Outline a detailed master deployment plan

This plan identifies what resources will be needed, as well as when they will be needed for training, equipment restoration and improvements, maintenance management systems and new technologies.

Step 6: TPM kick-off

TPM implementation begins at this stage.

Step 7: Improve the effectiveness of each piece of equipment

Operations and maintenance kaizen teams analyze each piece of equipment and implement necessary improvements on a continuing basis.

Step 7a: Develop an autonomous maintenance program for operators

Operators routinely clean, inspect and perform minor maintenance tasks that help stabilize and improve equipment conditions.

Step 7b: Develop a planned or preventive maintenance program

Create a schedule for preventive maintenance on each piece of equipment.

Step 7c: Identify losses/waste and implement a reduction plan

Create kaizen teams to eliminate or reduce waste.

Step 8: Conduct training to improve operations and maintenance skills

The maintenance department takes on the role of trainers or guides, providing training, advice and equipment information to operators (kaizen teams).

Step 9: Develop an early equipment management program

Lessons learned in operations and maintenance are communicated to the design process of new equipment development. Reliability and maintainability are then built into the new design.

Step 10: Continuous improvement

As in any lean initiative, the organization develops a continuous improvement mind-set.

6.4 Workplace Design 5S

An effective workplace design that includes a targeted list of activities also promotes organization and efficiency within a workspace. These activities are known as 5S.

5S is a technique to reduce waste and optimize productivity by maintaining an orderly workplace and using visual cues to achieve more consistent operational results. In short, 5S promotes a cleaner environment and a better organized workplace.

5S is a structured program to achieve total organization-wide cleanliness and standardization in the workplace. A well-organized workplace results in a safer, more efficient and more productive operation. 5S also boosts the morale of the employees, promoting a sense of pride in their work and a responsible ownership of their equipment.

Invented in Japan, 5S stands for five Japanese words that start with the letter S: *Seiri*, *Seiton*, *Seiso*, *Seiketsu*, and *Shitsuke*. An equivalent set of five "S" words in English has been adopted by many to preserve the 5S acronym in Japanese. They are:

S1 Sort (Seiri)

Sort is the first step in making a work area organized. It refers to the act of throwing away all unwanted, unnecessary and unrelated materials in the workplace and freeing up additional space. This step makes it easier for operators and maintainers to find the things they need. It requires keeping

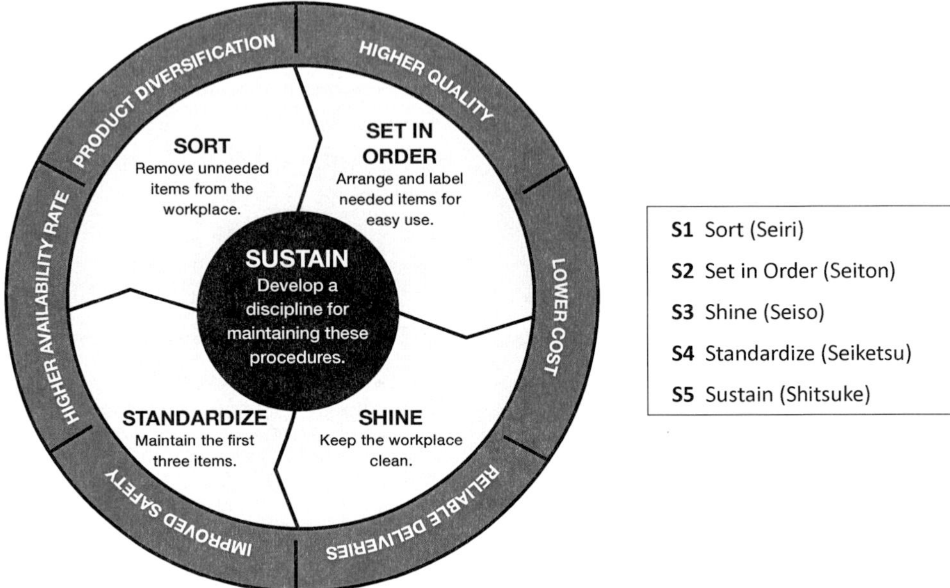

Figure 6.1: 5S process

only what is necessary. Any materials, tools, equipment and supplies that are not frequently used are moved to a separate, common storage area. Items that are not used are discarded. Don't keep things around just because they might be used someday.

As a result of the sorting process, you eliminate or repair broken equipment and tools. Obsolete fixtures, molds, jigs, scrap material, waste and other unused items and materials are discarded.

People involved in *Sort* must not feel sorry about having to throw things away. The idea is to ensure that everything left in the workplace is related to work. Even the number of necessary items in the workplace must be kept to its absolute minimum. Because of the *Sort* concept, the simplification of tasks, effective use of space and careful purchase of items will follow.

S2 Set in Order (Seiton)

Set in Order, sometimes called *Straighten*, is the second step of 5S and is all about efficiency. It requires organizing, arranging and identifying everything in a work area. Every item or material is given an assigned place so it can be accessed or retrieved quickly, as well as returned to that same place quickly. If everyone has quick access to specific items or materials, workflow becomes more efficient and the worker becomes more productive. The correct place, position, or holder for every tool, item, or material must be chosen carefully in relation to how the work will be performed and who will use which items. Every single item must be allocated its own place for safekeeping. Each location must be labeled for easy identification of its purpose.

Commonly used tools should be readily available. Properly label all storage areas, cabinets and shelves. Clean and paint floors to make it easier to spot dirt, waste materials and dropped parts and tools. Outline areas on the floor to identify work areas, movement lanes, storage areas, finished product areas, etc. Put shadows on tool boards, making it easy to quickly see where each tool belongs.

In an office environment, provide bookshelves for frequently used manuals, books and catalogs. Label shelves and books so they are easy to identify and publications can be easily returned to their proper place. Again, the objective in this step is to have a place for everything and everything in its place, with everything properly identified and labeled.

Many maintenance reliability professionals have started calling these practices of using labels and color-coded markings a "visual workplace." This practice helps operators and anyone unfamiliar with the asset or process to readily identify what is going on, understand the process and know what is to be done correctly and what is out of place. A visual workplace uses visual displays to relay information to operators and other employees and to guide their actions.

S3 Shine (Seiso)

Shine is all about cleanliness and housekeeping. The *Shine* principle says that everyone is a janitor. *Shine* consists of cleaning up the workplace and giving it shine. It's not about choosing a certain time to clean, but instead creating a habit to be clean all the time. Cleaning must be done by everyone in the organization, from operators to managers. Everyone should see the workplace through the eyes of a visitor and always ask themselves if it's clean enough to make a good impression.

While cleaning, it's easy to inspect the equipment, machines, tools and supplies you work with. Regular cleaning and inspection make it easy to spot lubricant leaks, equipment misalignment, breakage, missing tools and low levels of supplies. Problems can be identified and fixed when they are small. If these minor problems are not addressed while small, they could lead to equipment failure, unplanned outages, or long, unproductive waits while new supplies are delivered.

When done on a regular, frequent basis, cleaning and inspecting generally will not take a lot of time. In the long run, they save time.

S4 Standardize (Seiketsu)

The fourth step is to simplify and *Standardize. Seiketsu* translates to standards for all operational activities, including cleanliness. It consists of defining the standards by which personnel must measure and maintain operating and maintaining standards, such as lubrication plans, filter change out instructions, or measures of cleanliness. Visual management is an important ingredient of *Seiketsu.* The color-coding and standardized coloration of surroundings are used for easier visual identification of anomalies in the surroundings. Employees are trained to detect abnormalities using their five senses and to correct such abnormalities immediately.

One of the hardest steps is avoiding old work habits. It's easy to slip back into what you've been doing for years. That's what everyone is familiar with; it feels comfortable.

The good practices developed in earlier steps should be standardized and made easy to accomplish. As you learn more, be sure to update and modify the standards to make the process simpler and easier.

S5 Sustain (Shitsuke)

The final step is to *Sustain* the gain by continuing education, training and maintaining the standards. In fact, the word *Shitsuke* means discipline. It promotes a commitment to maintaining orderliness and practicing the first four steps as a way of life. The emphasis of *Shitsuke* is the elimination of bad habits and the constant practice of good ones.

Continue to educate people about maintaining standards. When there are changes, such as new equipment, new products and new work rules that will affect the 5S program, adjustments will be needed to accommodate those changes, modify changes in the standards and provide training that addresses those changes.

If your organization is planning to implement lean manufacturing, 5S is one of the first activities that needs to be carried out on your lean adoption.

Some organizations have added a sixth "S" to emphasize safety in their program and call it "5S Plus" or the "6S" program.

6.5 Key Performance Measures

Overall equipment effectiveness (OEE) is a key metric used in TPM and lean manufacturing programs to measure their effectiveness, as well as other initiatives. It provides an overall framework for measuring production efficiency. OEE is the traditional and most widely used metric to measure equipment and asset productivity based on actual availability, performance efficiency and product quality. However, true machine productivity is measured by total effective equipment performance (TEEP), which is based on twenty-four hours per day and 365 days per year operations. TEEP also considers equipment utilization.

OEE and TEEP measure the overall utilization of assets and equipment for manufacturing operations, directly indicating the gap between actual and ideal performance. OEE quantifies how well a manufacturing unit performs at its designed capacity during the periods when it is scheduled to run. TEEP measures how well an organization creates value from its assets by effective utilization based on twenty-four hours per day, 365 days per year availability. OEE and TEEP are joint responsibilities of operations and maintenance.

OEE and TEEP are calculated as:

OEE = Availability x Performance x Quality

TEEP = Utilization x Availability x Performance x Quality

TEEP = Utilization x OEE

OEE breaks the performance of an asset into three separate, measurable elements: availability, performance and quality. Each element points to an aspect of the process that can be targeted for improvement. OEE may be applied to any individual asset or a process. It's unlikely that any manufacturing process can run at one hundred percent OEE. Many manufacturers benchmark their industry to set a challenging target. Eighty-five percent is not uncommon.

Figure 6.2 illustrates the concepts of OEE and TEEP and how different production losses impact productivity.

There are several other measures and performance indicators that indicate efficiency of operations. Some of them are:

- Downtime as a percentage of scheduled hours (operating time):
    - Downtime due to operational issues;
    - Downtime due to maintenance;
    - Total downtime.
- 5S audits results tracking:
    - Percentage of assets covered by 5S Plus principles;
    - Asset condition and visual inspection:
        - Color-coded labels of piping, hoses, valves, etc.;
        - Checklists and PM instructions attached to the asset;
    - Required tools properly placed and labeled.

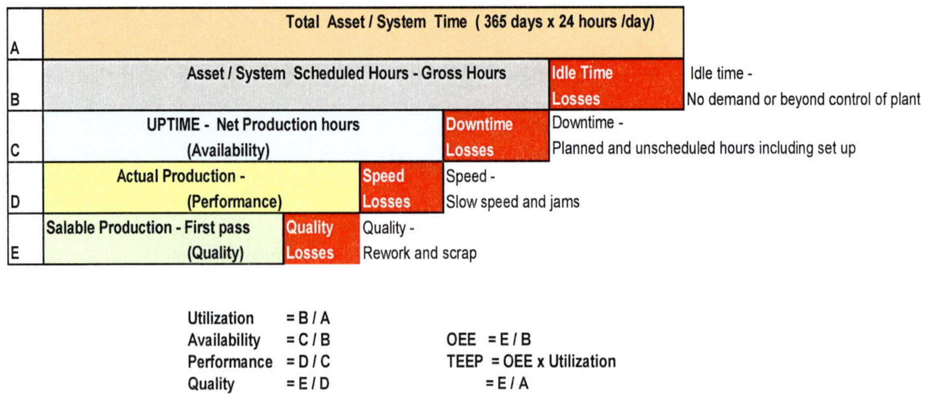

Figure 6.2: OEE and TEEP

- Asset performance and throughput:
  - Output as a percentage of designed/demonstrated capacity.
- Percentage of operational personnel involved with asset improvement projects:
  - RCM analysis support;
  - Design reviews;
  - Kaizen activities.
- Percentage of operators qualified/certified to operate assets and understand their roles, with one of the roles being to support maintenance);
- Percentage of assets ready and delivered on time to maintenance per agreed schedule.

It's good practice to track these performance measures on a regular basis to evaluate the improvements that have been made or to establish improvement goals.

Quality is pride of workmanship.

~ W. Edwards Deming

6.6 Operate It Right Summary and Checklist

6.6.1 Summary

Assets and plants are often the single largest investments for an organization. It makes sense, then, that asset reliability should be as important to the organization as the environment, health, quality and safety. But, asset reliability has not received its due emphasis in the past. Operator-driven reliability (ODR) and total productive maintenance (TPM) strategies encourage participation of all employees, specifically operators, and provide a framework for policies, procedures and structure to have assets available and operated at the lowest cost possible.

By making equipment more efficient, TPM and ODR are focused on keeping assets functioning optimally and minimizing equipment breakdowns and associated waste. Autonomous maintenance, a key pillar of TPM, seeks to eliminate major losses that can result from faulty equipment or operation by involving operators in the maintenance of equipment they operate. Under the TPM concept, equipment operators become owners of their assets. Working closely with maintenance, they take care of all details that will preserve the assets in the best possible condition.

Under autonomous maintenance, operators clean and lubricate the equipment and execute the recommended maintenance plan. They are empowered to modify the program according to the real needs and their personal observations. Operators have access to manufacturers' specifications and the support of maintenance technicians. Operators also become responsible for small adjustments, checking for parts that become loose and fixing them, as well as reporting small details, like noises, vibrations, or temperature changes, while operating the equipment.

An important factor in the success of the TPM program is the pride that operators experience from the optimal condition in which their equipment is preserved. A great deal of this improved effectiveness comes from the motivation given to employees through adequate training and education.

5S, a visual workplace system, has five elements: *Sort*, *Set in Order*, *Shine*, *Standardize* and *Sustain*. These elements are the most fundamental, but often overlooked, aspects in continuous improvement initiatives. 5S is a structured program. If properly implemented, it can achieve total organization-wide cleanliness and standardization in the workplace. A well organized workplace results in a safer, more efficient and more productive operation. It boosts the morale of employees, promoting a sense of pride in their work and ownership of their responsibilities.

Overall equipment effectiveness (OEE) is a key metric that quantifies how well an asset or a manufacturing process performs relative to its designed capacity during the periods when it is scheduled to run. It is calculated by multiplying asset availability, performance and the quality of products it produces. Another TPM-related metric is total equipment effectiveness performance (TEEP), which measures how well an organization creates value from its assets based on twenty-four hours per day, 365 days per year availability.

6.6.2 Checklist

Operate It Right Assurance Checklist		Check - √
1.	**Do asset operators perform some maintenance function as part of TPM/ODR?**	
	a. If not, do you have a plan to make this happen?	
2.	**Do operators have a good understanding on how the asset and system function?**	
	a. If not, do you have a plan to make this happen?	
3.	**Do operators take an ownership mentality when operating?**	
	a. If not, do you have a plan to improve this?	
4.	**Do operators support maintenance on major PMs and repairs?**	
	a. If not, do you have a plan to make it happen?	
5.	**Do operators support maintenance reliability improvement projects, such as RCM, failure eliminations, etc.?**	
	a. If not, do you have a plan to make it happen?	
6.	**Are operators and other operations personnel involved in implementing 5S?**	
	a. If not, do you have a plan to make it happen?	

7.	**Do operators get involved in providing input to capital projects?**	
	a. If not, do you have a plan to make this happen?	
8.	**Do you have an operator training program to assure operators have knowledge of current best practices to operate the asset efficiently and safely?**	
	a. If not, do you have a plan to make it happen?	
9.	**Do you have a training program for backup operators for specific assets to operate efficiently and safely?**	
10.	**Do you have appropriate metrics established to evaluate operations effectiveness?**	

6.7 References and Suggested Reading

1. *Operator-Driven Reliability* by Terry Wireman
2. *Making Common Sense Common Practice, Fourth Edition* by Ron Moore
3. *Secrets of Success with Procedures* by Jack Nicholas
4. *Maintenance and Reliability Best Practices* by Ramesh Gulati
5. *The Checklist Manifesto* by Atul Gawande
6. *The Visual Management Handbook* by Mary Jo Cherney and Robert Dapere

CHAPTER 7
MAINTAIN IT RIGHT

Learning Objectives to Understand

- Why do maintenance?
- Objectives of maintenance
- Types of maintenance and classification
- Value of planning and scheduling
- Maintenance optimization techniques
- Purpose of CMMS/EAM
- Need for MRO storeroom

7.1 The Importance of Maintaining It Right

All forward-looking, leading organizations understand that the best maintenance practices improve throughput and cut costs by minimizing downtime. However, the reality is that in many organizations in North America and elsewhere, up to ninety percent of the maintenance work is performed on a reactive basis rather than a proactive basis, as reported in a paper presented at the 2015 International Maintenance Conference (IMC) in Bonita Springs, Florida. Some blame the age of their equipment, the absence of spare parts, lack of a skilled workforce and lack of keeping pace with operations to meet market demands.

Catching or predicting failures before they happen and fixing them in a planned manner can yield significant cost savings and meet customer needs on schedule.

Maintenance enables an organization to keep its assets available to make products or provide needed services. The "right maintenance" ensures high asset availability, improved production yield, reliable production, improved quality, enhanced safety and improved environmental performance.

Maintenance strives to keep assets in good working condition to enable them to be used to their full productive capacity. Maintenance functions include both upkeep and repairs. The dictionary defines *maintenance* as "the work of keeping something in proper condition." A broader definition is to keep the asset in "designed" or an acceptable condition. This definition implies that the term *maintenance* includes tasks performed to prevent failures and tasks conducted to restore the asset to its original condition.

Unfortunately, literature related to maintenance practices over the past few decades indicates that most organizations do not commit the necessary resources to maintain assets in proper working condition. Rather, assets are allowed to fail, then whatever resources are needed become available to repair or replace the failed asset or components. In fact, the maintenance function has been viewed as the necessary evil and has not received the attention it deserves.

The new paradigm of maintenance relates to capacity assurance. With proper maintenance, the capacity of an asset can be realized at its designed level. The word *maintenance* has a negative connotation as something not desirable. Instead, maintenance should be referred to as "capacity assurance," which is a more positive way of looking at maintenance.

Maintenance practices have changed dramatically in the last few years. The corporate world has begun recognizing the reality that maintenance does add value. It is very encouraging to see that maintenance is moving from so-called "backroom" operations to the corporate boardroom.

Many leading organizations have started focusing and providing additional resources to improve maintenance and reliability efforts. This is also evident in the recent trend of increased attendance and participation at maintenance reliability conferences, not just across North America, but globally.

Top management of many leading organizations has started to recognize the value of good maintenance reliability programs, as well as continuous learning and sharing. Mike Harding, of Anheuser-Busch, said it very well: "As goes maintenance, so goes the business."

> *Failure is simply the opportunity to begin again, this time more intelligently.*
>
> *~ Henry Ford*

7.2 Maintenance Classifications and Prioritization

Organizations have different approaches to their maintenance programs. All approaches require keeping their assets at needed capacity levels to satisfy their current operational needs. Some of these maintenance programs are more structured than others. Some are based on reliability-centered maintenance (RCM) or reliability principles. Some organizations may develop an annual or multi-year maintenance program to guide their maintenance decisions strategically and tactically. The truth is all organizations have a maintenance plan, whether they admit it or not. Some programs are simply more costly than they need to be because organizations choose to operate in a reactive maintenance mode.

All assets require some form of care and maintenance. For example, belts and chains require adjustment; pump motor or blower motor shafts need to be properly aligned and maintained; filters need to be changed at regular intervals; and rotating machinery require proper lubrication. In some cases, individual components need to be replaced after a specified number of hours of operations, for example, a rubber coupling on a hydraulic pump to ensure uninterrupted operation. Any time you fail to perform maintenance activities on time, you may be shortening the operating reliability of the asset.

Over the past few decades, many cost-effective approaches have been developed to ensure an asset operates reliably or exceeds its design life. Instead of waiting for assets to fail and then fix them, maintenance actions are performed proactively to keep them in good working condition and obtain uninterrupted service.

Maintenance activities can be classified into two major categories: Preventive and Corrective.

Preventive Maintenance (PM) Types

- Time- or calendar-based maintenance (TBM): Primarily age related
- Run-based maintenance (RBM): Primarily usage related
- Condition-based maintenance (CBM) or predictive maintenance (PdM): Primarily health related
- Operator-based maintenance (OBM) or autonomous maintenance, a pillar of total productive maintenance (TPM): Primarily operations related

Corrective Maintenance (CM) Types

- Routine work resulting from PMs: Primarily planned and scheduled
- Major repairs/projects: Primarily planned and scheduled
- Reactive and primarily unplanned/unscheduled: Resulting from breakdowns or emergencies

This is just one way of categorizing maintenance work, but it doesn't actually matter how you categorize it. Your goal should be to collect asset performance and maintenance data and analyze it effectively to keep making improvements. Unplanned or unscheduled work usually costs three to six times more than planned work.

7.2.1 Preventive Maintenance

Preventive maintenance (PM) refers to a series of actions that are performed on an asset on schedule. That schedule may be either calendar-based or operating hours-based (e.g., run time or the number of machine cycles). These actions are designed to detect, preclude, or mitigate degradation of an asset and its components. PM work includes cleaning, adjusting and lubricating, as well as minor component replacement to extend the life of assets and facilities.

The goal of PM is to minimize asset and component degradation, thus sustaining or extending the useful life of the asset. Assets within a facility should not be allowed to run to the breaking point unless a run to failure decision has been made for each specific asset.

Preventive maintenance work can be further classified into four categories:

1. PM - Calendar-Based or Time-Based Maintenance (TBM)

TBM is typically performed based on calendar time. Maintenance personnel schedule periodic asset visits based on fixed time intervals, for example, every three or six months. Although better than no PM at all, calendar-based PMs are not the optimal way to run maintenance programs. Numerous visits to assets with "no data or abnormalities found" can be regarded as wasted maintenance dollars. If this happens, the PM periodicity should be reevaluated and adjusted. Nevertheless, time-based PMs are a good approach for assets having a fixed operating schedule, such as 24/7 or 80 hours/week operation.

2. PM - Run-Based Maintenance (RBM)

RBM is typically the next step up from calendar-based maintenance. It involves performing PMs based on asset duty cycles or run time. Intuitively, this approach makes more sense. An asset does not have to be repeatedly checked if it has not been used. In general, for many failure modes, it's the actual operation of the asset that wears it down, so the asset should be inspected after it has been working for a specified amount of time that may cause some wear. At that time, the adjustment or replacement of a component may be required.

3. PM - Condition-Based Maintenance (CBM)

Also known as predictive maintenance (PdM), this type of maintenance attempts to evaluate the condition of an asset by performing periodic or continuous asset health monitoring. The goal of CBM is to perform maintenance at a point in time when the maintenance activity is most cost-effective, yet before the asset fails in-service. The predictive component stems from monitoring the trend of asset health to determine at what point maintenance activities need to be planned and scheduled to be most cost-effective.

4. PM - Operator-Based Maintenance (OBM)

This practice uses the fact that operators are often the first line of defense against unplanned asset downtime. OBM assumes that operators who are in daily contact with the assets can use their knowledge and skills to predict and prevent breakdowns and other production losses. OBM is synonymous with autonomous maintenance and is one of the basic pillars of total productive maintenance (TPM). It involves operators taking over the asset's basic maintenance activities. The operators learn the maintenance skills through maintenance training programs and use those skills on a daily basis during operation.

7.2.2 Corrective Maintenance

Sometimes called repairs, corrective maintenance (CM) is performed to correct the deficiencies found during PM and CBM tasks, as well as after the asset has failed or stopped working. CM is also an action initiated as a result of an asset's observed or measured condition before or after the functional failure. CM activities can be further classified into three categories.

1. CM - Planned and Scheduled

This is a repair activity performed to mitigate potential asset failure or correct deficiencies found during PMs (e.g., TBM, RBM, CBM and OBM) and restore the asset's functions to its designed capacity or to an acceptable operating level. This work is generally well planned and scheduled unless an immediate failure occurs.

2. CM - Major Repairs/Projects (planned and scheduled)

In many organizations, all major repairs or improvement work, such as overhauls and turnaround projects valued over a certain threshold, are treated as capital projects for tax purposes. If these projects bring the asset back to its designed capacity and not to add additional capabilities, they are generally treated as corrective maintenance. In this case, they should always be planned and scheduled.

3. CM - Reactive (unscheduled) or Breakdowns/Emergency

This is basically repairing the assets after they fail. This work is also known as breakdown or failure repair work. Most of the time, completing this work interferes with the regular operating schedule. Unscheduled work costs much more than planned and scheduled work. This type of work should be avoided or minimized.

As noted earlier, it really doesn't matter how you classify maintenance work, as long as maintenance management systems can provide data in an appropriate format to help you make the right decisions. Your objective is to reduce failures and breakdowns and adjust maintenance activities accordingly.

Sometimes, the decision is made to take no maintenance actions or make no efforts to maintain the asset as the original equipment manufacturer (OEM) originally intended. Therefore, no PM program is established for that particular asset. This maintenance strategy, called run to failure (RTF), should be applied only after its risk to the business has been analyzed and its cost-effectiveness determined. In reality, this work should not be considered failure or reactive work because you made the decision in advance not to perform any PMs based on economic justification.

All maintenance work tasks need to be documented and classified in a CMMS/EAM system, as previously described. Then, to optimize resources, all tasks should be prioritized per the organization's priority system for execution. Every organization should establish a work and job task order priority system.

7.2.3 Work Priority

Do you have unlimited resources available to meet everybody's needs on time? Usually, you don't. Work needs to be prioritized for execution based on the availability of resources and its impact on the operation to maximize benefits of available resources.

Priority codes allow for the ranking of work orders to get work accomplished in order of importance. Too many organizations neglect the benefits of a clearly defined prioritization system. The organizational discipline that comes through communication, education and management support is key to the correct usage of priority codes. The drawbacks of not clearly defining priorities include:

- Wasted maintenance man-hours on tasks of relatively low importance;
- Critical tasks being lost in the maintenance backlog;
- Dissatisfied customers;
- Lack of faith in the effectiveness of the maintenance delivery system.

A disciplined method of prioritization eliminates tasks being done on a whim and instead allows work to proceed according to its true impact on the overall operations of the plant. It also allows the maintenance delivery function to be executed in a far more effective manner.

7.2.4 Priority System Guidelines

The system needs to cater to the following requirements equally and provide a universal method of coding all work orders:

- Plant-wide asset priorities, allowing for better plant-wide utilization of resources;
- Operations requirements;
- Improvement projects.

Accurate prioritization covers two distinct decision-making processes:

- Asset criticality;
- Impact of task or work to be done on overall operations.

The priority for work orders needs to be set by the originator of the work order and validated by someone, such as a coordinator, who has a better knowledge of operations requirements and budget/resources availability.

The work order originator is the most qualified to make an initial assessment of asset criticality and the impact of the work. Listings of major assets and their criticality help in decision-making for final priority ranking. Lower criticality items or areas are then easier to recognize.

The following criteria can be used to assign asset criticality and work impact if not corrected, which then can be used to make an objective assessment of overall job priority.

Asset Criticality Guidelines

Criticality #	Description
5	Critical safety-related items and protective devices
4	Critical to continued production/operation of primary product or service
3	Ancillary (support) system to main production/operation process
2	Standby unit in a critical system
1	Other ancillary assets

Work Impact If Not Corrected

Work Impact #	Description
5	Immediate threat to safety of people and/or plant assets
4	Limiting operations' ability to meet its primary goals
3	Creating hazardous situations for people or machinery, although not an immediate threat
2	Will affect operations after some time, but not immediately
1	Improve the efficiency of the operation process

Work Priority = Asset Criticality x Work Impact

The combination of the criticality and impact of the work can be cross-referenced to give a relative weight to each task when compared to all other work.

The asset criticality ranking could be 1-3, 1-5, 1-9, or L/M/H (low, medium, high), depending on your needs and the organization's guidelines.

The method described above is just one way of prioritizing work. You can modify it or use other approaches as long as you have a valid basis for prioritizing work.

7.3 Maintenance Optimization

Maintenance work can be looked at from two viewpoints:

a. **Work content**
   Work or maintenance activities that have been identified, such as PMs or CMs, are called work content. This work content is what you need to do to ensure assets keep working as designed.

b. **Execution of work content**
   How effectively work content is implemented is another viewpoint. This involves work planning, scheduling and managing asset data with a CMMS/EAM.

Identifying the right work and content by applying tools, such as reliability-centered maintenance (RCM) and asset health monitoring (i.e., predictive technologies) is called PM optimization. Some authors and subject matter experts include the execution of work content and call both viewpoints maintenance optimization.

7.3.1 Reliability-Centered Maintenance

Reliability-centered maintenance, more commonly known as RCM, is a process to ensure that assets continue to do what their users require in their present operating context. It's a structured process for developing an efficient and effective maintenance plan for an asset to minimize the probability of failures.

RCM is generally used to achieve improvements in all aspects of asset management, such as establishing safe minimum or optimum levels of maintenance, changing operating procedures and establishing an effective maintenance plan. Successful implementation of RCM promotes cost-effectiveness, asset uptime and a better understanding of the level of risk that the organization is presently managing.

It is also a systematic approach for developing new maintenance requirements where a program does not exist and optimizing an existing maintenance program. In both cases, the result of RCM analysis is a maintenance program composed of tasks that represent the most technically correct and cost-effective approach to maintaining asset/component operability. This operability, in turn, lends itself to improved system reliability and plant availability. Another important result of an RCM program is a documented technical basis for every maintenance program decision.

RCM development is an evolutionary process. Over forty years have passed since its inception, during which RCM has become a mature process. However, the industry has yet to fully embrace the RCM methodology in spite of its proven track record. Anthony (Mac) Smith, John Moubray and Jack Nicholas have been leaders in creating increased RCM awareness.

Reliability-centered Maintenance by John Moubray and *RCM: Gateway to World Class Maintenance* by Anthony M. Smith and Glenn R. Hinchcliffe are two leading books in this field. In recent years, other books by Jack Nicholas, Neil Bloom, Douglas Plucknette and Nancy Regan have appeared in this field with new implementation approaches.

It has been demonstrated that the best application of RCM is during the asset's design and development phases to eliminate or mitigate the effects of failure modes.

The objective of RCM is to maintain the inherent reliability of the system's function. A maintenance program can only maintain the level of reliability inherent in the system design—no amount of maintenance can overcome poor design. This makes it imperative for maintenance knowledge to be fed back to designers to improve the next design. RCM recognizes the difference between perceived design life, or what the designer thinks the life of the system is, and actual design life. RCM explores this through the age exploration (AE) process. RCM is driven by safety first, then economics. Safety must be maintained at any cost. It always comes first in any maintenance task.

7.3.1.1 The RCM Principles

Four principles define and characterize RCM and set it apart from any other preventive maintenance (PM) planning process.

Principle 1: The primary objective of RCM is to preserve system function

This principle is one of the most important and perhaps the most difficult to accept because it is contrary to our ingrained notion that PMs are performed to preserve asset operation. By addressing system function, you want to know what the expected output should be, as well as understand that preserving that output (function) is your primary task at hand.

Principle 2: Identify failure modes that can defeat the functions

Because the primary objective is to preserve system function, the loss of function is the next item of consideration. Functional failures come in many sizes and shapes. They're not always as simple as, "We have it or we don't." The loss of fluid boundary integrity in a pumping system illustrates this point. A system loss of fluid can be:

1. A minor leak that may be qualitatively defined as a drip.
2. A fluid loss that can be defined as a design basis leak. That is, any loss beyond a certain flow value will produce a negative effect on system function, but not necessarily a total loss.
3. A total loss of boundary integrity, which is defined as a catastrophic loss of fluid and loss of function.

In this example, a single function—preserve fluid integrity—led to three functional failures. The key point of Principle 2 is to identify specific failure modes in a specific component that can potentially produce those unwanted functional failures.

Principle 3: Prioritize function needs (failures modes)

All functions are not equally important. A systematic approach is taken to prioritize all functional failures and failure modes using a priority assignment rationale.

Principle 4: Select applicable and effective tasks

Each potential PM or CBM task must be judged as being applicable and effective. Applicable means that if the task is performed, it will accomplish one of three reasons for doing PM or CBM:

1. Prevent or mitigate failure;
2. Detect the onset of a failure;
3. Discover a hidden failure.

Effective means you are sure that this task will be useful and you're willing to spend resources to do it.

7.3.1.2 RCM Standard – SAE JA1011

The SAE International standard for reliability-centered maintenance, JA1011, describes the minimum criteria to which a process must comply to be called RCM. An RCM process answers the following seven essential questions:

1. What are the functions and associated desired standards of performance of the asset in its present operating context (functions)?
2. In what ways can the asset fail to fulfill its functions (functional failures)?
3. What causes each functional failure (failure modes)?
4. What happens when each failure occurs (failure effects)?
5. In what way does each failure matter (failure consequences)?
6. What should be done to predict or prevent each failure (proactive tasks and task intervals)?
7. What should be done if a suitable proactive task cannot be found (default actions)?

Any analysis that can answer these seven questions can be called an RCM process.

7.3.1.3 RCM Analysis Process

Although RCM has a great deal of variation in its application, most procedures or process include some or all of the following nine steps:

1. System selection and information collection;
2. System boundary definition;
3. System description and functional block diagram;

4. System functions and functional failures;
5. Failure mode and effects analysis (FMEA);
6. Logic (decision) tree analysis (LTA);
7. Selection of maintenance tasks;
8. Task packaging and implementation;
9. Making the program a living one by making continuous improvements.

Unlike other maintenance planning approaches, RCM results in all of the following tangible, actionable options:

a. Maintenance task schedules, which can include:
   - Time-directed (TD) tasks (i.e., calendar/run time based PMs);
   - Condition-directed (CD) tasks (i.e., CBM/PdM tasks);
   - Failure finding (FF) tasks (i.e., operator supported tasks);
   - Run to failure (RTF) tasks (i.e., economic decision-based).
b. Revised operating procedures for the operators of the assets, which might include service type tasks, such as changing filters, taking oil samples and recording operating parameters;
c. A list of recommended changes to the design of the asset that would be needed if the desired performance is to be achieved.

An RCM is summarized in Figure 7.1. Details of the RCM process can be found in any of the books listed in the References and Suggested Reading section at the end of this chapter.

7.3.2 Condition-Based Maintenance

Condition-based maintenance (CBM), also known as predictive maintenance (PdM) or asset condition management (ACM), attempts to evaluate the condition of an asset by performing periodic or continuous asset health monitoring. Based on asset health condition, maintenance is performed at a point in time when it is most cost-effective, yet before the asset fails in service.

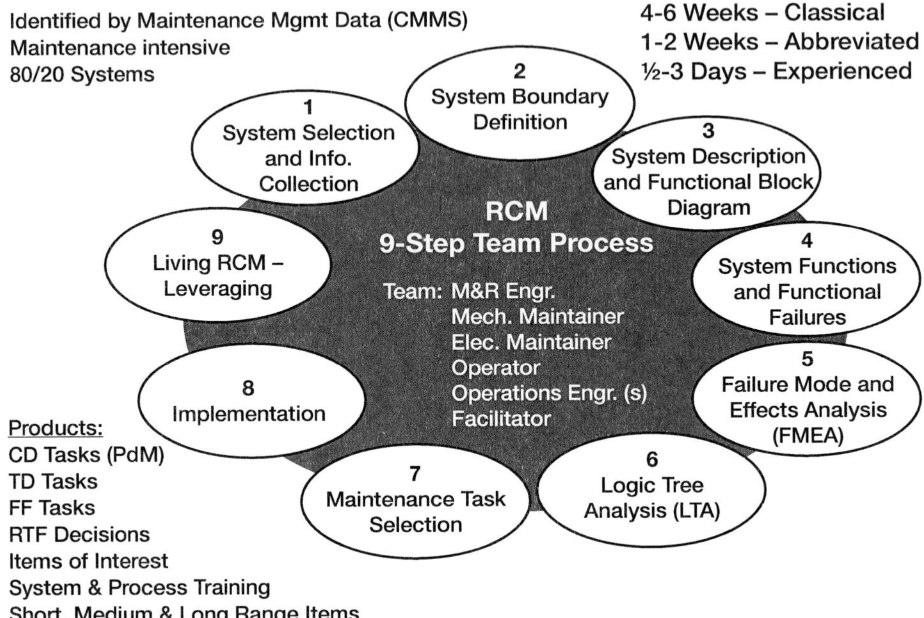

Figure 7.1: RCM process

CBM inspections mostly are performed while the asset is operating, thereby minimizing disruption of normal system operations. Adopting CBM/PdM in the maintenance of an asset can result in substantial cost savings and higher system reliability.

A number of different CBM/PdM technologies can be used to evaluate an asset's condition. A few of the more common technologies are:

a. Vibration Analysis (Vib);
b. Alignment and Balancing (Ab);
c. Ultrasonic Testing (Ut);
d. Infrared Thermography (Ir);
e. Machinery Lubrication (Lu);
f. Oil Analysis (Oa);
g. Motor/Electrical Testing (Mt);
h. Nondestructive Testing (Ndt);
i. Asset Condition Information (Aci).

Basically, in the CBM approach, the need for maintenance is based on the actual condition of the machine, rather than on some preset schedule. Activities, such as changing oil, are based on a predetermined schedule or time, such as calendar time or asset run time. For example, most people change the oil in their cars every 3,000 to 5,000 miles driven. This is effectively basing the need for an oil change on asset run time. No concern is given to the actual condition and performance capability of the oil. It is changed because it's time to change it. This methodology would be analogous to a preventive maintenance task.

On the other hand, if you ignore the vehicle run time and have the oil analyzed at some regular period to determine its actual condition and lubrication properties, then you may be able to extend the oil change until the car has been driven 10,000 miles, or maybe even more.

This is the advantage of utilizing condition-based maintenance. CBM is used to define needed maintenance tasks based on quantified asset conditions or performance data. The advantages of CBM are many. A well established CBM program can eliminate or reduce asset failures cost-effectively and helps in scheduling maintenance activities to minimize overtime costs. In addition, CBM allows you to minimize inventory and order parts as required, well ahead of time to support downstream maintenance needs.

Several CBM technologies can be used to assess the condition of an asset or system. In some instances, a number of technologies are used together to provide a more accurate picture of the asset's condition.

A short discussion on each technology is provided in Appendix D Maintenance – Condition-Based Maintenance in the back of this book.

7.3.3 Other Optimization Practices

a. Operator-Based Maintenance Program

Unlike what is typically assumed, the operator is actually one of the most important members of the maintenance team. Well-informed, trained and responsible operators ensure that assets are being kept in good working order.

Operators are the first line of defense against unplanned asset downtime. An operator-based maintenance (OBM) program assumes that operators who are in constant contact with the assets, because they are there to operate them, can use their knowledge and skills to predict and prevent breakdowns and other failures and losses.

The key objective of an OBM program, also known as an autonomous maintenance program, is to equip operators with the following asset-related skills:

- Ability to detect abnormalities;
- Ability to correct minor abnormalities and restore function, if they are able to;
- Ability to set optimal asset conditions;
- Ability to maintain optimal equipment conditions.

Operators learn the maintenance skills they need through a training program. They then perform the following tasks:

- Conduct general inspection;
- Keep assets clean and all areas accessible;
- Identify and eliminate problem sources;
- Support and create cleaning and lubricating standards and procedures;
- Standardize through visual workplace management;
- Implement autonomous asset management;
- Perform minor maintenance and service items, such as replacing filters, lubricating and changing the oil;
- Work with the maintenance team to repair what they are unable to perform.

Operators use the following four sensory tools to identify problem areas:

1. Look for any abnormalities: clean, in place, accessible;
2. Listen for abnormal noises, vibrations, or leaks;
3. Feel for abnormally hot or cold surfaces;
4. Smell to detect abnormal burning or unusual odors.

Operators can detect any abnormalities and symptoms at an early stage and then either fix them or request help to get the problems repaired before they turn into major failures.

Operations and maintenance (O&M) personnel ensure that all assets are properly secured and bolted, and support structures, such as piping, hoses, guards, etc., are not loose and vibrating, but rather properly fastened.

Another area is cleaning. Cleaning leads to inspection and timely detection of any incipient failures, like cracks and damaged belts. Dirt and dust conceal small cracks and leaks. If an asset is clean, you can assess if things are not working right, such as leaking, rubbing and bolt loosening, which may be an indication of an incipient failure.

Keeping assets and the surrounding area clean creates a good feeling and improves employee safety and morale.

This practice is also called operator-driven reliability (ODR), as discussed in Chapter 6.

b. Operating and Maintenance Procedures

All operating and maintenance procedures available at the site should be current. Are these procedures easily understood? Do operators know how to shut down or safely provide lockout/tagout for the asset in case of an emergency? Do they know what operating parameters (e.g., pressures, temperature, trip/alarm settings, etc.) to watch? Make sure operators and other support personnel have a good understanding of the answers to these questions. It's good practice and very desirable to have these operating instructions laminated and attached to the asset.

You need to ensure that maintenance/repair procedures are current when used. Maintenance personnel should have the right tools available to perform maintenance correctly and effectively. Having a current procedure is an ISO principle.

When an asset is ready to be repaired, all items identified in the work plan should be staged at the asset site for craft personnel to execute their work in the most effective and efficient manner. Specialized tools should be kept at or near the asset with proper markings.

It's good practice to laminate the procedures, drawings, parts list, wiring diagrams, logic diagrams, etc., and make them available at or near each asset location.

c. Repair Documentation

Repair documentation, which describes in some detail what repairs you performed to the asset, is very important when performing an analysis. You often see entries, such as "Pump broke, repaired" or "Mechanical seal replaced." Such entries merely help in maintaining failure statistics, but do not help in failure analysis.

The challenge is how to make data input easy for your crafts personnel. For a good reliability analysis, you need to have quality data to understand how the asset was found before and after the failure, what actions were taken to repair it, the parts used, the time taken to repair, etc.

7.4 Work Management and Maintenance Execution

Section 7.3 discussed maintenance tasks and work content optimization practices. This section explains how to execute those tasks effectively. Some of the key elements in task execution or work management are:

- Workflow Process;
- Work Planning Process;
- Work Scheduling Process;
- MRO Stores and Inventory Management;
- CMMS/EAM and the Maintenance Data System.

The following subsections discuss each one of these separately.

Maintenance tasks should be performed efficiently to ensure that plant capacity is sustained cost-effectively. Furthermore, to reduce overall operations and maintenance costs, these tasks must be executed efficiently and effectively. Basically, this is achieved by eliminating or minimizing avoidable delays and wait times.

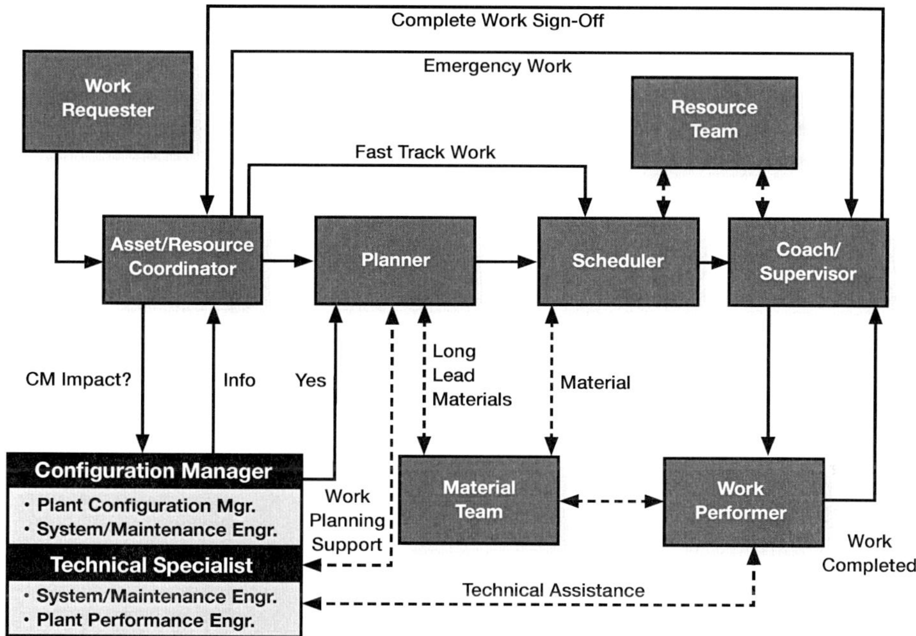

Figure 7.2: Workflow process and roles

7.4.1 Workflow Process

Figure 7.2 illustrates the workflow and key players in the maintenance workflow process. Key players in this process are:

- Work Requester;
- Coordinator - Asset/Resource;
- Planner;
- Materials Team or MRO Store;
- Configuration Specialist/Systems Engineer;
- Scheduler;
- Resource Team;
- Craft Supervisor;
- Work Performer;

Initially, the required or requested work task gets routed to an asset/resource coordinator. This person represents the asset owner and may work for maintenance or operations. The coordinator helps to prioritize the work, ensuring required resources are in the budget and scheduling asset outages, if necessary.

The coordinator forwards the work task to a planner, scheduler, or directly to the craft supervisor or maintenance crew, depending on the task's priority and planning needs. For example, PM-type work, which already should be planned, could go directly to the maintenance scheduler. The coordinator may also collaborate with the maintenance engineer or configuration management personnel for any technical help or if a configuration change request is needed.

The materials team or MRO store works with the planner and scheduler to arrange for required material.

The resource team supports the scheduler if additional people or other resources are needed temporarily from another part of the organization or via outsourcing.

The planner's and scheduler's roles are discussed in the next two subsections, respectively.

The craft supervisor and his/her team execute the task according to plan and document the work completed.

7.4.2 Work Planning Process

This is the process for determining what work needs to be done and how it will be performed. It involves identifying work that may need to be validated and determining the resources and methods needed, including tools, skills, safety precautions and time to perform the work effectively and efficiently.

Work (maintenance) planners plan the job and create a job or task package that consists of what work needs to be done, how it will be done, what materials, tools, or special equipment are needed, estimated time and skills required. The planners need to identify long delivery items and work with stores and purchasing personnel to ensure timely delivery. Planners may need to work with maintenance/systems engineers and craft supervisors for technical support to ensure the work plan is feasible with sufficient technical details.

The best method for determining the planners' workload is by the number of technicians for which work is planned. A good ratio of maintenance technicians to planner ranges from 10:1 to 20:1 (average 15:1).

In general, every hour invested in work planning saves one to three hours in work execution. Abraham Lincoln once said, "Give me six hours to chop down a tree and I will spend the first four sharpening the axe."

7.4.3 Work Scheduling Process

This is the process for determining when the work will be performed and by whom. It involves working with operations, production, maintenance and other resource owners to determine the best time to schedule the work based on resources availability, including materials.

Work (maintenance) schedulers, working with the craft technician supervisor, coordinator and other support staff, develop weekly, monthly and rolling annual long-range plans to execute maintenance work. They are more concerned with when the job should be executed in order to optimize the available resources with the work at hand.

Craft supervisors take the weekly schedule and assign who will do the job on a daily basis. In addition, they review work plans from an execution point of view and recommend necessary changes to the planner and scheduler. It is also their responsibility to ensure the work's high quality is maintained and the details of work completed are documented properly in the system.

7.4.4 MRO Stores and Inventory Management

The maintenance storeroom plays an important role in supporting the maintenance function. The objective is to provide the right spares, service parts and supplies at the right time, in the right quantities, at the right location. If the right part is not available when needed, the repairs have to be delayed. Any delay in restoring a failed asset increases maintenance and operations costs. Thus, a storeroom may be considered a very important enabler in reducing maintenance costs.

Also known as the maintenance, repair and overhauls or MRO storeroom, a maintenance storeroom is responsible for these functions:

- Providing the right spare parts, supplies and tools;
- Delivering the needed items to the right location at the right time.

These major responsibilities of a maintenance storeroom can be met with good advanced planning based on best practices. However, for certain parts, these expectations could be unrealistic due to cost, unexpectedly high failure rates and high lead time. Maintenance, engineering, purchasing and management must work together in developing a plan to determine the most economical stocking levels for critical items. Some items have small or negligible lead times and can be bought with very little lost time. As such, these items likely do not need to be stocked.

The right time to decide which parts and materials should be stocked and in what quantity is before placing an asset or system in service. The manufacturers of the assets and systems typically provide a recommended list of spare parts, as well as a preventive maintenance program based on a failure mode and effects analysis (FMEA). The failure modes and frequency of failures should optimize the spares list and provide a good estimate of what and how many are required to be stocked during a specified period.

Holding all critical parts in inventory can result in very high MRO storage expenses. Consider partnering with local industry and vendors for sharing some critical spares. Eliminating idle inventory is possible by negotiating delivery controls and establishing vendor trust.

Focus on implementing these best practices to improve MRO store effectiveness:

- Create a culture that emphasizes the storeroom as a service provider, with its objective to provide the right parts and materials at the right location at the right time.

- Ensure inventory accuracy:
    - Perform daily or weekly cycle counting as part of routine storeroom operations.
- Use bar codes or a radio-frequency identification (RFID) system to streamline data entry and reduce errors.
- Build PM/repair kits in advance.
- Establish shelf life and a PM program for stored items.
- Ensure all parts and materials get charged to the correct asset.
- Establish key performance indicators (KPIs) to measure and track performance.

7.4.5 CMMS/EAM and the Maintenance Data System

A maintenance management system is an essential tool for all maintenance organizations. It can help improve a maintenance department's efficiency and effectiveness and, ultimately, get more out of assets by streamlining critical workflows, work identification and work task planning, scheduling, and reporting.

There are two types of systems available. One is an enterprise-wide collection of modular applications, such as asset management, material resource planning, finance and human resources. These applications or systems interface with each other seamlessly and can work effectively across many locations and plants. Most of these systems, first developed in the mid-1990s and early this decade, are known as enterprise asset management (EAM) systems and typically can be expensive to install.

Other types of systems are stand-alone applications related to maintenance management. They can be interfaced with other enterprise-wide systems, such as finance or human resources systems. These systems are called computerized maintenance management systems (CMMS).

The CMMS name was coined in the late 1970s and 1980s when PM programs were automated using computers. New computerized maintenance management systems have a lot more capabilities and functionalities. They are easier to use compared to some EAM systems.

There are over a hundred systems available on the market, starting from $1,000 to over $250,000, depending on the number of users or the size of the plant. Most of the systems are now Web-based and a CMMS can be rented or leased on the Web for just a few dollars per asset. Today, there are basically no major differences in the way both types of systems function, so the terms CMMS and EAM are often used interchangeably.

7.4.5.1 Current Trends

One of the most important trends seen in CMMS/EAM is the improvement in user-centered design or usability during recent years. For those CMMS packages with rewritten software to become Web-based, the new, improved user interfaces have become more user-friendly. To compare prospective CMMS vendors, some users have even developed several scenarios to assess how many screens it takes to complete a given series of tasks and over what time. Some compare how many screens or clicks are typically needed to get the information they need.

Another key trend in user-centered design is the flexibility in customizing the application to the varying needs of individuals or tailoring it to different roles, such as maintenance planner, scheduler, supervisor, craftsperson and stockkeeper. This trend has been widely accepted by users as it decreases training time, simplifies the execution of day-to-day processes, improves accuracy and speed of data entry, and facilitates extraction of relevant information that leads to better and faster decision-making.

7.4.5.2 Data Analysis and Reporting

Users are slowly learning the incredible power of a CMMS to take raw data and turn it into information and knowledge that can improve maintenance effectiveness dramatically through the use of analysis tools. It's not enough to collect data and report on it. A CMMS can take the data and then, by using analysis tools, convert it to helpful information.

There are a few companies who can connect to your CMMS/EAM and provide very valuable information and reports to make decisions.

7.4.5.3 Mobile Technology

The popularity of mobile technology continues to rise as more users realize its power. Meanwhile, telecommunications networks continue to expand their geographic reach and their ability to handle interference.

Handheld devices are also improving in terms of functionality and affordability. Much of the functionality of a desktop computer can be put in the hands of a mobile user, including uploading and downloading work orders and spare parts inventory information, accessing equipment history and reports, and even viewing or redlining drawings and maps.

Mobile technology is one of the most important trends being adopted in the CMMS industry, just like tablets, notebooks and smartphones took the business world to a whole new level.

A CMMS/EAM is a valuable tool for ensuring that quality maintenance-related data is collected. It can help in enforcing good maintenance practices. The key is to select the correct, appropriate system to meet operational needs, then implement it correctly and provide the proper level of resources. The CMMS and control systems, including related software, are the key components of the asset(s). They should be considered a part of the asset and maintained appropriately with the right strategy.

The Internet of Things/Industrial Internet of Things (IoT/IIoT) is another emerging technology that connects assets, its components and devices to each other through a network of nodes that transmits data via the Internet to collect data and supporting decision-making. You need to ensure that IoT/IIoT is part of the asset maintenance management system.

IoT/IIoT is discussed in more detail in Chapter 10.

7.5 Performance Measures and Benchmarks

It's often said that, "what gets measured gets done" and "if you can't measure it, you can't improve it." Key performance indicators (KPIs), also called metrics, are an important management tool to measure performance and help you make improvement actions. However, too much emphasis on performance indicators or on the wrong indicators may not be the right approach. The selected performance measures shouldn't be easy to manipulate just to "feel good."

The following criteria are recommended for selecting the best KPI/metrics:

- Should encourage the right behavior;
- Should be difficult to manipulate;
- Should be easy to measure data collection and reporting.

Some key maintenance metrics with some benchmark data are listed in Table 7.1.

Table 7.1: Maintenance KPIs and Benchmarks

	Metric	Typical	Best of the Best (World-Class)
1.	**Breakdowns - CM Reactive** -- CM reactive/total PM+CM	40% - 60%	**< 10%**
2.	**Planned Maintenance Work** -- Planned work/total work (PM+CM+)	40% - 70%	**> 90%**
3.	**Production Loss Time** -- Downtime/total scheduled time	2% - 10%	**< 1%**
4.	**Overtime** -- Maintenance overtime (hours)/ total maintenance work (hours)	5% - 25%	**< 5%**
5.	**Schedule Compliance** -- Work (MHs) accomplished/total (MHs) scheduled	40% - 90%	**> 90%**
6.	**Parts and Kits Delivered on Time** -- Parts delivered on schedule/total parts delivered	70% - 95%	**> 95%**
7.	**Maintenance Inventory Turnover Ratio (Inventory Turns)** -- Inventory issued (year)/average inventory (year)	0.1 - 1.5	**> 1.5**

8.	**Maintenance Backlog - Weeks** -- Total maintenance work pending/ maintenance MHs available per week	0 - 30 weeks	**4 - 6 weeks**
9.	**Maintenance Personnel Certified/Qualified to Maintain and Operate Assets and Use Improvement Tools** -- Maintenance personnel certified and/or qualified/total maintenance personnel	0% - 30%	**> 30%**
10.	**Maintenance Cost Percent of Asset Replacement Value** -- Maintenance cost in a period/ total replacement value of assets in a period	2% - 10%	**2 % - 3.5%**

7.6 Maintain It Right Summary and Checklist

7.6.1 Summary

Maintain It Right is a practice that prevents an asset or item from failing and repairs it quickly if it *has* failed. The new paradigm for maintenance is capacity assurance, meaning that maintenance assures asset capacity as designed or to an acceptable level.

Maintenance activities can be classified into two major categories: preventive and corrective. Preventive maintenance (PM) is the basic asset maintenance strategy that many organizations use to begin their formal maintenance program. Most PM programs are either calendar time-based or asset run time based.

RCM and CBM/PdM are used to optimize maintenance tasks and activities. RCM is a process that determines what must be done to ensure assets continue to do what their users need them for in a certain operating context. RCM analysis provides the maximum benefits if it is performed during the asset's design/development phase. Condition-based maintenance (CBM) is based on using real-time health data to assess the condition of the assets utilizing predictive technologies, with maintenance performed only when necessary.

Corrective maintenance (CM) has two components: fixing failures (reactive) and repairing all other findings in a planned manner (proactive).

Run to failure (RTF) is another economically valid strategy for specifically identified assets and systems. This strategy must be deliberately selected for non-critical assets only. It should be documented and planned with the right level of support, such as spare parts.

Planning and scheduling (P&S) is a disciplined approach, both for utilizing maintenance resources effectively and executing maintenance tasks efficiently. Although planning and scheduling are closely related, they are two distinct functions.

- Planning: *what and how*
- Scheduling: *when and who*

Planning and scheduling have the highest potential impact on the timely and effective accomplishment of maintenance work.

Computerized maintenance management systems (CMMS) are essential data-based, decision-making tools for managing the asset. A CMMS or EAM supports a maintenance department to ensure assets and systems operate efficiently to minimize downtime.

Providing the right parts at the right location and at the right time is an important function of MRO stores. Managing inventory/material and parts storage effectively is a key strategy that can't be overlooked. The decision concerning what spares to stock should not be based on vendors' recommendations, but rather on FMEA/RCM analysis, the stocking costs, the lead time to procure and the impact on operations if spares are not in stock.

Skilled, trained and motivated maintenance personnel are essential for achieving a quality maintenance program. Selecting the right performance indicators to measure maintenance performance is critical, while implementing best practices is also important. The indicators should encourage the right behavior.

The purpose of maintenance is to keep the asset or equipment running. But more to the point, maintenance is all about managing risk. Assets provide function(s). Some examples, a pump provides or transfers a certain quantity or volume of fluid at a certain pressure; a valve diverts or stops the fluid flow; a motor provides a rotational or linear motion with some torque. Several functions together produce a product or service that you deliver to your customers. Maintenance's task is to keep those functions working.

To determine the right amount of maintenance, you need to do risk management. This depends on what you and/or the asset owner/organization values. If an organization only cares about throughput, it may not do required maintenance and only fix the asset when it breaks. Another organization may put value in delivering quality product on time. That means it has to have a good, robust (i.e., right) maintenance program to ensure all asset functions work reliably within tolerances to produce a quality product. The organization is taking less risk and putting more value in

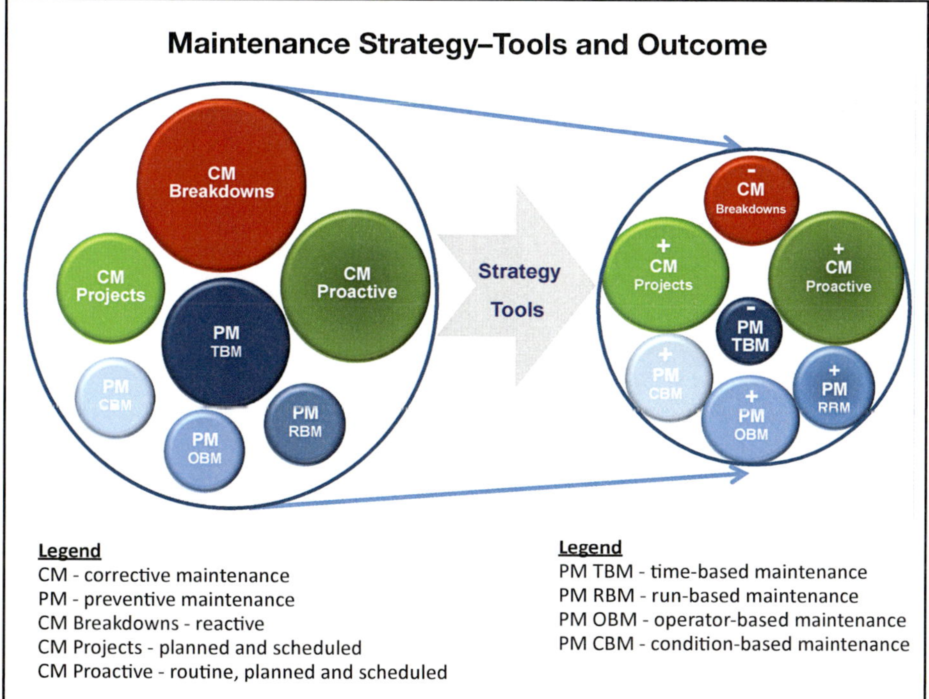

Figure 7.3: Application of strategies and tools to optimize maintenance

customer satisfaction by consistently delivering a quality product on time. This organization will stay in business, whereas other organizations may do well for a short period of time, but may not last for long.

The right applications of strategies and tools discussed in this chapter should improve uptime and reduce total cost of maintenance, as shown in Figure 7.3 (See page 137). Some elements will reduce and some will increase. However, the total impact will be in the reduction of maintenance costs.

7.6.2 Checklist

Maintain It Right Assurance Checklist		Check - √
1.	**Is every asset accounted for (i.e., listed) in the CMMS's asset register?**	
	a. If not, do you have a plan to make this happen?	
2.	**Has asset criticality analysis been performed?**	
	a. If yes, has a criticality number been assigned to each asset in the CMMS?	
	b. If not, do you have a plan to accomplish this?	
3.	**Have you used an appropriate naming structure (i.e., taxonomy) and hierarchy for the asset and its components?**	
	a. If not, do you have a plan to improve?	
	b. Do you have a standard policy/procedure to establish taxonomy and hierarchy?	
4.	**Do you have the right CMMS/EAM to support the maintenance reliability function? Are you satisfied with its performance?**	
	a. If not, do you have a plan to improve or replace it?	
5.	**Do you have a PM plan, including RTF, for every asset in the CMMS/EAM?**	
	a. If not, do you have a plan to improve?	

6.	**Do you measure/evaluate PM effectiveness on a regular basis?**	
	a. If not, do you have a plan?	
7.	**Does every PM task link to a failure mode?**	
	a. If not, do you have a plan to improve?	
8.	**Do you have a work planning process?**	
	a. If yes, is planned work less than 90 percent? If yes, do you have a plan to improve?	
9.	**Do you have a scheduling process?**	
	a. If yes, is scheduling compliance less than 90 percent? If yes, do you have a plan to improve?	
10.	**Do you have appropriate metrics established to evaluate maintenance effectiveness?**	
	a. If not, do you have a plan to establish them?	

7.7 References and Suggested Reading

1. *Maintenance Reliability Best Practices* by Ramesh Gulati
2. *Operator-Driven Reliability* by Terry Wireman
3. *Lean Maintenance* by Ricky Smith and Bruce Hawkins
4. *Making Common Sense Common Practice, Fourth Edition* by Ron Moore
5. *Secrets of Success with Procedures* by Jack Nicholas

CHAPTER 8

IMPROVE/MODIFY IT RIGHT

Learning Objectives to Understand

- Improvement is essential
- Defect elimination process
- Asset data management
- Improvement tools and applications

8.1 The Importance of Improve It Right

The questions you need to be asking yourself are:

Why and where/what needs to be improved?
What right things should I be doing to stay and thrive in business?

Staying in business means keeping your stakeholders, including shareholders, happy. The majority of improvement initiatives fail or don't produce required results. One of the foremost reasons for failures is not having the right environment for improvement and change. To make improvement successful, you need to have a "burning platform" or a "perfect storm" situation. Either of these situations forces you to make some changes and improvements to get better. Humans and organizations tend to become complacent if things are going well and then they fall behind.

The burning platform metaphor is perhaps one of the most pervasive in the world of business. It was coined by consultant Daryl Conner more than twenty-five years ago and popularized by Professor John Kotter of Harvard Business School. It comes from the true story of Andy Mochan, a worker on the Piper Alpha offshore oil and gas platform when it exploded in July 1988, killing 167 of his colleagues.

Burning platform is now a business lexicon that emphasizes immediate and radical change due to dire circumstances. Today, we all live in a global society and information age. Forward-looking businesses, wherever they are located, try to do better and compete to increase their market share by providing better quality products at very competitive prices, and deliver them on time. They do this by continuous improvement in their processes. They are creating a quick and lasting change environment in their organization to compete worldwide.

The second consideration is where to make improvements. Are you collecting and analyzing operational and performance data on a continual basis? The data should indicate to you where defects are being introduced in your processes, or what area you need to be focusing your efforts to improve. You need to have a strategy and the right tools in place to make effective improvements.

> *Orchestrating pain messages throughout an institution is the first step in developing organizational commitment to change.*
>
> ~ *Rosabeth Moss Kanter,*
> former editor, *Harvard Business Review*

Improvement should not be a onetime or as needed strategy. Organizations should establish a *continuous* improvement strategy. Continual improvement is a type of change that is focused on increasing the effectiveness and efficiency of an organization to fulfill its policy and objectives on a continual basis. It is not limited to quality initiatives. Business strategy and business results, customers and employees, and supplier relationships can be subject to continual improvement. Put simply, it means getting better all the time.

8.2 Don't Just Fix It, Improve It!

Organizations must continually improve processes, reduce costs and cut waste to remain competitive. Data from operations and maintenance (O&M) should be analyzed using various techniques and tools to develop and implement effective plans that can lead to improvements in assets and processes.

Recent industry surveys have indicated that although many organizations have started investing time and effort to improve their processes, it isn't unusual to see the same problems popping up over and over again. The impact of these challenges on both internal and external customers, employees, profitability and competitiveness has been documented. One factor making such problems highly visible is the formalized management systems guided by documents, such as ISO9000, ISO51000, etc. A new continuous improvement requirement in International Organization for Standardization (ISO) standards and other industry standards requires organizations to collect and analyze data on process performance using audits, internal performance indicators and customer feedback. Any problems that are identified must have corrective action taken to prevent recurrence.

Unfortunately, insufficient effort has been placed in providing guidance on how to carry out an effective diagnosis to identify the causes of problems. Organizations usually try to fix the symptoms of the problems instead of fixing the root causes. They often try to implement what could be called a "duct tape solution," hoping it will address the problems. Meanwhile, the risks associated with repeat problems have significantly increased.

Also, assets and their systems are getting very complex. Although identifying challenges is more rigorous, the ability to solve them has not necessarily improved at the same rate. Much of the training that is normally provided is too high-level and philosophical or is not focused on analytical problem-solving. People aren't being taught how to think logically and deductively. They lack the knowledge of what tools to use and how to apply them appropriately.

Improvement should not be about using a set of tools and techniques. It is not about going through the motions of organizing improvement by changing teams and training people. Improvement is a result that only can be claimed after there has been a beneficial change in an organization's performance.

8.2.1 Asset Data Management

Tom Peters, author and leading business management consultant, said in 2001 that, "Organizations that do not understand the overwhelming importance of managing data and information as tangible assets in the new economy will not survive." This statement is still true today and will be in the future.

Money and people have long been considered as assets in an organization. Physical assets (e.g., machinery, steam plants, compressors, buildings, etc.) are resources with recognized value under the control of an individual or organization, so they are called tangible assets. These physical assets help to achieve the goals of the organization and, therefore, need to be thoughtfully managed to achieve organizational objectives. Broadly speaking, tangible or physical assets and people are simply called assets nowadays because of their support in creating value for the organization.

Data and the information created or collected from assets and other sources to manage them effectively are now being recognized as an asset, too. As an asset, data should be managed appropriately. No organization can be effective without high quality data. Today's leading organizations rely on their data to make more informed and effective decisions. Thus, data has to be managed properly.

8.2.2 Data to Information to Knowledge

Data is the representation of facts, such as numbers, graphics, images, text, sound, or video. Technically, data is derived from the Latin word *datum*, meaning "a fact." Facts are captured, stored and expressed as data.

Data is a raw material that is interpreted by applying different tools to create information and knowledge on demand or continually. This information and knowledge then guides your decisions. But, you need to be cautious in understanding that the information is data in context. Without context, data is meaningless. You create meaningful information by interpreting the context around the data. The context includes:

- The business meaning of data elements and related terms;
- The format in which the data is presented;
- The time frame represented by the data;
- The relevance of the data to a given usage.

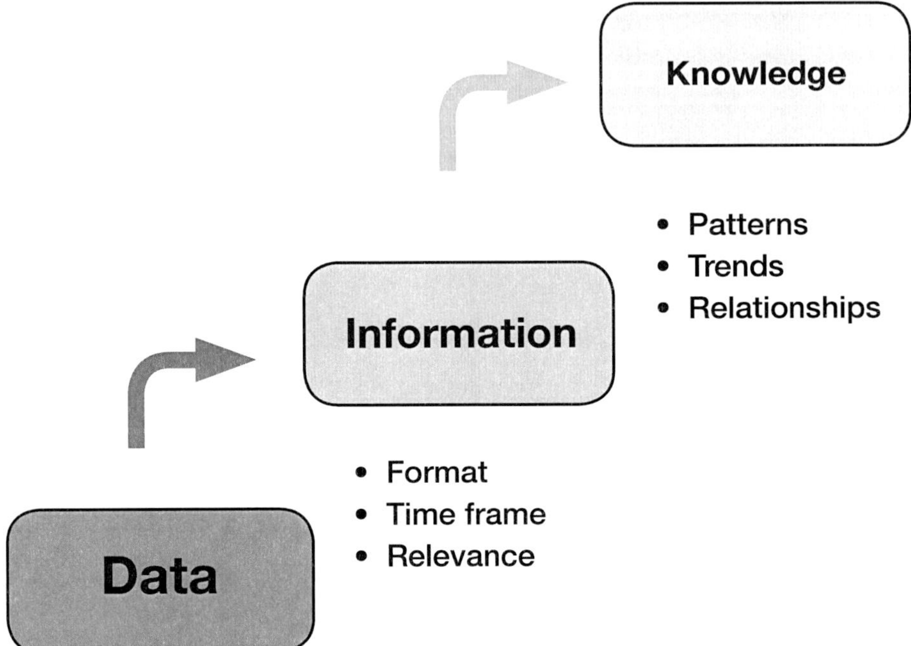

Figure 8.1: Data to information and knowledge creation

As shown in Figure 8.1, by managing data, you get the information and that information contributes to knowledge.

Knowledge is understanding, awareness, the acknowledgment of a situation and familiarity with its complexity. It is based on the recognition and interpretation of patterns, such as trends, formed with other information and experience. It may also include assumptions and theories about causes. You gain knowledge when you understand the significance of the information.

For example, let's say you have several types of pumps in your plant facility and investigating the data shows there is one type of pump manufactured by one company that is showing a lot of failures. Also in the investigation, you find that the seal material used in this pump is not compatible with the pumping medium. This information is knowledge.

Data is the foundation of information, knowledge and ultimately, wisdom and informed action. But is data always the truth? Not necessarily. Data can be inaccurate, incomplete, out-of-date and misunderstood. On a practical level, the quality of data that is available may not be relevant, complete, accurate, consistent, meaningful, timely, usable, or understood. Organizations that recognize the value of real data can take concrete, proactive steps to increase the quality of data and information.

8.2.3 Asset Data Lifecycle and Management

Like physical assets, data has a lifecycle. Data is created or acquired, stored, used, maintained and eventually destroyed when its need is over. In the course of its life, data may be extracted, exported, imported, migrated, validated, edited, updated, cleaned, transformed, converted, integrated, aggregated, referenced, reviewed, reported, analyzed, mined, backed up, recovered, archived and retrieved before eventually being deleted.

Data is fluid. It flows in and out of asset control systems and asset condition databases to a plant's IT infrastructure databases and then packaged for delivery in information products.

Data is stored in structured formats, such as databases, flat files and tagged electronic documents, as well as in many less structured formats, such as e-mail and other electronic documents, paper documents, spreadsheets, reports, charts or graphics, electronic image files, and audio and video recordings. Typically, eighty percent of an organization's data assets reside in relatively unstructured formats.

Data has value only when it is used or can be useful in the future. All data lifecycle stages have associated costs and risks, but only the "use" stage adds business value. When effectively managed, the data lifecycle begins even before data acquisition, with organizational planning for data, the specification of data and the enablement of data capture, delivery, storage and controls.

The asset data lifecycle has the following elements or phases that need to be managed:

1. **What data or information do you need?**
   It should be based on how the asset will be managed and the metrics needed to report its performance. You should think about this during the planning of an asset's acquisition and the design phase of the asset.

2. **How will data be collected?**
   Will it be part of the control system and automatically collected, part of the PdM/CBM route by a maintenance technician, or will an operator be collecting it as part of pre- or post-operations activities?

3. **How will data be retrieved and stored for analysis?**
   Will data be stored in a common shared drive that can be accessed by an individual asset analyst or manager? Can this data be transferred or linked directly to a CMMS/EAM or other databases?

4. **How and what format will the data/information be displayed?**
   What tools will you be using to analyze the data and in what format will you present the information? In what time frame does information need to be shared and with whom?

5. **Is data quality all-encompassing?**
   What are your plans to ensure that data quality is good, consistent, reliable and timely?

6. **How long do you need to keep the data/information?**
   Are there any regulatory or management system requirements to maintain data or information for a given period? When do you need to purge the data/information?

First-hand observations indicate that organizations don't do a good job with managing data. Either they collect too little or too much. Many times, it's too much and even then, they don't know what they have. Sometimes, they have very little data because they didn't plan. Then, it's too late and costs a lot more to collect it.

Managing data and information is crucial. It should be done right from the beginning of a capital project or asset acquisition, otherwise wrong or untimely data can force you to make bad improvement decisions.

8.3 Defect Elimination

Do assets perform reliably as expected, without any failures, all the time? No, they don't. Assets don't produce products or provide service without any failures. They stop randomly or you have to stop them to do repairs or make them safer to operate. One of the reasons assets fail unexpectedly is because you introduce defects in them when designing, fabricating, building, installing, operating, or maintaining them. You do it by error, omissions, unintentionally and sometimes intentionally due to budget constraints or lack of knowledge.

What can you do when the asset is already installed and operating at a high rate of failures? You need to establish a defect elimination or asset improvement program to eliminate or reduce errors (i.e., failures and defects) in assets so they operate reliably and cost-effectively.

Defects are introduced during the:

- Specifications/requirements phase;
- Design phase;
- Procurement/sourcing phase;
- Building/fabricating phase;
- Installation phase;
- Operations and maintenance phase.

However, these defects become evident or identified during the commissioning or operational phase. These defects need to be eliminated or minimized by defect elimination or an improvement program.

The objective of a defect or error elimination program is to have zero defects. In other words, "do it right the first time." It becomes part of the continuous improvement process. Defects are eliminated or minimized by using improvement tools and techniques in a structured method.

Strive for continuous improvement, instead of perfection.

~ Kim Collins

8.4 Improvement Program Types and the Process

Every organization has some form of improvement program in effect today. Some of these are organization-wide and some are focused on mission critical processes. Most are somewhere in between. Some are driven by new technologies, new applications, or new strategic direction, objectives, goals and initiatives.

However, studies have shown that about seventy-five percent of improvement projects and programs fail in some way or don't meet expectations. They may be over budget, take too long, become too complicated, or fail to deliver results. Many of them fail as a result of not having a proper culture or environment conducive to change. The change management should not be overlooked when implementing an improvement or change initiative.

Improvement efforts can be classified into three categories:

- Gradual – continuous;
- Incremental – continual;
- Breakthrough.

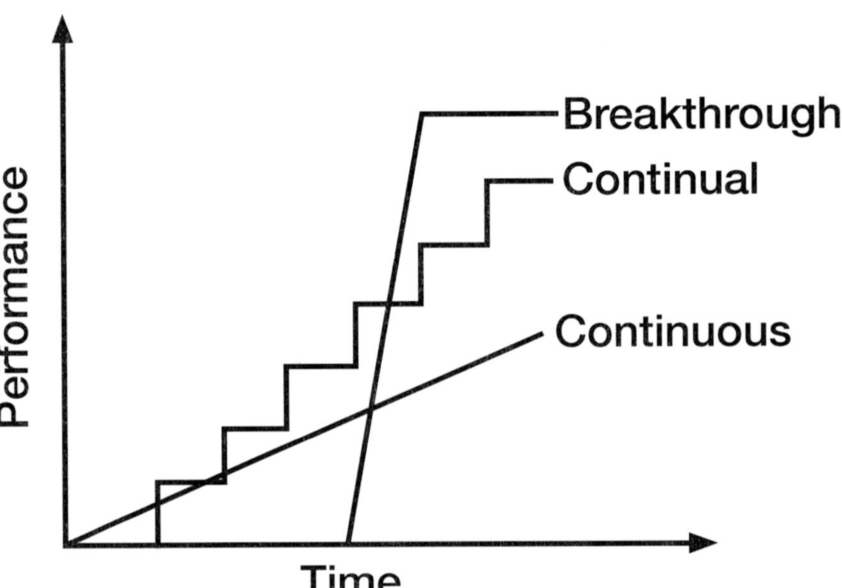

Figure 8.2: Types of improvement processes

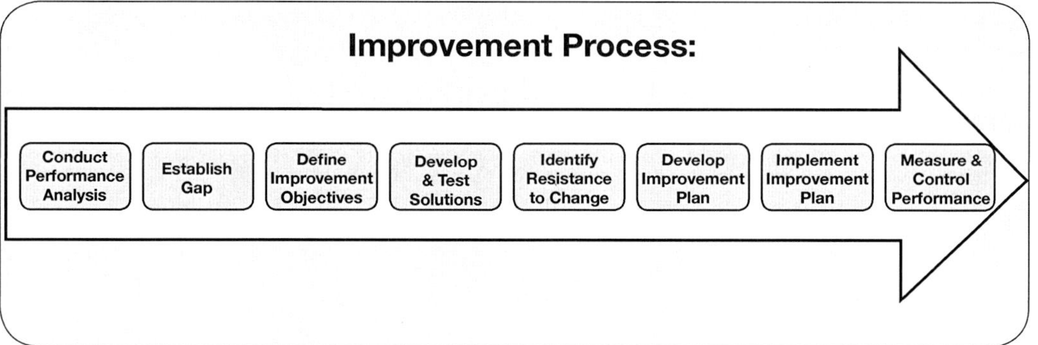

Figure 8.3: Improvement process steps

Continuous improvement is a gradual, never-ending change, whereas continual improvement is incremental change. Both types of improvements are what the Japanese call *kaizen*. Breakthroughs are improvements, but in one giant leap change. Although the method of achievement is the same, breakthroughs tend to arise out of discoveries and could take a long time before being made.

There are eight steps to an improvement initiative:

1. Conduct performance analysis to identify current performance level.
2. Perform gap and opportunity analysis. Use benchmarking and other strategies and problem-solving tools to establish performance gaps and opportunities.
3. Define the improvement objectives and obtain a commitment from stakeholders.
4. Develop and test solutions that will accomplish improvement objectives.
5. Identify and plan to overcome any resistance to change. Remember, improvement is a change.
6. Develop an improvement plan that specifies how and by whom the changes will be implemented. Communicate the plan with stakeholders.
7. Implement the improvement plan, including overcoming resistance to change.

8. Put in place controls to sustain new levels of performance and start the improvement process again.

Every asset, system, or project should have a provision for an improvement process. Therefore, when an objective has been achieved, work should begin on identifying better ways of doing it.

8.5 Tools for Improvement

The portfolio of tools and practices used for continual improvement should be those that enable an organization to execute the eight steps to an improvement initiative. They include:

1. Strategy Tools and Practices

- SWOT (Strength, Weakness, Opportunities, Threats)
    - A structured planning method that evaluates four elements: *strengths*, *weaknesses*, *opportunities* and *threats* of a process or project to make improvements.
- SIPOC (Supplier, Input, Process, Output, Customer)
    - A high-level flowchart of a process that lists all *suppliers*, *inputs*, *outputs* and *customers*. It identifies key elements and provides a quick, broad view of the process.
- Change Management
    - A process of managing change that can have positive or adverse effects on the success of improvement and change. It helps to identify issues concerning implementation and to develop a mitigating plan.
- Core Competencies Analysis
    - An analysis that identifies what the organization or people around the process are good at and can grow fast. They focus on these core competencies and switch away from the area where they are weak.
- Deming's PDCA Cycle (Plan, Do, Check, Act)
    - A systematic series of steps for gaining valuable learning and knowledge for the continual improvement of a process. The cycle

starts with a *Plan* to identify a goal and is then followed by the *Do* step in which the plan is implemented. Next is the *Check* step, where outcomes are monitored to check the validity of the plan for success. The last step, *Act*, closes the cycle by integrating the learning of the entire process and making adjustments, if needed.

- Asset Management Strategy
  - A strategy for the implementation and documentation of asset management practices, plans, processes and procedures within an organization.

2. Decision-Making Tools

Decisions are usually made in a situation of some uncertainty because you can never be entirely sure what tomorrow will bring. According to statistician George Chacko, decision-making is the "commitment of resources today for results tomorrow." Deciding which decision-making tool to use can be a puzzle in itself. Some of the tools you can use are:

- Monte Carlo Analysis
  - A computer simulation technique that uses random samples and other statistical methods to find approximate solutions to mathematical or physical problems.

- Linear Programming
  - When you have limited resources, it's helpful to calculate how to maximize those resources using this tool.

- The Vroom-Yetton-Jago Decision-Making Model
  - This model helps you to make the most efficient and effective means of reaching the decision. You don't want to make autocratic decisions when team acceptance is crucial for a successful outcome. Nor do you want team involvement in every decision you make because that is an ineffective use of time and resources. This model provides a useful framework for identifying the best leadership style to adopt for the situation you're in.

- OODA Loop Model
  - This model outlines a four-point decision loop that supports quick, efficient and proactive decision-making. The four stages are:
    - Observe – Collect current information from all sources;
    - Orient – Analyze this information and use it to update your current reality;
    - Decide – Determine a course of action;
    - Act – Follow through on decisions.
- The Ladder of Inference to Avoid Jumping to Conclusions
  - The Ladder of Inference describes the thinking process that you go through, usually without realizing it, to get from a fact to a decision or action. It involves reviewing reality and facts, and interpreting reality, assumptions, conclusions, beliefs and actions. This reasoning process helps to remain objective.

3. Creativity Tools

- Brainstorming and Affinity Diagram
  - Brainstorming is used to come up with creative solutions to problems. Brainstorming combines a relaxed, informal approach to problem-solving with lateral thinking. It encourages people to come up with thoughts and ideas that can, at first, seem a bit crazy. Some of these ideas can be crafted into original, creative solutions to a problem, while others can spark even more ideas. An affinity chart/diagram helps organize ideas into their natural relationship groups.

- Metaphorical Thinking
  - A direct comparison between two unrelated or indirectly linked things is called a metaphor. Metaphorical thinking can be used to improve communications and add impact or explain a difficult concept by association with a more familiar one. It also can be used to help solve problems and generate new ideas for solutions.

4. Problem-Solving Tools

- Deductive and Inductive Reasoning
  - Deductive reasoning is used to reach a valid logical conclusion. It starts with a general statement or hypothesis and examines the possibilities to arrive at a specific, logical conclusion. The opposite of deductive reasoning is inductive reasoning. It makes broad generalizations from specific observations. You make many observations, discern a pattern and make a generalization, then infer an explanation or theory.

- 5 Whys
  - The 5 Whys is a simple, practical tool that is very easy to use. When a problem arises, you simply keep asking the question "why" until you reach the underlying source of the problem and until a robust countermeasure becomes apparent.

- Heuristic Method: Rule of Thumb
  - People use rules of thumb in all sorts of areas in their daily lives. For example, "When the needle on the fuel level indicator in my car gets to red, I know it'll last at least another twenty miles." These rough rules, based on experience, are invaluable because they help us make decisions without further detailed fact-finding.

- Failure Mode and Effects Analysis (FMEA)
  - The FMEA tool identifies potential problems before a solution is implemented (i.e., proactive). It predicts failure and prevents its occurrence by supporting mitigating actions.

    When things go terribly wrong, it's easy to say with hindsight, "We should have known that would happen." And with a little foresight, perhaps problems could have been avoided if only someone had asked, "What could go wrong?"

    By looking at all the things that could go wrong at the design stage, it can cheaply solve problems that would otherwise take enormous effort and expense to correct if left until the solution has been deployed in the field. FMEA helps you to do this.

More than this, FMEA provides a useful approach for reviewing existing processes or assets so problems can be identified and eliminated.

- Root Cause Analysis/Root Cause Failure Analysis (RCA/RCFA)
  - This tool is for tracing a problem to its roots. Root cause analysis (RCA) is a popular and often used tool that helps answer the question as to why the problem occurred in the first place. It seeks to identify the origin of a problem using a specific set of steps, with associated tools, to find the primary cause of the problem so you can:

1. Determine *what* happened;
2. Determine *why* it happened;
3. Figure out what to do to reduce the likelihood that it will happen again.

RCA assumes that systems and events are interrelated. An action in one area triggers an action in another, and another, and so on. By tracing back these activities, you can discover where the problem started and how it grew into the symptom you're now facing.

Usually, you will find three basic types of causes:

1. Physical Causes: Tangible, material items failed in some way.
2. Human Causes: People did something wrong or did not do something that was needed. Human causes typically lead to physical causes.
3. Organizational Causes: A system, process, or policy that people use to make decisions or do their work is faulty.

RCA looks at all three types of causes. It involves investigating the patterns of negative effects, finding hidden flaws in the system and discovering specific actions that contributed to the problem.

- Cause and Effect Analysis (Fishbone Diagram)
  - When you have a serious problem, it's important to explore all the things that could have caused it before you start to think about a solution. This way, you can solve the problem completely the first time around, rather than just addressing part of it and having the problem run on and on.

    This diagram that examines cause and effect is also known as an Ishikawa diagram, named after its creator, Kaoru Ishikawa. Because it looks like the skeleton of a fish, it's also called a fishbone diagram. The effect (i.e., the problem) is always stated in the head of the fish and the rest of the skeleton (i.e., the bones) are used to state causes.

- Kaizen
  - The practice of continual improvement originated in Japan. The word translates to mean *change* (Kai) *for good* (Zen). Kaizen is based on the philosophical belief that everything can be improved. Some organizations look at a process and see that it's running fine, but organizations that follow the principle of kaizen see a process that can be improved.

    Kaizen means that nothing is ever seen as status quo; there are continuous efforts to improve that result in small, often imperceptible, changes over time. These incremental changes add up to substantial changes over the longer term without having to go through any radical innovation. It can be a much gentler and employee-friendly way to institute changes that must occur as a business grows and adapts to its changing environment.

- Bottleneck or Theory of Constraint (ToC)
  - A bottleneck in a process occurs when input comes in faster than the next step can use it to create output. For example, when liquid is poured out of a bottle, it has to pass through the bottle's neck. The wider the bottle's neck, the more water (i.e., input/assets) you can pour out. The smaller or narrower the bottle's neck, the less you can pour out, so you end up with a backup or bottleneck. It's also called theory of constraints, originally discussed by Eliyahu Goldratt in his book, *Goal.*

- Pareto Analysis: Resource Optimizing/Focus
  - Pareto analysis helps you focus on the right things to make the best use of your resources.

- Barrier Analysis
  - A technique that is used for tracing energy flows in an asset or process. It focuses on barriers to those flows and helps identify how and why the barriers did not prevent the energy flows from causing damage.

5. Lean Six Sigma and Other Tools

Lean Six Sigma is a rigorous, focused and highly effective implementation of proven quality tools and techniques. Incorporating elements from the work of many quality pioneers, Six Sigma aims for virtually error-free performance.

Sigma is a letter in the Greek alphabet used by statisticians to measure the variability in any process. If you can keep the output of that process within a Six Sigma-wide band – in effect, no more than 3.4 defects per million outputs – you can be confident that your assets and processes are operating as they should.

Six Sigma focuses on improving quality and, therefore, reducing waste, by helping organizations produce products and services better, faster and cheaper. In more traditional terms, Six Sigma focuses on defect prevention, cycle time reduction and cost savings. Unlike mindless cost cutting programs that reduce value as well as quality, Six Sigma identifies and eliminates wastes (i.e., costs) that provide no value to customers.

Some of the Six Sigma tools include:

- DMAIC Framework
  - DMAIC, which stands for define, measure, analyze, improve and control, is an improved version of PDCA. *Define* the goal and objectives of the improvement activity, then *Measure* the existing performance to establish valid and reliable metrics to monitor progress toward objectives. *Analyze* the asset and process to eliminate the gap between current performance and desired goals. Develop and implement an *Improvement* plan to find new ways to perform better and faster by applying statistical and other tools or practices. *Control* the new process by institutionalizing policy and procedures.
- Flowcharts and Swim Lane Diagrams
  - Flowcharts make understanding and communicating how the process works easier. If you want to improve your asset or process, you need to understand what's done at each stage along the way. Flowcharts visually show the steps, decisions and activities involved in a process, and they represent them in a format that's easy to understand.

    Swim lane diagrams are a unique form of a flowchart that make visualizing processes easier. The diagrams are set up and put in various lanes, making the process and flowchart clearer. Typically, one lane is used for each step of a process, which is labeled at the top, making it easy to follow.
- Value Stream Mapping (VSM)
  - A visual representation of how work flows through a process to identify value-added and non-value-added activities. The objec-

tive of this tool is to eliminate or minimize waste or non-value-added activities.

- Variance Analysis/SPC
  - Variance analysis is the quantitative investigation of the difference between an actual and a planned activity. This analysis is especially useful when reviewing the amount of a variation on a trend line or graph so sudden changes in the variance level from a period to another are more readily apparent.

    Variance analysis also involves the investigation of these differences so the outcome is a statement of the differences from expectations and an interpretation of why the deviation occurred.

    In the statistical process control (SPC) method, data is analyzed using statistics to understand process variation. This information is graphically displayed in histogram and stratification formats.

Other Tools:

- Checklists
  - A structured, pre-prepared form for collecting, recording and analyzing data as work progresses. The generic tool can be developed for a wide variety of purposes, such as an operator's start-up checklist, a preventive maintenance checklist and a maintainability checklist used by the designers, etc.
- Force Field Diagram
  - Force field analysis is a simple, but powerful technique for building an understanding of the forces that will drive and resist a proposed change. It consists of a two-column form, with driving forces listed in the first column and restraining forces in the second.

8.6 Performance Measures and Metrics

Management consultant Peter Drucker once famously said, "If you can't measure it, you can't improve it."

To manage the effectiveness of your work, you must create metrics (i.e., measurable details of a process or assets) to gather data before and after a change/improvement is introduced. Analyzing these metrics provides data and information that communicates how much the change improved the process, if at all. To get started, it's important to select the appropriate metrics for your processes. Some of the metrics for the improvement process include:

- Percent of kaizen events finished:
    - Number of kaizen events completed/number of events planned;
- Percent of employees involved in the improvement process;
- Percent of time employees are spending on the improvement process;
- Percent of training time spent on improvement tools as a total of training time.

> *Almost all quality improvement comes via simplification of design, manufacturing, layout, processes, and procedures.*
>
> *~ Tom Peters*

8.7 Improve/Modify It Right Summary and Checklist

8.7.1 Summary

Most improvement initiatives fight a constant tide of challenges, from budget constraints at the top to employees on the front lines who are reluctant to change. Improvement is a change.

To improve, you need to measure. This requires collecting good, quality data, using tools to analyze and implementing time-tested strategies and proven best practices to align process improvement efforts with business goals. It's important to understand these terms in this context:

- Measures: What you measure is right and matters;
- Benchmark: Find where you stand;
- Best Practices: Going from good to great to excellent;
- Tools: Applying the right tools for the right application;
- Stakeholders: Understand why you are doing or executing it and what's in it for them;
- Culture: Creating the right environment for sustainable improvement.

The 8-step improvement process involves:

1. Conducting performance analysis to identify current performance levels.
2. Performing gap and opportunity analysis. Use benchmarking and other strategies and problem-solving tools to establish performance gaps and opportunities.
3. Defining improvement objectives and obtaining a commitment from stakeholders.
4. Developing and testing solutions that will accomplish the improvement objectives.
5. Identifying and planning to overcome any resistance to the change (i.e., improvement is a change).
6. Developing an improvement plan that specifies how and by whom the changes will be implemented. Communicate the plan with stakeholders.
7. Implementing the improvement plan, including overcoming resistance to change.
8. Putting in place controls to sustain new levels of performance and starting the improvement process again.

The improvement process doesn't end here, however. Only through successive iterations of the improvement program can you sustain operational excellence. As such, it becomes necessary to ingrain the tools and best practices to employees who are daily charged with performing the good work of the organization.

Every asset, system, or project should have provisions for an improvement process. Therefore, when an objective has been achieved, work should commence on identifying better ways of doing it again. It's a journey that never ends.

8.7.2 Checklist

Improve/Modify It Right Assurance Checklist		Check - √
1.	**Have you conducted a performance analysis to identify current performance level?**	
	a. If not, do you have a plan to make this happen?	
2.	**Do you know the performance gap? Where do you need to be?**	
	a. If not, do you have a plan to accomplish this?	
3.	**Have you defined improvement objectives to meet corporate goals?**	
	a. If not, do you have a plan to accomplish this?	
4.	**Do you have stakeholders buy-in for this change/ improvement?**	
	a. If not, do you have a plan?	
5.	**Have you developed and tested solutions to meet improvement objectives?**	
	a. If not, what's the plan and when will it be accomplished?	
6.	**Have you identified any resistance to this improvement/change?**	
	a. If not, do you have a plan?	
7.	**Have you communicated the improvement plan to all stakeholders?**	
	a. If not, do you have a plan? Is this plan a part of the overall implementation plan?	

8.	**Have you established appropriate metrics to measure/trend progress?**	
	a. If not, do you have a plan?	
9.	**Have you established controls to sustain new performance levels?**	
	a. If not, do you have a plan to do it and by when?	

8.8 References and Suggested Reading

1. *Fire in the Night: The Piper Alpha Disaster* by Stephen McGinty
2. *Where Do We Start Our Improvement Program?* by Ron Moore
3. *Don't Just Fix It, Improve It!,* by Winston P. Ledet, Winston J. Ledet and Sherri M. Abshire
4. *The Relativity of Continuous Improvement* by Klaus Blache
5. *Root Cause Analysis* by Robert J. Latino, Kenneth C. Latino and Mark A. Latino
6. *Air Force Process Improvement Guide* by the Air Force Quality Center
7. *Start with Why: How Great Leaders Inspire Everyone to Take Action* by Simon Sinek
8. *Quality Toolbox* by Nancy R. Tague
9. *Understanding Variation: The Key to Managing Chaos* by Donald J. Wheeler

If you want to make the right decision for the future, fear is not a very good consultant.

~ Markus Dohle

CHAPTER 9

DISPOSE/ DECOMMISSION IT RIGHT

Learning Objectives to Understand

- Disposal issues
- The disposal and decommissioning process
- Various types of waste and their disposal

"A good plan which everyone knows is better than the best plan no one knows."

9.1 The Importance of Dispose/Decommission It Right

Do you have a junk area or yard where old, unused assets are stored in the plant or factory? Is every asset you have on the plant floor needed? Maybe some of them are just kept for spares, but are not maintained properly. Others may be getting rusty or leaking with hazardous material little by little, or perhaps a significant amount. If they are indeed leaking, you have a problem. This can already be or become a hazardous situation.

Many people are junkies at home and that can spill into their professional life, too. Some people love to keep things for "just in case" situations. Those situations may not happen for years, but they keep accumulating things in the garage or in the attic that they really don't need. The garage or another area in the home gets filled with unnecessary things and they can easily create safety hazards.

Most people have old computers, data collectors, or other electronic equipment, including software. How are they disposing of them? Some of the devices may contain valuable data that could be harmful if it gets into the wrong hands or places.

The plants in which you work also generate various types of wastes. Waste generated by a plant's processes can be:

- Hazardous and toxic chemicals;
- Used oil;
- Toxic and hazardous gases;
- Wastewater or untreated water;
- IT waste/computers, including software that is obsolete and outdated;
- Electrical devices, circuit boards and printed circuit boards (PCBs), wirings, etc.;
- Batteries;

- Biomedical waste;
- Nuclear waste;
- X-ray and radiation-exposed materials.

There must be a process in place to take care of these wastes. You cannot and should not just throw away waste in junk areas or unapproved disposal sites, exposing it to the environment without proper care or treatment. Some of these wastes are governed by regulatory requirements for their safe disposal. In many cases, you may be liable for legal actions.

We also live in a very different world today. Changes in the economic environment to various factors, such as technological advancement in communications, transport and policies of states, such as low entry tariffs, encouragement for foreign direct investment and tax incentives, create new challenges every day. The product lifecycle undergoes a change when the external environment changes. If you look at events in the last few years, it becomes apparent that the economic boom and bust cycle happens at a much faster rate, unlike in the past where plants or facilities could adjust to the environment over a period of a decade or so.

In the present economic climate, there may be times when assets that make products need to be decommissioned. It could be because of technological obsolescence, various regulatory requirements, taxation, cost pressures, or even pressures from third parties. Such a situation may also arise due to a buyout or bankruptcy because of severe economic conditions, or from a change in market geography.

In all these cases, there is a need to decommission an asset or an entire existing plant. The fixed assets need to be utilized for other products or just disposed of to recover part of the investment. Alternatively, they can be relocated to a new site to set up a new facility, which could be several thousands of miles away or even in a different country.

Decommissioning assets or a whole plant and relocating them to a different site, or disposing of unused assets that have passed their useful life must be taken care of in a proper or “right” manner.

9.2 Dispose of, Decommission, or Replace

Deciding whether to fix a broken asset or replace it with a new one is often a tough decision. In fact, to repeatedly repair broken assets or to keep them going as long as possible isn't always the best practice. There's no need to throw away good money on a bad asset.

Determining when an asset has reached the end of its useful lifecycle in the organization's overall reliability strategy often can be difficult if not looked at in the proper perspective. This is especially true in today's business environment, where the impetus is placed on the reduction of operations/ manufacturing costs and improving overall plant reliability. After all, asset reliability directly relates to profitability and, in the end, overall customer satisfaction, which is the only true indicator of increasing profitability.

So how do you know when an asset has actually reached or is approaching the end of its useful lifecycle? The key is not the *age* of the existing asset, but its *condition*. Plant assets may be old from the standpoint that it was purchased many years ago. However, many assets have been continually upgraded and maintained in order to keep up with evolving manufacturing and production requirements. Replacement considerations should not emphasize the capabilities of the assets when initially specified and purchased, but their capabilities and reliability in their existing current configuration. With all this taken into account, there are but a few actual reasons to change or replace an asset. Some of these reasons are:

1. **Safety:** Is the asset safe to operate and maintain? If the asset creates an unacceptable risk of causing a major accident, loss of life, or environmental incident, these are all good reasons to replace it.

2. **Asset requires a high cost to maintain:** A good reason to replace an asset is that it is no longer cost-effective to maintain. This not only includes any changes in the original features of the asset, but also externally imposed changes, such as those required by new government legislation, including emission levels, waste disposal requirements, noise levels, etc. In addition, maintenance costs associated with maintaining an accept-

able reliability level may be far too expensive or the cost/availability of spare parts could become unacceptable from a business standpoint.

3. **Asset is unable to meet product specifications:** When an asset can't meet customer specs, it is no longer viable to keep producing. It's not unusual for a client to ask for a product produced to a tighter tolerance than what is actually required for its intended use. You don't need to keep an asset that can't meet customers' needed requirements.

4. **Asset is unable to meet production needs:** An asset should be replaced if it can't meet production requirements. Every organization looks for ways to reduce manufacturing costs while, at the same time, increasing production. When an asset can't meet production requirements regarding either throughput or manufacturing cost, it should be replaced.

Caution: It is not advisable just to buy a new asset. Rather, you must do a detailed study of the reliability of the new asset. There should be a lifecycle reliability strategy developed and adhered to at every stage, from initial concept to decommissioning/disposal.

In some cases, the need for an asset is temporarily over, but the same asset may be needed at a later date, maybe in five or ten years or so. In this case, the asset should be appropriately decommissioned and packaged for safe storage so it can be brought back into operation when needed in an efficient manner and at a reasonable cost. This situation is also known as asset, plant, or facility "mothballing." Mothballing is the closure of a plant/facility with a plan to:

- Maintain buildings, structure and assets in a state where deterioration is minimized and reuse is possible upon reactivation.
- Manage contamination on the site, ensuring it is stabilized, treated and removed, or controlled as necessary to ensure compliance with applicable regulations.
- Ensure access to the site is controlled to minimize pilfering.

So, in a decommissioning process, the asset(s) or entire plant is taken out of service in a proper way to transfer to other locations. Or, assets may be sold or disposed of according to local or national regulations, or could be stored for later use. The decommissioning process could be one or a combination of any of these situations.

9.3 Decommissioning/Disposal Practices

Decommissioning is defined as a "planned shutdown or removal of an asset, building, plant, etc., from active service or usage." Decommissioning becomes very important for assets in the chemical process industry, power plants with coal or nuclear sources, or in any plant where assets have hazardous material or energy sources that need to be removed and properly disposed of.

Decommissioning in industries, such as chemical and hydrocarbon processing, pharmaceutical, power plants, coal, nuclear and the like, is much more challenging than other industrial sectors, such as metal or automotive, because of the nature of the chemicals and other hazardous materials handled. Many of these may be explosive, toxic, or in other ways harmful to the environment. In plants where chemicals are toxic, flammable, or corrosive, a sound methodology is needed to ensure proper care is taken to dismantle the assets.

The decommissioning and disposal process involves:

1. **Understanding the objective of decommissioning and disposing of, which may include:**
    a. Transferring asset(s) to another location;
    b. Selling the asset(s) or the entire plant;
    c. Storing the asset(s) for later use;
    d. Disposing of asset(s) to a junkyard.

Each of these objectives may have a different strategy and plan. Also, the decision has to be made regarding who will be leading this effort. Will it be done by the internal workforce or outsourced? There are many organizations that specialize in decommissioning and dismantling processes. Be sure to select an organization that can meet the organization's objectives.

2. Performing FMEA/risk analysis

Risk analysis using failure mode and effects analysis (FMEA) becomes important if assets have various energy sources and hazardous material. FMEA helps in developing an efficient and safe decommissioning plan. A FMEA analysis provides a better understanding of how the asset operates and how to safely remove energy sources and hazardous material from it.

3. Developing a plan based on decommissioning/disposal objectives

As previously stated and based on the type of asset(s), the plan should consider these six factors:

1. Power/energy source disconnect and removal;
2. Decontamination;
3. Dismantling;
4. Packaging for transfer, storage, or safe disposal;
5. Disposal of remaining material and waste;
6. Area/site clearance.

Let's take a look at each one separately.

1. **Power/energy source disconnect and removal:** The first step in the process is to ensure that the asset(s) to be decommissioned are appropriately disconnected from the electric power and other energy sources, such natural gas, other gases, oils, chemicals, etc. Everything should be at the fail-safe position.

   If you have to leave behind some piping, referred to as "dead leg," you need to ensure that it's blinded properly and free of any liquid or gas. Sometimes, even water in the dead legs can cause hazardous situations when they freeze in cold weather and cause pipes to crack.

2. **Decontamination:** The removal of contaminants from the asset/system by washing, heating, chemical treatment and mechanical cleaning is important, if needed. The term *contaminant* denotes the undesirable

chemicals and hazardous materials, such as asbestos, Freon, PCBs, etc., that are present in the asset. The internal and external surfaces of the asset or system can be exposed to chemicals during service. Thus, the objectives of any decontamination process are to:

a. Reduce occupational exposure;
b. Salvage the assets, plant and materials as far as possible;
c. Restore the site for future use, which may be an alternate use (e.g., commercial rather than industrial).

Note: Additional information on decontamination and types of contaminants and their safe handling can be found at: https://www.osha.gov/SLTC/hazardouswaste/

3. Dismantling

The process of dismantling an asset or a whole plant, specifically an oil and gas facility or a chemical or pharmaceutical plant, starts with the selection of a proper internal staff or contractor who has experience in dismantling plants in stages for the facility and infrastructure.

The contractor should have sufficient engineering expertise to carry out surveys, make as-built drawings, track the dismantled parts and carry out associated tasks so nothing gets lost or misplaced, especially if the same plant is to be assembled again at another location.

The dismantled equipment has to be secured with special protective packing (e.g., a compressor or a reactor with a stirrer can be transported, provided the stirrer is locked). Different packing arrangements may be needed for different types of assets. Also, the computerized maintenance management system (CMMS) may have asset data that needs to be cleaned or removed.

4. Packaging for transfer, storage, or safe disposal

The disposal process may consist of either complete disposal of the dismantled plant, complete shifting of the decommissioned plant to another location, or a partial disposal of some equipment. There are several variations possible in the break up of assets, such as those that are to be disposed of outright versus the equipment that is to be reused.

Disposal of waste should be carried out only after ensuring a valid consent from the environmental authorities is available and the characteristics of effluent are well within the norms specified.

Packaging assets becomes an important consideration if they have to be shipped internationally. Also, packaging needs special attention if it has rotating types of assets.

5. Disposal of remaining material and waste

Various pieces of asset equipment or components may no longer be useful and should be disposed of. Some components and material in this category would be piping, ducting, gearboxes, steel structures, electrical and electronic control cables, printers, fax machines, etc.

There also may be a lot of printed material, technical manuals, operating instructions, drawings, etc., that need to be destroyed or stored at the appropriate place.

6. Area/site clearance

This is the last step in the process. The area or site needs to be cleaned and cleared for reuse if required by the plan.

After a plant shuts down, the site progresses through decommissioning, remediation and redevelopment. Though it is not always possible, it helps to know site's reuse options early in the process in order to make cleanup decisions and determine the appropriate level of work needed in each stage of the assessment, cleanup and redevelopment process.

Understanding the range of reuse options and needs associated with each helps in the development of realistic schedules and cost estimates. Time and costs associated with permits, approvals of permits, plans and funding, and public involvement should be factored into the redevelopment plans as well.

9.4 Practices of Waste Disposal

There are four kinds of material waste that need to be disposed of properly.

1. Mechanical/electrical (electronic components)
Most of the material and components in the mechanical-type waste category would be piping, ducts, gearboxes, tanks, cylinders, etc. They're bulky, but not difficult to handle. You need to ensure that tanks, gearboxes, cylinders and bottles are empty and not filled with fluid or gases. If they are in good shape, they could be refurbished and reused. If not, a recycling dealer may pick them up at no cost.

Electrical and electronic components have computer monitors and picture tubes, camcorders, circuit boards and other electronic devices. A standard old computer monitor (i.e., glass tube type) contains a few pounds of lead. This toxic metal is utilized to line the glass in the cathode ray tube to shield the user against radiation exposure. Small amounts of mercury, a highly regulated toxic metal, can be found in some of the computer's printed wiring boards, switches, relays and batteries. Cadmium compounds, which are metals suspected as persistent carcinogens, are utilized in the computer's batteries, wiring boards and plastic stabilizers. Toxic metals are also found in the circuit boards of other devices, such as microwave ovens, VCRs, DVD/CD players, stereo equipment, cell phones, printers, cordless phones and electronic lab equipment.

If these devices are disposed of in a municipal landfill, they can potentially contaminate the soil, which can lead to a costly contamination of water supplies. Proper disposal of these items must be done in the "right" way.

2. Computers (software-related)
Industry best practices should be used to correctly secure the removal of data and licensed data from all computer disks. It is crucial to ensure that all sensitive and internal files are deleted from computers before they are transferred to other departments, locations, or to salvage. There will be asset-related data stored in the CMMS, so this data needs to be removed from the CMMS and other databases.

Decommissioning a computer or asset control system is not as easy as it may sound. A variety of issues could be encountered before and after it is decided that a system is to be decommissioned and disposed of.

The process of decommissioning a computer system consists of these steps:

- **Assessing** what's involved;
- **Planning** what will be done, including data removal, storage and system disposal;
- **Decommission planning** and **data archive scheduling**;
- **Reporting** who should be informed and coordinated with.

When it has been decided that a system will be decommissioned, coordination needs to be performed with the network architects, system owners, the information technology operations group, information security and external entities.

3. Hazardous (chemical/nuclear material waste)

Decommissioning large chemical plants, offshore oil platforms and power plants, specifically nuclear plants, gets very complicated and challenging. To ensure the decommissioning of a nuclear plant is safe and environmentally sound, the Nuclear Regulatory Commission (NRC) has established regulations and associated guidance in outlining the requirements and process organization that must be followed.

The NRC's decommissioning process facilitates participation by state and local authorities at several points along the way. The process involves:

- Decontaminating the facility to reduce residual radioactivity;
- Dismantling the structures;
- Removing contaminated materials to appropriate disposal facilities;
- Storing used nuclear fuel until it can be removed from the site for disposal or consolidated storage;
- Releasing the property for other uses.

The owner remains accountable to the NRC until decommissioning has been completed and the agency has terminated the plant's license.

There may be some old equipment containing asbestos, lead, or some other dangerous material. You need to ensure that you're removing the hazardous material in a safe manner and meeting all regulatory requirements.

4. Non-hazardous (industrial/construction waste)

Non-hazardous waste can be disposed of quickly and easily. The management of waste is an essential aspect of sustainability. Managing waste means eliminating it where possible, minimizing waste where feasible and reusing materials that might otherwise become waste.

Solid waste management practices should identify the reduction, recycling and reuse of wastes as essential for sustainable management of resources. You should be looking for opportunities to reduce and recover materials that would otherwise be destined for disposal as waste.

Perhaps a cliché, but still valid: "ALWAYS EXPECT THE UNEXPECTED."

9.5 Dispose/Decommission It Right Summary and Checklist

9.5.1 Summary

The decommissioning/disposal process for a plant or site is complex in nature. It is not a simple "demolish and exit" job, hence, a structured approach is essential for success. However, each decommissioning/disposal may have certain unique features that require the development of special procedures.

Industrial assets have hazardous/toxic waste and cannot be disposed of with the regular trash in the plant's dumpster. Much of this equipment contains chemicals and toxins that can cause severe health problems and irreversible environmental damage. These assets need to be decommissioned and disposed of in the right manner.

A decommissioning/disposal process is important in every industry, but becomes critical for assets in the chemical process industry, power plants with coal or a nuclear source, or in any plant where assets have hazardous material or energy sources that need to be removed and properly disposed of.

The decommissioning/disposal process includes the following steps:

a. Understand the objective of decommissioning/disposing of;
b. Perform FMEA/risk analysis to understand the risks involved;
c. Develop a plan to meet decommissioning/disposal objectives and mitigate the associated risks, which include these six factors:

    1. Power/energy source disconnect and removal;
    2. Decontamination;
    3. Dismantling;
    4. Packaging for transfer or storage;
    5. Disposal of remaining material and waste;
    6. Area/site clearance for future use.

Every organization, small or large, faces the problem of generating and disposing of hazardous waste. Everything from gases, solvents and oils used in the manufacturing process to pesticides and other commercial chemicals can result in hazardous waste that must be properly contained and disposed of. As these types of industrial chemicals can cause damage to both humans and the environment, the U.S. Environmental Protection Agency (EPA) places restrictions on how organizations must dispose of hazardous waste. Typical disposal methods include incineration, land disposal and underground injection wells.

Imagine a world where you could simply throw away your old equip ment and, in doing so, have its composite materials recycled for reuse in the construction of brand new industrial assets, effectively reclaiming the metals and plastics for use in totally new products. Sounds like an unachievable dream, right? Far from it! Sustainability is now a reality and it comes at no or very little cost to the environment, our health, or our industry. Progress is being made thanks to forward-thinking organizations that make an effort to recycle the "right" way.

The act of decommissioning a system should not be taken lightly. There are many considerations and it could take a long time. Only careful planning leads to success and the avoidance of many problems and headaches.

9.5.2 Checklist

Dispose/Decommission It Right Assurance Checklist		Check - √
1.	**Have you decided the purpose of decommissioning?**	
	a. If no, do you have a plan when this will happen?	
	b. If yes, is it to transfer or move to another site/location?	
	c. If yes, is it due to selling to a third party?	
	d. If yes, will the asset be put in storage for later use?	
	e. If yes, will the asset be disposed of to a salvage yard or a recycling dealer?	
2.	**Have you decided who will be performing the decommissioning/disposal process?**	
	a. If no, do you have a plan?	
	b. If yes, and the internal staff will perform it, do they have a plan?	
	c. If yes, and it will be outsourced, is a third party and RFP in the process?	
3.	**Is the plan based on a FMEA/risk assessment analysis for safe decommissioning and dismantling?**	
	a. If no, do you have an alternate plan?	
4.	**Do any of the assets have hazardous material or chemicals in them?**	
	a. If yes, do you have a plan to dispose of them properly, in the right manner and meeting regulatory requirements?	

5.	**Have you taken care of the safe disposal of data and documents?**	
	a. If no, do you have a plan, including a schedule?	
6.	**If any of the assets are being relocated to other locations, have you packaged them appropriately?**	
	a. If not, do you have a plan? Who will be doing this?	
7.	**After asset removal, do you need the site cleaned/ cleared from a sustainability perspective?**	
	a. If yes, do you have a plan? Who will be doing it?	

9.6 References and Suggested Reading

1. "Best Decommissioning Program" paper/presentation, Iluka Resources Inc., 2015 *Uptime* Awards, Special Recognition Award Winner http://reliabilityweb.com/uptimeawards/docs/pdf/2015_iluka.pdf
2. *Decontamination* by the U.S. Department of Labor, Occupational Safety and Health Administration (OSHA), www.osha.gov/SLTC/hazardouswaste/training/decon.html
3. *National Guidelines for Decommissioning Industrial Sites*, CCME-TS/WM-TRE0113E, March 1991, http://www.ccme.ca/files/Resources/csm/pn_1074_e.pdf
4. Miscellaneous conference papers, IMC http://www.cvent.com/events/the-31st-international-maintenance-conference-imc-2016-/event-summary-edcf52161d43408bb71d9f1b952a1b30.aspx and SMRP https://smrp.org/

CHAPTER 10

MANAGE IT RIGHT

Learning Objectives to Understand

- Why managing is important
- The role of leadership
- The importance of training
- AM-related standards and their application
- Managing change
- A culture of excellence
- The importance of continuous learning and improvement

10.1 Introduction

To ensure the 9 Rights explained so far are implemented appropriately, you need to manage them right. Managing these rights involves ensuring that you have:

- **The Right People** with the right skills and talent in every role they are given;
- **The Right (Robust) Processes** that are repeatable and deliver quality products and services by deploying standards and other best practices;
- **The Right Technology** to get high productivity and more value.

Having the right people, processes and technology creates a conducive environment that will lead to a culture of excellence. In this culture, the entire workforce works together to ensure that assets are performing and exceeding expectations in delivering high quality products and services on a continuing basis at much lower costs.

Terrence O'Hanlon, coauthor, calls this a "culture of business excellence." Achieving excellence in what you do is all about the "Manage It Right" concept.

10.2 The Importance of Manage It Right

One of the key factors that dictates the financial success of an organization is how assets are managed in a company. In a keynote address, Robert DiStefano, a renowned maintenance reliability professional and a retired CEO of Management Resources Group (MRG, now part of Emerson Process Management), said that in many asset-intensive companies around the world, corporate executives are more focused on achieving financial results instead of the technical aspects of running a company. They know they have highly talented, technical people who worry about the technical aspects. But what they often don't understand is the impact those "technical" asset management practices have on the financial performance of the company.

Asset management affects financial performance, as well as all other enterprise-level benefits, such as safety, quality, industrial security and sustainability, all of which executives tout as important to the company. What has been learned over the last couple of decades is that good asset management is not just about managing assets properly, but is linked directly to financial success. When asset management is done in the right manner, it not only impacts the bottom line, but also affects safety, quality and sustainability as well.

Ron Moore, another renowned author and reliability guru, said in his presentation at the 2016 International Maintenance Conference (IMC), that his research data from manufacturing companies around the world shows that omissions and errors and not providing sufficient resources (due to cost cutting measures) during the procurement, design, installation, operations and maintenance phases of assets have (and will) cause high failure rates and an increase in cost of ownership. Our own experience validates these findings.

If you implement the 10 Rights detailed in this book in the right manner, they will make assets more reliable and safer to operate and maintain, while the total cost of ownership will go down.

In this chapter, you will learn what it takes to implement all the 9 Rights appropriately. This will ensure that assets are designed and built right, as well as reliably and safely operated and maintained. In doing so, your assets will deliver maximum value and reduce total cost of ownership.

10.3 People Development

So many leadership courses and books, and so few leaders!

~ Terrence O'Hanlon

10.3.1 Key Roles and Functions

Generally, there are four roles and functions in an organization:

- A **Performer** who does the particular task;
- A **Guru**, also known as a **Subject Matter Expert (SME)**, who provides the expert advice;

- A **Manager/Supervisor** who manages the people and takes care of resources, budgets, etc.;
- A **Leader or Leadership** who inspires, motivates and guides in achieving the vision of the organization.

Each of these roles is crucially important in any organization. These roles can be played by one person or many, depending on the size of the organization and its complexity.

Let's take a more in-depth look at each one.

Performer

Individuals in this position perform assigned work or tasks, including a duty or function often to be finished within a certain time frame. A task could be anything, such as cleaning the area, lubricating bearings, operating a machine, assembling or repairing components and assets, planning the work, developing a preventive maintenance (PM) plan, performing a failure mode and effects analysis (FMEA) or a root cause analysis (RCA), and so on. It could be anything to meet the customers' needs.

The performer needs to have the following attributes:

- Performs the assigned task safely:
    - Has a knowledge and understanding of how work will be performed;
    - Follows the written and verbal instructions;
    - Knows and uses the right tools;
    - Produces quality work.
- Takes ownership of the work, including quality of the work being performed;
- A learner who understands new methods and tools to perform the task efficiently;
- A thinker and a proactive doer.

The performer also should have good personal traits to perform the work, which include:

1. A positive attitude;
2. Ethics with high moral and integrity standards.

Basically, everyone starts out as a performer and then some become gurus, managers, or leaders, while many stay performers. It is vital to maintain a workforce of good performers. In fact, there wouldn't be any managers or leaders without performers.

Guru

Individuals viewed as gurus are pundits, masters, experts, or specialists who people trust to have a lot of experience in knowledge—insights not obvious to others—of a particular subject.

Guru is a Sanskrit language word that has been adopted in the English language many years ago and has a very deep meaning. In the past, it was used in a spiritual sense, but now it is used very broadly to describe any expert in a particular field. In Sanskrit, the word *guru* suggests "gu," which means darkness and "ru," which means dispeller, as in a dispeller of darkness.

The guru is the person who dismisses darkness (i.e., ignorance) and brings light (i.e., knowledge, insight, wisdom and understanding) to the darkness. In other words, darkness is the absence of light.

Those who have a great passion to become an expert in a specific field should choose to become a guru. It brings great pleasure and satisfaction to help others, as well as respect. It's not a title you get, but others start valuing your advice and teachings.

Manager/Supervisor

Managers or supervisors are individuals in charge of a particular group of tasks or a certain subset of an organization. Managers often have a staff of people who report to them.

A manager's title in the workplace can cover a realm of duties, most of them supervisory in nature. In larger organizations, you may find tiers of management levels, each with specific duties. But in small businesses, the manager is often a jack-of-all-trades. Though managers may oversee aspects of the business, their responsibilities may be hands-on as well. They enable others to do their skilled work.

Management guru Peter Drucker wrote in his 1954 classic, *The Practice of Management*, about management as a profession and described five key roles of a manager:

1. Set objectives and establish the goals that employees need to reach;
2. Organize tasks, coordinate his/her allocation and arrange the right roles for the right people;
3. Motivate and communicate to mold staffers into cooperative teams and to convey information continually up, down and around the organization;
4. Establish targets and yardsticks that measure results and clarify outcomes to ensure the firm is moving in the right direction;
5. Develop people through finding, training and nurturing employees, an organization' primary resource.

Since Drucker's *The Practice of Management*, thousands of books have been written about management and leadership, yet somehow new and experienced managers still often lack a clear understanding of their roles and essential functions.

Research and experience shows that managers' roles have been expanding and essentially now have more functions. Dan McCarthy, Director of Executive Development Programs at the Peter T. Paul College of Business and Economics at the University of New Hampshire, lists fourteen functions and roles of managers.

1. **Hiring great people.** It all starts here with great talent. For some reason, managers often take shortcuts when it comes to sourcing, screening and selection. Or, they overly rely on human resources or recruiters instead of seeing the selection as a critical part of their job.

2. **Managing performance.** This covers the people management aspect of a manager's job. It includes clarifying and setting expectations and goals, coaching, measuring and monitoring employees' work, addressing performance problems, providing feedback and recognition, coaching, developing, training and doing performance reviews.

3. **Managing resources, including time management.** Managers have to make sure their team members have the resources they need to do their work, while at the same time, making sure a team does not overspend or waste resources.

4. **Improving processes and quality.** While individuals should take responsibility for the quality of their own work, managers are usually in the best position to see the overall workflow, make adjustments and remove performance barriers.

5. **Setting overall direction.** A manager sets the long- and short-term direction of the team or organization. This includes the vision, mission, goals and objectives. In other words, strategy. Managers need to ensure that every team and all team members are going in the right direction, aligning with the organization's vision and mission.

6. **Communicating information.** Managers must make sure information is flowing from above, sideways and upwards. They shouldn't be the bottleneck in the information highway. A manager also should be more of a listener than a talker.

7. **Developing and training people**. Managers need to ensure that team members are properly trained in their job duties. Team members must have the proper skills to perform the assigned tasks.

8. **Empowering people and teams.** Managers empower people and teams so they are able to take the initiative without any hindrance or bureaucratic obstacles, make the best decisions to solve problems and improve service and performance. Empowerment builds confidence, creates satisfaction, encourages innovation and is a great morale booster.

9. **Supporting peers and teams.** The manager should be supportive of his or her peers (i.e., other managers and their teams) in order to meet the organization's overall objective. Working together always wins.

10. **Doing unique work that no one else could (or should) do.** Managers should be very careful in making sure that they are doing work that only they can do and not work that they like to do, are good at, or don't trust their team to do.

11. **Self-development.** Although managers are not responsible for the development of their employees and teams alone, they are responsible for their own personal development as a manager.

12. **Create a culture of excellence and continuous improvement.** Managers should be building an environment where all people work together (i.e., not in silos) to develop the best solutions to the problems without any consequences of an adverse outcome. They are willing to take the appropriate risk without any fear and ensure continuous improvement becomes the norm.

13. **Respect and recognition.** Managers treat their people and teams nicely and respectfully, as they would want to be treated. They recognize them for their good work and celebrate successes with them. Remember, you are all in this together.

14. **Communicate.** Managers remove rumors and "fake news."

When I talk to a manager, I get the feeling that they are important. When I talk to a leader, I get the feeling that I am important.

~ Anonymous

Leader or Leadership

The words *leader* and *manager* are often used interchangeably, but they mean two completely different things. For example, a manager tells his or her employees what to do, while a leader encourages and inspires his or her employees. A manager accepts the status quo, while a leader challenges it.

Manager (management) and leader (leadership) are not the same. Not all leaders are managers and not all managers are leaders, but sometimes they play both roles. You can be good at one and lousy at the other, or you can be good or bad at both.

In his article, "What Leaders Really Do," published in the *Harvard Business Review*, John P. Kotter, author and management guru, says:

- Managers plan and budget, organize and staff, control and solve problems, and produce predictability and order.
- Leaders establish direction, align people, motivate, inspire, mentor and produce change.

While leadership and management are different, they are complementary and equally important. One is not better than the other. Organizations need both great leadership *and* best management. To what degree of each depends on the extend of change needed.

Neither management nor leadership is hereditary traits. Both need to be learned and developed over time. Contrary to what was believed many years ago, leaders are not born. They are made. For most people, leadership tends to be harder and takes longer to develop. You need to remember that leadership is earned and does not come with a title.

While everyone has some potential to lead, some have more potential than others. Organizations need to cast a wide net to find these individuals and invest in their development. The role of a manager can be appointed, but the title of a leader must be earned. A manager can inherit or hire employees, while a leader has to be "elected" by followers to be their leader.

You can *do* management to manage, but you have to *be* a leader to lead. Management can be a 9 to 5 job, while leadership is transformational. There is no on and off switch.

The following quotes offer some great wisdom from gurus and leaders about leadership:

"A leader is best when people barely know he exists, when his work is done, his aim fulfilled, they will say: we did it ourselves."
~ Lao Tzu

"If your actions inspire others to dream more, learn more, do more and become more, you are a leader."
~ John Quincy Adams

"Leadership is lifting a person's vision to high sights, the raising of a person's performance to a higher standard, the building of a personality beyond its normal limitations."
~ Peter Drucker

"A leader takes people where they want to go. A great leader takes people where they don't necessarily want to go, but ought to go."
~ Rosalynn Carter

"Great leaders are almost always great simplifiers, who can cut through arguments, debate and doubt, to offer a solution everybody can understand."
~ General Colin Powell

"Before you are a leader, success is all about growing yourself. When you become a leader, success is all about growing others."
~ Jack Welch

"A leader is one who knows the way, goes the way and shows the way."
~ John C. Maxwell

As you can see from these quotes from leading experts in the field, leadership plays a very crucial role in any organization. Some of the characteristics of a manager and a leader are compared in Table 10.1.

Table 10.1: A Comparison of the Attributes of a Manager and Leader

MANAGER	LEADER
Has subordinates	Has followers
Has objectives	Has or helps in developing vision
Plans the details	Sets the direction
Minimizes risks	Takes risks
Directs/tells employees what to do	Sells, encourages and influences to let employees do
Accepts status quo	Challenges status quo
Obstacles are problems	Obstacles are opportunities
Meets expectations	Charts new growth
Concerned about bottom-line	Eyes the horizon
Approves	Motivates
Thinks short-term	Thinks long-term
Establishes rules	Breaks the rules
Relies on control	Inspires trust
Assigns duties	Fosters ideas
Does things right	Does the right things

10.3.2 People Development: Education and Training

People get things done. Managers may have detailed plans and amazing processes, but if the right people with the right skills aren't in place, these plans and processes can't be carried out effectively. Developing people or the workforce at every level and empowering them to do their best is the key to success.

Employees may have some weaknesses in their workplace skills, or they may need to acquire new skill sets to meet new requirements. A training program allows them to strengthen the skills they need to improve. Training presents a prime opportunity to expand the knowledge base of all employees.

A good training program should reduce any weak links within the organization who rely heavily on others to complete basic work tasks. Providing the necessary training creates overall knowledgeable employees who can take over for one another as needed, work on teams, or work independently without constant help and supervision from others.

Employees who receive the necessary training are better able to perform their tasks. They become more aware of safety practices and proper procedures for basic or specialized tasks. Training also may build employees' confidence because they have a stronger understanding of the assets, system, or processes and the responsibilities of their job. This confidence may push them to perform even better and think of new ideas that help them to excel.

Training in continuous improvement also keeps employees on the cutting edge of industry developments. Employees who are competent and on top of changing industry standards help the organization hold a position as a leader and a strong competitor within the industry. Training also sends the message that employees are valued and that management is interested in their development and betterment.

The types of training or training curriculum should include:

a. The asset and system operations and maintenance to increase understanding of how it works;
b. The asset and its component repair methodology;
c. Regulatory and standards to understand regulatory requirements and application of standards;
d. Specialized or new technology-related topics;
e. Professional development, for example in FMEA, RCA, reliability-centered maintenance (RCA), etc.;
f. Organization specific, such as process-related, company safety, diversity related, etc.

Training of any kind should be relevant to the work or responsibilities of the individual and delivered by any appropriate method. For example, it could include:

- On-the-job learning, especially broadening assignments;
- Mentoring approaches;
- In-house training;
- Individual study through universities and training organizations;
- Short courses or seminars organized by professional societies or universities;
- Conferences organized by professional societies and universities.

Additionally, blended learning (BL) is becoming more and more popular as an effective combination of online learning and classroom learning.

Measuring training effectiveness is also important. Many times, questions are raised about how good the training is: Are people being taught the right things? Are people grasping the knowledge? Are training delivery methods effective?

These are all good questions and an evaluation of training effectiveness should be measured. Some of the methods could be:

- Reviewing training evaluation sheets after training is performed to ensure the right questions to ask are on the evaluation sheets;
- Feedback via a focus group;
- Professional certifications, with employees encouraged to take a certification examination, such as CLS, MLT, CRL, CPMM, CMRP, CMRT, IAM-AM, CAMA, etc.

Achieving certifications are proud accomplishments and should be celebrated by peers, managers and leaders. Employees should be recognized for their achievements.

Certification also can be used to assess the knowledge of employees, which can help in developing an appropriate or "right" training plan.

Developing people within an organization should be viewed as an investment, not overhead. A *Harvard Business Review* study shows that capable, ambitious young employees want training, mentoring and coaching. They want to gain skills. They want to become more versatile and valuable to the organization. Some of the benefits of training are:

- Increased employee performance and productivity;
- Fewer failures;
- Reduction in operations and maintenance (O&M) costs;
- A safe environment;
- Boosted employee engagement;
- Enhanced innovation and nimbleness;
- Improved employee satisfaction and morale;
- Increased employee retention rate.

"Training isn't just important to any organization, it is vital."

10.3.3 Communication

Communication is important in achieving productivity and maintaining strong working relationships at all levels of any organization. It doesn't matter what role you are playing—leader, manager, guru, or performer. Your communications, whether instructions, directions, or whatever you want to communicate, always should be clear, concise and easy to understand.

Poor communication in the workplace inevitably leads to unmotivated, demoralized employees who may begin to question their own confidence in their abilities. Organizations that invest time and energy into delivering clear lines of communication rapidly build trust among employees, leading to increases in productivity, output and morale.

Communication is today's most important skill, but schools don't teach it. They teach math, science and history, and give routine instructions about rigid grammatical rules, but give very little guidance on how to express ideas clearly. When you enter your professional life, you immerse yourself in the jargon and principles of your chosen field and obediently follow company rules and precepts laid out for your respective role. Yet, professionals rarely put serious effort toward expressing themselves in a language that can be understood by those outside their tribe. Think about financial professionals. Does the maintenance reliability/asset management tribe talk or understand their language and try to work with them, or just ignore them in frustration? Yet we wonder why our efforts and achievements fail to resonate. Stephen Covey's two habits—"seek first to understand, then to be understood" and "begin with the end in mind"—are excellent concepts to follow to achieve good communication.

Effective communication is an important life skill that enables you to better understand and connect with the people around you. It allows you to build respect and trust, resolve differences and foster environments where problem-solving, caring, affection and creative ideas can thrive. Lack of effective communication inadvertently leads to conflict and frustration in both professional and personal relationships. It takes time, effort and patience to develop effective communication skills, but the more effort you place into doing so, the more natural your skills will become.

A crucial, but often overlooked, function of leadership is creating a culture in which effective communication can flourish. Communication is bidirectional, requiring both a transmitter and a receiver. Both need to be effectively engineered. Be aware of obstacles or noises in your communication and try to minimize them. Feedback from the receiver becomes imperative to ensure the intent of the message being received is correct and properly understood.

Good communication skills involve:

- Listening carefully and attentively;
- Nonverbal communication, which includes paying attention to nonverbal indicators, facial expressions, etc.;

- Emotional awareness, meaning and respecting the emotional stage of a person, such as stress level.

In order to effectively communicate, you must clearly organize the thoughts in your mind before sharing them. The only way to properly share valuable ideas is by first shaping them coherently to yourself. You need to remember that communication is collaborative, not competitive. As noted earlier, communication is a two-way process that involves the exchange of ideas. If communication is only one-way, the exchange is prevented, which leads to frustration. An adequate knowledge of communication skills significantly improves the ability to exchange thoughts and ideas with others.

Some key areas where you can improve and enhance your communications are:

a. Define goals and expectations

You need to deliver clear, achievable goals and tasks to both teams and individuals, outlining exactly what is required. Ensure the message is clear and accessible to the intended audience. To do this, it is essential that you speak plainly, politely and get your message across clearly without causing confusion or offense.

b. Choose the medium carefully

Once you have created your message, you need to ensure that it's delivered in the best possible format. While face-to-face communication is by far the best way to build trust with employees, it is not always an option. Take time to decide whether information delivered in a printed general memo would work better than an e-mail.

c. Keep everyone involved

Ensure lines of communication are kept open at all times. Actively seek and encourage progress reports and task updates. This is particularly important when communicating with staff working remotely.

d. Listen and show empathy

Communication is a two-way process and no leader, manager, or any individual for that matter can survive long if they don't listen and encourage dialogue with the other party. Listening shows respect and allows you to learn about any outstanding issues that you may need to address.

10.3.4 Ethics, Honesty and Integrity in the Workplace

A key component to workplace ethics and behavior is integrity: being honest and doing the right thing at all times. The dictionary defines ethics as "moral principles that govern a person's or group's behavior." Among many other things, ethics includes integrity and honesty. Both are values that are essential to succeed.

This section does not address asset or data integrity— although both are very important—but rather personal integrity or honesty related to people.

Integrity, honesty and strong moral ethics should saturate every part of your workplace, both internal and external. They should make up the foundation by which the business is built. They should govern how you treat people, including employees, competitors, clients and customers. Your value system should be based on doing everything with respect toward others and with the utmost integrity.

These words of wisdom on honesty and integrity come from gurus and well-known leaders (See page 198).

Leaders know that honesty and integrity are the foundations of leadership. Leaders stand up for what they believe in. Take Jon Huntsman, Sr., a multi-billionaire who started a chemical company from scratch and grew it into a $12 billion enterprise. His book, *Winners Never Cheat*, is filled with stories taken from his own experience in which he steadfastly refused to compromise his principles. Huntsman says that integrity is the reason why he has been as successful as he is. "There are no moral shortcuts in the game of business or life," he writes. "There are, basically, three kinds of people, the unsuccessful, the temporarily successful, and those who become and remain successful. The difference is character." Great leaders never compromise their honesty and integrity.

Workplace ethics is integral in fostering increased productivity and teamwork. It helps align the values of the organization with those of the employees. Achieving this alignment requires that you encourage consis-

"The glue that holds all relationships together, including the relationship between the leader and the led, is trust, and trust is based on integrity."
~ Brian Tracy

"Honesty is the first chapter in the book of wisdom."
~ Thomas Jefferson

"Speak with integrity. Say only what you mean. Avoid using the word to speak against yourself or to gossip about others. Use the power of your word in the direction of truth and love." ~ Don Miguel Ruiz

"Real integrity is doing the right thing, knowing that nobody's going to know whether you did it or not."
~ Oprah Winfrey

"Moral authority comes from following universal and timeless principles like honesty, integrity, treating people with respect." ~ Stephen Covey

"Whoever is careless with the truth in small matters cannot be trusted with important matters."
~ Albert Einstein

tent dialogue about the values of the organization. This enhances community, integrity and openness among employees. Ethics enables employees to feel a strong alignment between their values and those of the organization. They show such feelings through increased productivity and motivation.

10.4 Process: Managing the Application of Standards

10.4.1 Standards and Standardization: Value and Benefits

A *standard* is an established norm or requirement generally presented in a formal document that establishes uniform technical criteria, methods, processes, or practices.

BusinessDictionary.com defines a *standard* as a "written definition, limit, or rule approved and monitored for compliance by an authoritative agency (or professional or recognized body) as a minimum acceptable benchmark." Standards may be classified as:

1. Government or statutory agency standards and specifications enforced by law;
2. Proprietary standards developed by a firm or organization and placed in public domain to encourage their widespread use;
3. Voluntary standards established by consultation and consensus and available for use by any person, organization, or industry.

The General Agreement on Tariffs and Trade (GATT) defines *standard* as "technical specifications contained in a document that lay characteristics of a product, such as levels of quality, performance, safety, or dimensions. Standards may include or deal exclusively with terminology, symbols, testing and methods, packaging, or labeling requirements as they apply to a product."

The most important application of standards helps demonstrate that products or services meet regulatory and sometimes contractual requirements—though standards themselves are voluntary. The use of standards and practices make processes robust and repeatable, therefore, they reassure customers that products and services maintain a high level of quality, reliability and consistency.

Based on the prevalence of standards, it's safe to assume that they offer considerable value to economies, businesses and people. The economic impact of standardization is far from negligible. In recent years, a range of studies from the United Kingdom, Australia, Canada and Germany discovered the hard macroeconomic benefits of standards. In the U.K., this has been quantified at an annual contribution to gross domestic product (GDP) of £2.5 billion per year. The same study found that thirteen percent of the growth in labor productivity between 1948 and 2002 is attributable to standards, as reported on the BSI Group's website.

You may not be aware of them, but standards are in use every day, in all aspects of our daily lives: in communications, the media, healthcare, food, transportation, construction, furniture, energy and more. Standards support:

- **Improved environment, reliability and safety.** Adherence to standards helps ensure safety, reliability and environmental care. As a result, users perceive standardized products and services as more dependable.
- **Improved productivity and reduced costs.** Standards make processes robust and improve asset performance, resulting in lower failures, improved quality and lower cost of operations.
- **Support of government policies and legislation.** Standards are frequently referenced by regulators and legislators for protecting users and business interests, and to support government policies.
- **Interoperability.** The ability of devices to work together relies on products and services complying with standards.
- **Business benefits.** Standardization provides a solid foundation upon which new technologies can developed and existing practices enhanced.

Standards also:

- Open up market access;
- Provide economies of scale;
- Encourage innovation;
- Increase awareness of technical developments and initiatives;
- Offer consumer choices.

Standards provide the foundation for new features and options, thus contributing to the enhancement of our daily lives.

Also, think about what the world would be like without standards:

- Products might not work as expected;
- They may be of inferior quality;
- They may be incompatible with other equipment; in fact, they may not even connect with them.

10.4.2 Asset Management Related Standards

Specifications and code standards help in standardizing parts, components for interchangeability and safety of products and assets. The management standards are sometimes referred to as "management best practices" to help improve the processes. The application of management standards, such as ISO9001 and ISO55001, makes processes more robust, repeatable and consistent. Some of the management standards that relate to asset management include:

- ISO9000 – Quality management (to ensure product and process quality);
- AS9100 – Quality management (for the aerospace industry);
- ISO14000 – Environment management (to reduce environmental impact);
- ISO26000 – Social responsibility (guidelines for social responsibility);
- ISO27000 – Information security management (to ensure IT information security);

- ISO31000 – Risk management (to manage risk);
- ISO45001 – Occupational health and safety (to help in reducing health and safety incidents);
- ISO50000 – Energy management (to manage and reduce energy usage);
- ISO55000 – Asset management (to manage assets to realize more value);
- ISO14224 – Petroleum, petrochemical and natural gas industries -- Collection and exchange of reliability and maintenance data for equipment (taxonomy and codes).

In addition to this family of standards, the Global Forum on Maintenance & Asset Management (GFMAM), a worldwide association of several professional asset management bodies, has published two documents: *Asset Management Subjects* and *Asset Management Landscape*, which is proposed as guidance to achieve a unified overview of asset management and thirty-nine linked subjects. The list of the thirty-nine subjects in six groupings published by GFMAM is included in Appendix E.

Another important and valuable document related to asset management is, *An Anatomy of Asset Management*, published by the Institute of Asset Management (IAM). This provides an appreciation of asset management: what it is, what it can achieve, the scope of the discipline and a description of the underlying concepts and philosophy. The first version was published in 2011 and the second in 2014 to align it with the published ISO55000. It's available on the IAM website.

There are two types of ISO management standards: requirements and guidelines. Together, they make up what is known as the ISO family of standards. For example, in the ISO55000 Asset Management family of standards, ISO55001 is the requirement standard and the other two standards, ISO55000, provides the overview, principles and terminology, and ISO55002, provides guidelines for the application of ISO55001.

There are eight principles of quality management that underpin the ISO management standards, which also need to be embedded within any management system to provide a sound foundation for achieving the organization's goals and objectives. These principles are derived from the collective experience and knowledge of international experts who participate in the ISO Technical Committees, which are responsible for developing and maintaining the ISO standards.

The *quality* term referenced has a much broader meaning. It doesn't mean a quality management or department; it means a system that produces (i.e., forces) a highly disciplined process with fewer failures (i.e., nonconformities). Under this quality system, everything is done **right** with proper procedures and instructions, resulting in zero or a very minimum numbers of errors.

The Eight Principles of Quality Management are:

1. **Customer-focused organization.** The very relevance of any organization relies on its customers, both internal and external. As such, it must understand and meet their needs.

2. **Leadership.** Sound leadership is fundamental to the success of an organization. The leadership must establish a vision or a desired future for the organization. The leadership also must clearly demonstrate in a practical manner the ongoing commitment to the quality management system. They must also create an environment that encourages people to achieve the organization's objectives.

3. **Involvement of people.** All organizations rely on their people, so they should ensure that they are involved, as is appropriate, in the delivery of their products or the services they provide. However, to ensure the quality of their products, organizations should equip their people with the appropriate skills and knowledge to ensure this occurs.

4. **Process approach.** An organization is more efficient and effective when it uses a process approach to the delivery of its products and services. The processes should provide clearly defined standards and structured formats for all its activities, including product delivery. This enables the efficient management of resources.

5. **System approach to management.** The organization must use a systems approach that requires the identification, understanding and management of interrelated processes.

6. **Continual improvement.** This should be an ongoing commitment of any organization to continually improve its overall performance by engaging its stakeholders and providing them with the right tools.

7. **Factual approach to decision-making.** Organizations perform better when they make informed decisions based on facts. They should measure and evaluate their products, processes and performance. Analysis of this data and information enables informed decision-making and improvement in service delivery.

8. **Mutually beneficial supplier relationships.** Organizations must establish mutually beneficial relationships with internal and external customers, partners, specific community sectors, international and national organizations, and the various levels of government. These relationships should be appropriately managed and nurtured to ensure benefits to the organization.

These principles are the backbone of any standard and adherence to them will create a very conducive environment and culture.

10.4.3 Implementing Asset Management and Other Standards

This section outlines the 12-step process to implement asset management or any other standard. The section also covers how to achieve certification.

1. **Understand the standard.** Get acquainted with the standard(s). As previously mentioned, the ISO55000 family of standards has three standards in it. ISO55001 is the key standard and is called the "requirement standard." It has "shall" statements that you need to comply with. The two other standards, ISO55000 and ISO55002, are guidance and clarification standards. Try to understand how the implemen-

tation of this standard would help improve your organization's asset management process so it achieves higher reliability of plant assets and reduces the overall cost of ownership. It means getting more value from your assets. Remember that the ISO55000 standard is a framework, so you need to tell the system what and how you are going to take care of the assets and process.

2. **Perform gap analysis**. It's a good idea to perform a gap analysis with the support of internal or external resources to identify major shortcomings in implementing an asset management standard.

3. **Acquire management support.** This is crucial. Without the support of management, the standards implementation will almost certainly fail. Plan a strategy well to convince management that an ISO standard is not just a good idea, but required to get more value from the assets. The management/leadership is responsible for creating an asset management policy, which should state how assets will be managed based on lifecycle management and the 10 Rights principles. An example of an asset management policy is shown in Appendix F.

4. **Identify requirements.** Another important step is to ensure that all the requirements that exist for an asset management process have been identified. These include customer requirements, as well as other requirements, such as regulations and the need for having the **right** culture. Performing a SWOT analysis (see Chapter 8) may be helpful in determining weaknesses, threats and opportunities in the process, system, or department area. They may become part of the requirements.

5. **Define the scope.** Defining the scope of asset management helps ensure the limits and boundaries of what assets and area are covered in the asset management process and which areas of the organization might not have an effect on the asset management process. The key tool for defining the scope is the strategic asset management plan (SAMP), sometimes just referred to as the asset management plan (AMP).

6. **Define processes and procedures.** It's very helpful to understand or identify who the customers and suppliers are to the asset management process before starting procedure development and beginning work instructions. Performing a SIPOC analysis (see Chapter 8) is a best practice for developing good policies, procedures, work instructions, metrics, and so on.

   The key is to define all the processes and procedures in the asset management process and look at how they interact with other processes and procedures in the organization. It is in these interactions where problems can occur. You also need to ensure that all policies and procedures are fulfilling the requirements of the standard's "shall" statements. Where all the documents will reside also needs to be identified. A good practice is that all processes and standards compliance documentation reside in one organization-wide system, sometimes called a quality management system (QMS) or management documentation system (MDS).

7. **Implement processes and procedures.** In this step, you put all documentation in an appropriate system, such as an MDS, QMS, or CMMS. Many procedures and instructions already may be in place, but they need to be linked appropriately to ensure that only the **right** and current procedures and instructions are released to the performer. Also ensure that all problems are being documented, including failures and what corrective actions are being taken. This corrective action system or database could be part of a CMMS or a separate stand-alone linked to the CMMS.

8. **Training and awareness programs.** It is important for everyone in the organization to know what they are doing and how they fit into the overall plan. Some of the stakeholders would have been involved from Step 1 or 2. But, it's good practice to have all employees go through awareness and process training, as well as the important training on any changes to the processes and procedures in which they're involved. Everyone should be aware of why they are doing this.

9. **Choose a certification body or registrar.** This can be a very important step in determining the effectiveness of your implementation. The certification body is a company that comes in to audit the system and decides if it is compliant with ISO55000, or whatever standard requirements you are implementing, as well as whether it is effective and improving. It may be beneficial if the certification body is selected early so they can provide guidance in the implementation process.

10. **Conduct internal audits.** Before the certification body audits the system, they will first want you to audit each process internally. This affords you the opportunity to make sure the processes are doing what was planned. You will also have an opportunity to implement the necessary corrective actions to fix any problems that may be found.

11. **Certification audit.** The first step of an external audit is the review of documentation by the certification body auditors to verify that, on paper, all the necessary requirements of the ISO standard have been addressed. The auditors issue a report outlining where there is compliance and where there are problems. You will have a chance to implement any corrective actions to address the problems.

    The second step of the external audit is the main audit. The certification body auditors review the records that have been accumulated about operating asset management processes, including records of internal audits, management review and corrective actions. They may visit the site where work is being performed. From this review, which may take several days, they will issue a report detailing their findings and whether they have found the asset management system to be effective and in compliance with the ISO55000 requirements. The auditors will also make a recommendation for certification if all requirements are met. If there are any major nonconformances, then corrective action will need to be taken for these problems before certification can be recommended.

12. **Maintaining the certification.** The key to maintaining the certification is keeping the gains. This means not just remaining compliant, but ensuring that the system is continually improving.

When trying to implement any standard and work toward certification, a good plan helps. So, take the time to plan and know what resources are needed. This will save time and resources later on.

Some organizations, especially those who already embrace ISO9001 or ISO14001, are aware of how ISO managing system standards work with their own processes. Others use publicly available frameworks, like the newly revised Uptime® Elements™ A Reliability Framework and Asset Management System™ by Reliabilityweb.com. This framework connects the technical asset management activities with the leadership domain. All these areas connect through the line of sight to the business process through a detailed asset management system aligned to ISO55001.

Organizations, such as the Metropolitan Transportation Authority (MTA), Bristol-Myers Squibb and the Central Arizona Project, have started using the Uptime Elements A Reliability Framework and Asset Management System to establish their asset management process. ATA-Jacobs at the U.S. Air Force's Arnold Engineering Development Center in Tennessee used a tailored ISO9001 framework to very successfully implement an asset management process since 2004, even before PAS55/ISO55000 was introduced. Its reliability journey is another great example of how all stakeholders, including an organization's leadership, are involved in creating a culture of excellence in asset management.

10.5 Managing the Application of Breakthrough Technology

In the last couple of years since we started writing this book, we have noticed the emergence of some new breakthrough technologies, such as drones, the Industrial Internet of Things (IIoT), the smart camera and data analytics, just to name a few. The right application of these technologies can have a big impact in reducing maintenance costs and improving the reliability of assets.

From wind turbine inspections to long-range deliveries, unmanned aerial systems (UAS), also called unmanned aerial vehicles (UAV) or most commonly known as drones, are becoming more and more present in the daily life of maintenance professionals. Drones are flying beyond visual line of sight to help maintain power lines, inspect infrastructure and even do work inside towering boilers. No wonder why the idea of skyways for drones—along with a recharging infrastructure that can serve thousands or millions of drones—is beginning to take shape across the world. New opportunities and ways to use this technology are starting to be recognized by everyone in the industry, specifically those in the power, petrochemical and the oil and gas industries. In fact, these industries are a hotbed for development opportunities.

Because the Pacific Gas and Electric Company (PG&E) sees drone technology as an opportunity with safety and reliability benefits, it has begun testing how it can use drones to help monitor and survey its gas and electric infrastructure. Currently, PG&E is in the research and development phase of drone use for its nearly 160,000 miles of electric lines in northern and central California.

"Drones have incredible potential for improving the safety and reliability of our systems," says Eric Back, PG&E Director of Compliance and Risk Management. "We want to roll out this program methodically and in alignment with the industry, and are partnering with a number of industry organizations to help design requirements to ensure the safe operations of drones. These partnerships provide a valuable resource for identifying safe applications of this promising technology."

Speaking at an ARC Advisory Group's Industry Forum, Bentley Systems CEO Greg Bentley shared his insights on how new reality modeling software can dramatically enhance productivity by turning a simple series of digital photos taken with a smart camera mounted on a drone into a 3-D reality mesh model. The result is a compact, intelligent representation of the asset in its current operating context. He confidently predicted there would be a drone in every major infrastructure maintenance organization. Using drones and normal digital photography, inspectors can observe existing conditions, then track and trend the conditions over time, with the ability to compare to the design basis or any point in the asset's life. In fact, there are a growing number of drones being used in industrial maintenance, reliability and integrity inspections.

New opportunities and ways to use this technology are starting to be recognized everywhere in the industry today. Infrared cameras, gas detection sensors, and multi- and hyperspectral cameras are several additional capabilities of a drone. Using the cameras above and sensors, elevated work can be minimized or even eliminated. Drones, coupled with these advanced technologies, also help narrow the focus to specific areas so maintenance crews know exactly what they're dealing with before they leave the ground. This is especially useful for turnaround planning. Areas that were once only accessible with scaffolding or rope now can be accessed using drones at a fraction of the time and cost. Moreover, equipment can remain in service during drone operations; flare stacks are a good example of this. Other applications include inspecting insulation for damage and early detection of hazardous material on difficult to reach operating columns, reactors and piping, just to name a few.

Many existing plants have no information model, no accurate records and, possibly, some unreliable or outdated 2-D drawings. If you are operating in an existing plant with poor engineering records, you can now capture a precise 3-D model using simple digital photographs taken from drones using software to render an information model that you can maintain going forward. You can then take updated photos to observe the current state and compare them to the model as time goes on.

10.5.1 Interoperability Standards and IIoT/IoT

According to a World Economic Forum study, if the first Industrial Revolution was driven by steam, the second by electricity and the third by digitization, we are now in the midst of a fourth: one driven by data. In this Industrial Internet of Things (IIoT) era, an explosion of Internet of Things (IoT) connected devices has created a new level of big data possibilities for enterprises of all types.

While many consumer-facing industries, such as retail and healthcare, make bold attempts to keep up with the changing times, manufacturing generally lags behind in capitalizing on data-driven strategies. Granted, because of the technical complexity of data analysis, gaining meaningful business insights from the IIoT is far from easy. However, that doesn't need to be the reason manufacturers fall behind.

The use of standard Internet-based technology with IIoT enables unlimited interconnection and exchange of data between physical and logical industrial systems that are accessible via the Web to deliver new business processes.

Using technology to drive a predictive maintenance approach, organizations can stream data from sensors mounted on their machines to uncover key usage and performance patterns in real time. This allows them to identify potential malfunctions in the making and avoid the hefty costs of unexpected breakdowns.

In addition, data analytics examines large data sets containing a variety of data types—structured, time series, transactional, media—to uncover hidden patterns, unknown correlations, manufacturing issues, performance improvements, customer preferences and other useful business and manufacturing information. This helps you to take quick actions and do fast repairs, eventually cutting down lost downtime and reducing operations and maintenance (O&M) costs.

10.6 Change and Safety Management

> *The world we have created is a product of our thinking. It cannot be changed without changing our thinking.*
>
> *~ Albert Einstein*

10.6.1 Change Management

With varying customers' needs and the economy, technological changes and growth opportunities are reasons for all organizations to make improvements in their processes if they want to stay in today's fast-moving, globally competitive environment. Improvements are a change for the better and necessary in both personal and work life.

Change is a necessary part of life. Without it, there would be no life at all. Our lives are actually fueled by change, though most of us want a certain amount of stability. Many of us don't like change and want to stay with the status quo. However, if you can learn to accept change as helpful rather than something to be avoided, you may experience better results and less stress.

Change is important for any organization because, without it, the business would likely lose its competitive edge and fail to meet the needs of its customers. Organizations benefit from change that results in new ways of looking at customer needs, innovative ways of strengthening customer interactions and novel products that might attract new markets. New employees joining an organization are especially valuable because they can often point to areas of opportunity for improvement that those who have been long involved in the organization might have overlooked. But even existing employees should be encouraged to question why things are done a certain way and look for new ways to get work done faster, better and with higher levels of quality and service.

Implementing change is not as straightforward as it sounds. You can't just tell your employees about it and they simply do it. It doesn't work that way because employees will resist the change. The majority of them will want to keep things the way they are. For it to be successful, change has to be accepted by the people for whom it is going to impact. Change—improvement—needs to be managed.

Who Moved My Cheese?: An A-Mazing Way to Deal with Change in Your Work and in Your Life by Dr. Spencer Johnson, who also co-authored *The One Minute Manager*, is an amusing story that illustrates the vital importance of being able to deal with unexpected change. This book is a timeless business classic, using a simple parable to reveal profound truths about dealing with change so you can enjoy less stress and more success in your work and personal life.

In a nutshell, the wisdom you can gain from this book is:

- Anticipate change;
- If you do not change, you can become extinct;
- Adapt quickly;
- Enjoy change;
- Be ready to change quickly, again and again;
- Ask yourself: "What would I do if I weren't afraid?";
- When you move beyond your fear, you feel free;
- The more important your cheese is to you, the more you want to hold on to it;
- Smell the cheese often, so you know when it's getting old;
- Movement in a new direction helps you find new cheese;
- When you see that you can find and enjoy new cheese, you change course;
- Noticing small changes early helps you adapt to the bigger changes that are to come;
- Read the handwriting on the wall;
- Change happens. They keep moving the cheese;
- Move with the cheese and enjoy it!

There are several change models that can be adopted to implement change. Among them are:

- Prosci's ADKAR Model:
  - **Awareness** of the need for change;
  - **Desire** to participate and support the change;
  - **Knowledge** on how to change;
  - **Ability** to implement the required skills and behaviors;
  - **Reinforcement** to sustain the change.

- Kotter's 8-Step Change Model:
  1. Create urgency;
  2. Form a powerful coalition;
  3. Create a vision for change;
  4. Communicate the vision;
  5. Remove the obstacles;
  6. Create short-term wins;
  7. Build the change;
  8. Anchor the change in the corporate culture.

- Kurt Lewin's Change Management Model: Unfreeze - Change – Refreeze;
- The McKinsey 7-S Model;
- Stephen Covey's 7 Habits Model.

Choose a model or process that best meets your environment and culture to implement the change. It could even be a hybrid approach. Use whatever makes sense to implement the improvement change.

The 10 Rights we have been discussing are improvements. Therefore, implementing them is a significant change. It requires very careful planning, engagement of all stakeholders and a conducive environment, meaning a culture where change takes place naturally without any fear and frustration.

10.6.2 Time Management

Time management plays a critical part in the workplace. It can have a big impact on your success, no matter what industry you're in. Whatever your role or function, managing time is crucial. It allows you to take control of life, rather than follow the flow of others. By managing time, you can accomplish more, make better decisions and work more efficiently. This leads to a more successful life.

The art of arranging, organizing, scheduling and budgeting one's time for the purpose of generating more effective work and productivity is known as time management. Time management involves exercising conscious control over the amount of time you spend on specific activities, with a focus on increasing effectiveness, efficiency, or productivity.

Poor time management can be related to procrastination, as well as problems with self-control. A good time management practice can improve the ability to plan and control how you spend the time in a day to effectively accomplish your goals. Good time management practices are:

- Plan efficiently;
- Be efficient;
- Schedule efficiently;
- Be organized;
- Prioritize tasks;
- Be relaxed and less stressed;
- Have a clarity of objectives;
- Focus on achieving the set objectives;
- Be self-disciplined;
- Have time for yourself.

Hence, time management helps you to be more organized and productive. The following are key steps that you should follow for effective time management:

Step 1: Set goals;
Step 2: Develop a schedule;
Step 3: Revisit and revise your plan.

Another essential trait of good time management is to delegate tasks. Delegation is one of the most important time management skills.

- Proper delegation saves time, develops a team, grooms a successor and motivates individuals.
- The primary purpose of delegating is time management so you can concentrate on bigger and main assignments (i.e., assignments that need your attention).
- Poor delegation causes frustration. It demotivates people, confuses others directly involved and fails to achieve the task or purpose.

Other tips for effective time management are:

1. Keep a to-do list and review and update it regularly.
2. Plan and organize.
3. Prioritize and put first things first.
4. Estimate the time for tasks properly.
5. Set clear objectives and deadlines.
6. Get clear instructions and be focused.
7. Avoid interruptions and idle chitchat.
8. Always keep additional time for emergencies.

Managing time makes you work smarter, not harder, and reduces stress levels and conflicts.

10.6.3 Safety Management

Workplace injuries account for approximately $20 billion in direct costs each year and $100 billion in indirect costs, as reported in several studies. Sixty-three hundred people die each day globally due to workplace injuries and work-related diseases.

In implementing the 10 Rights in whatever your role—performer, guru, manager, or leader—you need to ensure that you do your tasks safely. Safety of your people is paramount.

Safety features also include ergonomics, which should be specified and designed into your assets. Ergonomics is the science of fitting workplace conditions and job demands to the capabilities of employees. Ergonomic principles are used to improve the "fit" between the employee and the workplace. A practical approach to ergonomics considers the match between the person, the asset the person uses, the work processes and the work environment.

The most common workplace injuries are related to:

- Cumulative Trauma Disorders (CTDs)
    - Repetitive stress injuries (RSIs);
    - Repetitive motion injuries (RMIs);
    - Musculoskeletal disorders (MSDs).

All these types of injuries can be avoided or minimized with the right ergonomic design of assets. In addition, various considerations must be taken into account to apply ergonomic principles to the workplace:

- Adjust the workstation/work area;
- Correct the environment and choose the right tools;
- Improve posture, work techniques and habits.

Ergonomic principles also can be applied in industrial settings to develop a safer, healthier and more productive work environment. Organizations need to know how to minimize risk factors by choosing the best tools and work techniques for a given task. Everyone doing all tasks as safely as possible leads to a safety culture—a culture of operational excellence.

10.7 Manage It Right Summary and Checklist

10.7.1 Summary

To ensure the 10 Rights are implemented appropriately, you need to manage them right. Managing these rights involves ensuring that you have:

- The right people;
- The right, robust processes;
- The right technology.

Organizations are run by people who perform one of four functions/roles: performer, guru, manager, or leader. Each of these roles is important in every organization. These roles can be performed by one person or many, depending on the size of the organization and its complexity. You need to ensure that every person, regardless of the role they are performing, has right skill set.

Training is not a onetime event. Assets keep changing with new technology and people keep moving to new and challenging jobs, so the skills of people need to be upgraded on a regular basis.

Effective communication is an absolute essential attribute of all roles. Likewise, ethics, honesty and integrity in everyone, including all stakeholders, is a must to sustain a culture of excellence.

Processes and methods should be robust to ensure that outputs, products and services are of high quality and repeatable. The application of standards and standardization can ensure this. The asset management standard, ISO55000, and other standards can help any organization put discipline in its activities.

Although a constant challenge, leveraging technology to improve people productivity is also a necessity.

All 10 Rights and many other topics discussed in this book are part of an improvement strategy. Although implementation of them becomes necessary, they are all change. Implementing change is difficult and challenging. You need to have a strong, solid plan to ensure stakeholders buy-in for improvement (i.e., change).

And don't forget about safety. You need to make sure that every task you or your people do is done safely.

Having the right talent, robust processes and the right technology mix, along with stakeholders working together, will create a culture of excellence. This conducive culture will support continuous improvement and sustain the gains.

10.7.2 Checklist

Manage It Right Assurance Checklist		Check - √
1.	**Have training needs of your people been identified, including all roles for the current year and beyond?**	
	a. If not, is there a plan to make this happen?	
2.	**Are soft skills (e.g., communication, ethics, integrity, etc.) training included in the plan?**	
	a. If not, is there a plan to accomplish this?	
3.	**Do you have the appropriate level of resources for training? (Benchmark is about 5%.)**	
	a. If not, is there a plan to accomplish this?	
4.	**Is there a plan to get your people (e.g., technicians, professionals and managers/ supervisors) certified?**	
	a. If not, is there a plan?	
5.	**Are you encouraging your people to get involved in professional societies and associations, and to present papers, etc.?**	
	a. If not, is there a plan?	
6.	**Are you planning to comply or get certified in a standard (e.g., ISO55000, ISO14000, etc.)?**	
	a. If not, do you have a plan?	

7.	**Are you investigating to implement new technology, including software to improve productivity, such as mobile applications, smart sensors, IIoT, or drones?**	
	a. If not, do you have a plan?	
8.	**Do you engage people and get buy-ins when implementing improvements?**	
	a. If not, do you have a plan to manage change?	
9.	**Do you have an effective safety program to ensure people do their tasks safely?**	
	a. If not, do you have a plan to accomplish this?	
10.	**Do you have appropriate metrics established to evaluate safety effectiveness?**	
	a. If not, do you have a plan?	

10.8 References and Suggested Reading

1. *The importance of good communication* by Michael Page, http://www.michaelpage.co.uk/advice/management-advice/development-and-retention/importance-good-communication
2. *Jack Welch and the 4 E's of Leadership: How to Put GE's Leadership Formula to Work in Your Organization* by Jeffrey A. Krames
3. *The Extraordinary Leader: Turning Good Managers into Great Leaders* by John H. Zenger and Joseph Folkman
4. *Leadership Excellence* by Pat Williams
5. *Tribal Leadership: Leveraging Natural Groups to Build a Thriving Organization* by Dave Logan, John King and Halee Fischer-Wright
6. *True North* by Bill George with Peter Sims
7. *Maintenance and Reliability Best Practices* by Ramesh Gulati
8. *ISO55000 Asset Management: A Biography* by Rhys Davies and Danielle Humphrey

9. *ISO55000:2014 Asset management – Overview, principles and terminology*, www.iso.org/standard/55088.html
10. *Why we need standards* by ETSI, www.etsi.org/standards/why-we-need-standards
11. *Inspectioneering Journal,* March/April 2015 issue, https://inspectioneering.com/journal/2015/03
12. *Occupational Safety and Health Administration* (OSHA), https://www.osha.gov/
13. *United States Environmental Protection Agency* (EPA), https://www.epa.gov/

EPILOGUE

Asset management (AM) is becoming a frequently used term in the industry around the world. It is a term being used more often by engineers, facility planners, designers and regulators, as well. Unfortunately, the term is developing the initial symptoms of becoming a buzzword.

This tendency is dangerous in several respects. First, asset owners and managers may view it as something new and, therefore, a potentially costly additional task they may be required to perform. Secondly, and perhaps more importantly, the concept loses cogency and impact as a buzzword. It becomes just another annoying fad that will hopefully go away. With asset management, neither could be further from the truth.

Asset management is neither something new, nor, hopefully, a temporary trend. AM is the science of making the right decisions and optimizing the delivery of value. There are tangible benefits to be realized in both the short and long term through the adoption of a coordinated AM strategy to get more value from assets. AM is a best practice and a real value creator if done right.

Also, we have found that the majority of companies who used to be in the equipment maintenance and reliability field now have become asset management companies or have added AM in their name.

If you do an online search for asset management, you'll get over 101,000,000 hits, with ninety percent or more of those sites related to financial companies or finance-related service providers.

So, what is asset management? Why are so many ignorant about AM, while, at the same time, some are vigorously trying to join the "AM bandwagon?"

Performance vs. Value-Based Strategy

In the past, our maintenance strategy has been to manage equipment (i.e., assets). We perform preventive maintenance (PMs) on assets to reduce failures or get them repaired quickly when they break. Also, we try to use condition-based maintenance (CBM) wherever it's feasible. Our goal in this strategy is to ensure the equipment keeps performing. Some call this a *performance-based* strategy. We keep fixing equipment at whatever it costs to ensure it keeps producing products or providing services. In reality, this is challenging and may be expensive.

If we, the maintenance reliability tribe, get involved early in the asset acquisition phase, we could provide valuable input in writing specifications and supporting design to ensure assets are designed from a reliability, availability, maintainability, safety and sustainability (RAMS^2) perspective.

We also could get involved in the machine build, installation and commissioning phases. Our operators and maintainers need to be engaged and appropriately trained before assets become operational. They need to know how to operate or maintain assets properly, in the right manner, and have a good understanding of what not to do to damage or misuse the asset when being operated.

Studies indicate that over forty percent of asset failures are caused by operational errors and omissions. A good understanding of how asset functions can reduce these types of failures to a minimum is a necessity.

The important thing is to create a culture that includes an asset ownership concept. In this concept, operators become "owners" of the assets (e.g., machine, equipment, facility, etc.). This creates a different mind-set of caring for the assets as if they own them. The assets are maintained from a lifecycle cost perspective of doing the right things to get more value from them. This concept or strategy of managing equipment is called asset management.

Asset management is a systematic process of deploying, operating, maintaining, upgrading and disposing of assets cost-effectively. ISO55000 defines asset management as, "coordinated activities of an organization to realize value from assets." This is a *value-based* strategy. It means we try to do the right things to assets so we get more value out of them. We build, operate, maintain, etc., them right so it costs less during their whole life. Whereas in old strategies, we do things on assets based on performance at whatever it costs. Operators may abuse assets to produce more to meet production requirements, or we may experience more failures from poor design, bad installation, etc.

To implement a good asset management strategy on assets, you should deploy a "10 Rights of Asset Management" strategy as discussed in this book. These rights are:

1. Specify It Right by providing the right requirements and specifications;
2. Design It Right by designing it with $RAMS^2$ to minimize failures;
3. Source It Right by purchasing the best value components;
4. Build It Right by fabricating and assembling it with quality workmanship;
5. Install/Commission It Right by installing with precision quality;
6. Operate It Right by operating it with care and safely;
7. Maintain It Right by performing the right maintenance;
8. Improve It Right by applying the right tools and practices to improve;
9. Dispose/Decommission It Right by disposing of it in an environmentally safe manner;
10. Manage It Right by ensuring the right skilled talent at every role and in establishing an asset management process.

But, we must not only recognize the right things to do, we must daily encourage, educate, remind and embrace these rights. We must be on the lookout for efforts that have not been considered yet and be the champion in the use of the science of asset management.

The implementation of the 10 Rights will ensure a robust AM process that results in:

- Low or minimum failures and high reliability;
- High uptime and availability;
- Low injury rates and a safe operation;
- Process repeatability;

- Lower overall lifecycle cost of ownership;
- High morale;
- Very satisfied stakeholders.

Furthermore, implementing *The 10 Rights of Asset Management* will help improve your organization's bottom line. Also, it will support your compliance with the ISO55001 standard. The application of standards ensures discipline in the processes and organization's activities. *The 10 Rights of Asset Management* process engages stakeholders and the workforce, encourages teamwork and becomes a value creator by making or supporting the right decisions.

Finally, we strongly believe that implementing the 10 Rights discussed in this book will improve the performance of your organization. You will be able to realize more value from your assets. They will also help you in creating a culture of excellence.

You may have to tailor these 10 Rights to meet your specific needs and environment. Again, don't forget, it's not a program, it's a journey… and it takes time to get the right results.

~ Ramesh Gulati

Case Study from Coauthor Terrence O'Hanlon

I was fortunate to play a small role in the leadership lessons learned by Ramesh Gulati and the team he was an essential part of at Arnold Engineering Development Complex (AEDC), a mission critical U.S. Air Force facility in Tennessee.

As the CEO and Publisher at Reliabilityweb.com and *Uptime* Magazine, I was one of the judges on the Uptime Awards, an annual event that has included some of the best reliability and asset management programs in the world since 2006.

I paid many visits to AEDC since 2001 and learned a great deal about best practices for reliability and asset management, but what I learned most about was leadership.

In the Uptime® Elements™ A Reliability Framework and Asset Management System™, we state that a reliability leader is someone who creates a future that was not going to happen anyway. The origins of that idea were heavily influenced by the reliability team we worked with at AEDC.

In publishing a major industry magazine and as conference organizers, my team gets to meet a lot of reliability teams, many of whom manage the technical and tactical elements of reliability and asset management in what could be classified as the top quartile or world-class. They are capable managers who deliver their teams and organizations to what, in Uptime Elements language, is called the "default" future.

The default future is the future that is hurling toward us. It is the future we know will arrive tomorrow if we do not do something different. In many cases, the default future is perfectly fine to deliver the results that the asset owners desire. Other times, for instance, like the mission-critical focused and highly patriotic team at AEDC, they make decisions to create a future that definitely would not happen without reliability leadership.

Many of the systems and assets at AEDC present a huge challenge as they predate World War II (ended 1945) and are unlike assets found anywhere else. The base changes leadership every few years and the new leader arrives with his or her own ideas about reliability and asset management and the budget. The economics are firm, as the government does not provide much flexibility regarding budget expansion. There is a constant pressure to improve performance with fewer resources.

My coauthor, Ramesh Gulati, and several key team members not only deliver best practices in managing reliability and asset management, they also lead everyone from the front line to the base commanders to a new future that was not going to happen anyway. While other similar agencies suffer setbacks and restarts, the team at AEDC has been consistently creating a culture of reliability leadership for almost 20 years, with improvement each and every one of those years.

They gain a great deal of industry acknowledgment by hosting plant tours and being invited to speak at every major industry conference. The AEDC team won several Uptime Awards for Best Overall Reliability Program over the years and are recognized by many other institutions, including being the first U.S. organization to earn independent certification of their asset management process under ISO9001 (prior to ISO55001). Members of the team won both the first Certified Maintenance and Reliability Professional Next Generation Award and the second Certified Maintenance and Reliability Professional Veterans' Award.

Of course, good, competent reliability management plays an important role. However, I attribute the sustainability and success of that program to reliability leadership.

Failing organizations are usually over-managed and under-led.

~ Warren Bennis

In the 21st century, leading organizations recognize that success is achieved through leadership. However, they also realize that results are only delivered through engagement and empowerment of everyone in the workforce. Leadership does not come from one person, it comes from everyone. This is especially true for reliability.

Moreover, they understand that such engagement and empowerment lead to the enlightened awareness that "reliability" is a holistic system of interactive and interrelated elements. They appreciate the roles that culture and leadership play in the delivery of performance. Finally, they are aware of the nature of the journey.

The following chart summarizes the big picture differences between reliability management and reliability leadership.

Traditional Reliability Management	Reliability Leadership
Manages to the future	Creates a future that was not going to happen anyway
Performance through threats and incentives	Performance through leadership fundamentals, including integrity, authenticity and responsibility
Planning	Creating a Vision (Aim)
Organizing the hierarchy	Empowering people
Measuring and controlling	Aligning the web of relations
Continuous improvement	Inspiring and coaching

Reliability Leadership as a Context

As I mentioned earlier, we see a lot of very good reliability management programs, but when you meet a team that operates in the context of reliability leadership, you know it right away.

Context is something that clarifies meaning.

Context is also a fundamental set of assumptions. Many of these assumptions are accepted as fact and they go unquestioned, which is likely to limit the ability of people to even realize that there might be another context from which to choose.

There was a time when the context of earth was that it was flat. The worldview or context limited humankind, as it prevented worldwide sailing trips of discovery that created huge benefits once a new context was "invented."

Management Is Important

Well managed reliability programs tend to focus on rearranging the content of their programs. In other words, choosing a different software solution or replacing an old consultant with a new one. They may change the sequence of improvement efforts and add investment that was missing prior. These are all important decisions and they will create change, but do they make a difference?

As humans, we tend to think things are the "way they are" or are the "way they appear," however history is filled with examples of people who "saw through" the way things were to create a new context that dramatically changed the way the rest of us experienced life.

To return to the example of reliability leadership at AEDC, they created a context called *high performance reliability*, even with the circumstances of rigid government budgeting and procurement, ever changing top management, a skeptical workforce and unique aging assets that had no possibilities for replacement.

How did they create this highly improbable context?

1. The people at the center of the AEDC team had remarkably high integrity. They did what they said they would do and they cleaned up the mess they made when they chose not to keep their word or could not keep their word. This element of leadership went a long way toward creating an environment of trust. Of course, everyone on the team did not like every decision. However, they often remarked on how they valued working in an environment where they could count on other members of the team to do what they said they would do.
2. The people at the center of the AEDC team had remarkably consistent authenticity. The values of the team were wide and varied, but the thing they had in common was that the values the team members said they had were aligned with the way the team members acted. This went a long way toward building trust because when people share their values transparently, the people closest to them know how closely their stated values match their actions.
3. The vast majority of the people on the AEDC reliability and asset management team did not have job titles that made them responsible for the outcomes of the reliability program. However, almost all of them took a stand for reliability and declared their commitment to be a highly reliability organization.

4. The team also was acutely aware of the importance of the AEDC mission to United States national security. Working on an aim that is bigger than one's self creates a solid foundation for reliability leadership.

In other words, the context of reliability leadership was created because a group of people said it was so. This special group of people had built up their "reliability leadership bank accounts" with deposits of integrity, authenticity and responsibility, so when they made their declaration, they had their ***word*** solidly in place. These reliability leaders created a future that was not going to happen anyway.

Failing to pay attention to these laws of reliability will generate painful consequences, just as failing to pay attention to the law of gravity will generate painful consequences for those who ignore it.

The Managing System Framework

At the time of the AEDC journey, there were very few established frameworks for them to follow. They had to make up their own. Luckily for the world, there has been some significant work done to institutionalize the journey. They chose ISO9001 (a tailored quality management system standard) for their asset management framework and got certified in 2004.

Since then, one of the most significant advances is the release of the ISO55000 series of standards relating to a managing system for asset management. This is discussed in detail in Chapter 10.

Uptime Elements A Reliability Framework and Asset Management System

Some organizations, especially those that have already embraced ISO9001 or ISO14001, are aware of how ISO managing system standards work with their own processes. Others use publicly available frameworks, like the new revised Uptime® Elements™ A Reliability Framework and Asset Management System™ by Reliabilityweb.com.

This framework connects technical asset management activities with the leadership domain. All those areas connect through a line of sight to the business process through a detailed asset management system aligned to ISO55001.

Several organizations, such as the Metropolitan Transportation Authority (MTA), Bristol-Myers Squibb, Honda Motor Company, Medtronic, DC Water and the Central Arizona Project, are applying the Uptime Elements A Reliability Framework and Asset Management System.

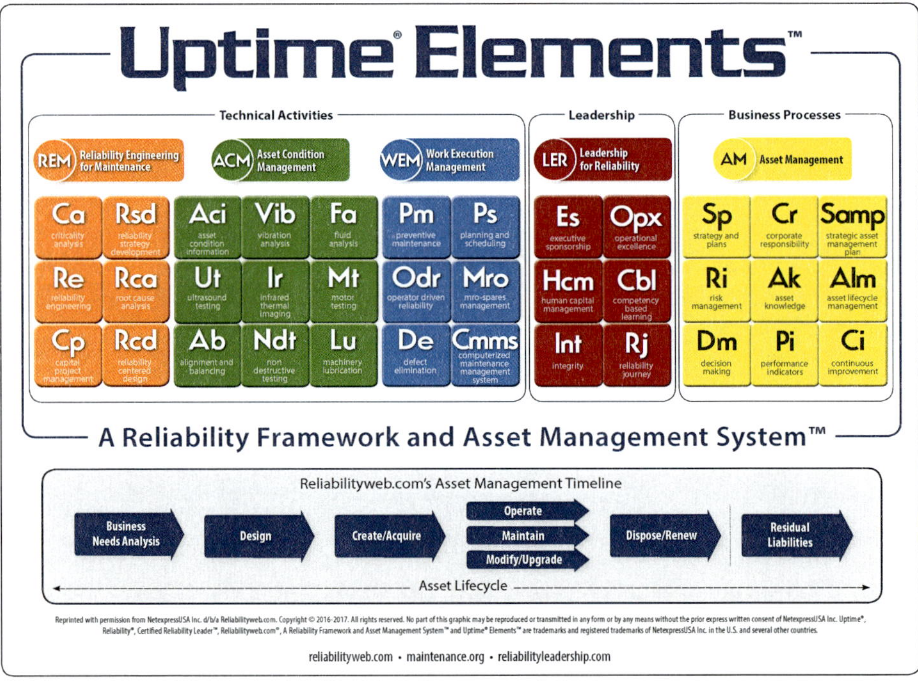

There are many other frameworks, such as the Institute of Asset Management's An Anatomy of Asset Management and the Society for Maintenance & Reliability Professionals' 5 Pillars, available in the public domain.

The Benefits of a Framework

All things that can be mastered begin with the acquisition of a specialized language that contains words, concepts and ideas. An example would be a doctor who begins medical training by studying the specialized words, phrases and concepts related to the practice of medicine.

At Ross University School of Medicine, they provide the following advice for medical students: "Clear use of language is essential for communication with both colleagues and patients—you cannot succeed as a physician without a good command of language. You are about to start learning a new language, the language of medicine. ***The more you think about what words mean, the more fluent you can become, and the more effectively you will be able to think in this new language***. Your task as a medical student will be much harder if you do not pay close attention to language, both technical and non-technical."

A Pennsylvania Academy of the Fine Arts instructor relates this musical mastery wisdom: "So, what is the goal of a music education? I would say to 'communicate' musically or, in other words, to learn and to speak the 'language' of music. Using the word 'language' in this context does not refer to reading the written musical language (although that is good) but instead means speaking a language in the broader sense of understanding, as well as communicating the grammar, vocabulary and syntax so that 'ideas' and 'creativity' can be shared."

Uptime Elements A Reliability Framework and Asset Management System creates a common foundational language of words, phrases, sentences and concepts to minimize communication errors that can undermine traditional reliability efforts.

ISO55001 provides a consistent management system framework across enterprises to ensure that all supporting aspects that are required to be managed and asset management business approaches are in place.

Frameworks make it easier to align teams and organizational silos. When combined with powerful organizational objectives, they empower teams to achieve much more together than any of the individual parts could have produced independently.

Time to Bend the Universe

Yes, that is the term I like to use for calling forth something that previously did not exist and creating something new – like a new future, a new way to move through each day, a new way to create results.

I have come to realize this even though for years I had some strongly held beliefs and thought some really deep thoughts about advancing reliability and asset management. The fact is my beliefs and thoughts did not change anything. The universe is one hundred percent ambivalent to what I think and what I believe about reliability and asset management. Nothing will change as a result of your thoughts or beliefs, no matter how pure they are.

If you doubt what I am saying, I suggest you go outside on the next clear evening and look up at the stars and let them know what you think and what you believe about advancing reliability and asset management. Let me know what changes result the next day from your deeply held beliefs and incredibly brilliant thoughts.

My point is that the universe will only bend, will only allow change and will only allow something new to be called forth from committed action.

Mahatma Gandhi said, "Be the change you wish to see in the world," and I offer a few steps in that direction:

1. Take a stand for something, like reliability and asset management.
2. Find others who may share that stand and create a declaration (e.g., for reliability and asset management).
3. Follow that declaration with committed action.
4. Practice integrity. Keep your word and do what you say you will do.
5. Restore your integrity by cleaning up the mess you make at the earliest possibility when you do not keep your word.
6. Align stakeholders on the destination (i.e., aim) and organizational objectives.
7. Lead by engaging, empowering and enlightening stakeholders.

How will you bend the universe now that you know the 10 Rights of Asset Management?

~ Terrence O'Hanlon

APPENDIX A

HOUSE OF QUALITY TOOL

The house of quality tool is a diagram that resembles a house and is used for defining the relationship between a customer's desires and an asset's or product's capabilities. It utilizes a planning matrix to relate what the customer's needs are and how that product is going to meet those needs. It looks like a house with a correlation matrix as its roof; customer's wants versus product features as the main part; competitor evaluation as the porch; etc. It is based on the belief that products should be designed to reflect the customer's desires and tastes. It is reported that the tool can increase cross-functional integration within organizations using it, especially between marketing, engineering and manufacturing.

The basic structure of the house of quality is a table with "Whats" as the label on the left and "Hows" across the top. The roof is a diagonal matrix of "Hows vs. Hows," and the body of the house is a matrix of "Whats vs. Hows." Both these matrices are filled with indicators, showing whether the interaction of the specific item is a strong positive, a strong negative, or somewhere in between. Additional annexes on the right side and bottom hold the "Whys" (e.g., market research, etc.) and the "How Much." Rankings based on the "Whys" and the correlations can be used to calculate priorities for the Hows.

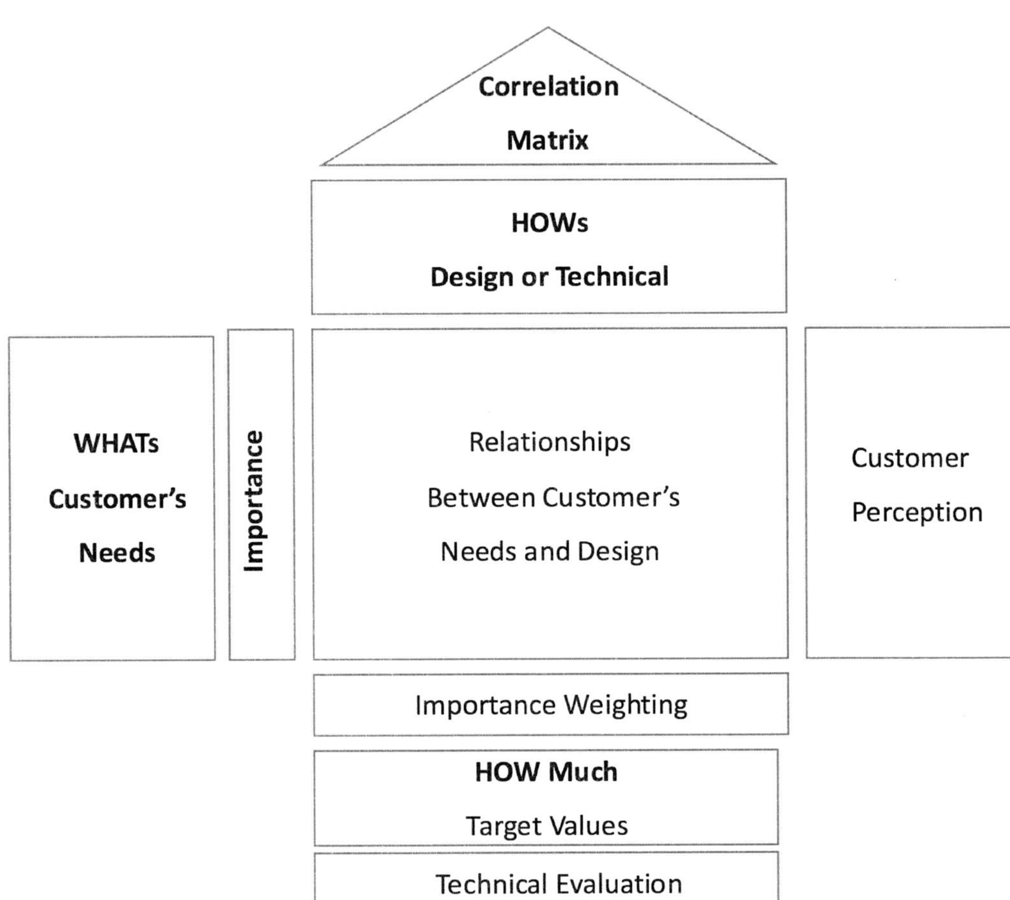

Figure 1: Building blocks of the house of quality

A house of quality analysis also can be cascaded, with "Hows" from one level becoming the "Whats" of a lower level. As this progresses, the decisions get closer to the engineering and manufacturing details.

Basic building blocks or areas of the house of quality are shown in Figure 1 and a description of each block is given in Table 1.

Table 1: Description of Areas in the House of Quality

House of Quality Areas	Description of Areas
Rows	Listed left of the central matrix as customer requirements; they are *what* the customer thinks are important about the asset
Importance to customer	The *whats*, with ranking by customer preference
Columns	Along the top of the central matrix, listed in columns, are the technical attributes of the asset; this is *how* an asset can meet the customer's requirements
Central matrix	Inside the central matrix, showing the strength of the relationship between the *whats* and *hows* (e.g., strong positive, positive, negative, strong negative)
Importance weighting	The weighting of the relationship in each column is summed up to determine the importance of the technical attributes
Roof - gabled	The roof on the house shows the correlation among the technical attributes
Target values	The numerical or qualitative descriptions are shown in the basement of the house and are design targets set for the technical attributes
Technical evaluation	The graph in the sub-basement compares the new design with others – current and competitors' alternate designs
Customer's competitive evaluation	The graph on the right rates new design and competitors' designs in terms of customer requirements; these ratings are based on customer surveys and input

House of quality, also known as quality function deployment (QFD), is a very powerful tool as it incorporates the customer's needs into design parameters so that the final asset is better designed to meet customer–owner expectations.

APPENDIX B

10 STEPS TO CONDUCT A DESIGN FAILURE MODE AND EFFECTS ANALYSIS (DFMEA)

Assemble a cross-functional team of individuals with diverse knowledge about the process, asset, or service and customer needs. Functions often included are design, operations and manufacturing, quality, reliability, maintenance, purchasing and suppliers, and customer service.

- Identify the scope of the failure mode and effects analysis (FMEA). Is it for concept, system, design, process, or service? What are the boundaries? How detailed should it be? Use blueprints, schematics, drawings, or flowcharts to identify the scope and make sure every team member understands it in detail.
- Review to identify each component and interface. Document the function(s) of each component and interface on a DFMEA/FMEA form.

Reasons for the review:

- Helps assure all team members are familiar with the asset, system, or process and its design;
- Identifies each of the main components of the design and determines the function(s) of those components and interfaces between them;
- Makes sure you are studying all components defined in the scope of the DFMEA;
- Adds reference numbers to each component and interface;
- Invites a subject matter expert, if needed, to clarify questions.

Brainstorm and list potential failure modes, review existing documentation and data for clues.

- Consider potential failure modes for each component and interface.
- A potential failure mode represents any manner in which the asset or component could fail to perform its intended function(s).
- Remember that many components have more than one failure mode. Document each one. Never leave out a potential failure mode because it rarely happens. Don't take shortcuts here; this is the time to be thorough.
- Prepare for the brainstorming activity.
- Before starting the brainstorming session, review the documentation for clues about potential failure modes.
- Use operators' complaints regarding the asset's performance, including downtime issues, downtime or lost time reports, and reports that identify things that have gone wrong, such as hold tag reports, scrap, damage and rework, as inputs for the brainstorming activity.
- Additionally, consider what may happen to the asset under difficult usage conditions and how the asset might fail when it interacts with other assets or systems.

List potential effects of failure; there may be more than one for each failure.

- The effect is related directly to the ability of that specific component to perform its intended function.
- An effect is an impact a failure could make should it occur.
- Some failures have an effect on the asset itself, other assets, or the whole process, while other failures have an effect on the environment or the safety of operators.
- The effect should be stated in terms that are meaningful to asset performance. If the effects are defined in general terms, it will be difficult to identify and reduce true potential risks.

Assign severity rankings based on the severity of the consequences of failure. The ranking scales are mission critical for the success of a DFMEA because they establish the basis for determining the risk of one failure mode and its effect relative to another.

- The same ranking scales for DFMEAs should be used consistently throughout an organization. This makes it possible to compare the risk priority numbers (RPNs) from different FMEAs to one another.
- The severity ranking is based on a relative scale ranging from 1 to 10. A "10" means the effect has a dangerously high severity leading to a hazard without warning. Conversely, a "1" severity ranking means the severity is extremely low. The scales provide a relative, not an absolute, ranking.
- The best way to customize a ranking scale is to start with a standard, generic scale and then modify it to be more meaningful to the organization.

By adding organization-specific examples to the ranking definitions, DFMEA teams will have an easier time using the scales. The use of examples saves the team time and improves the consistency of rankings from team to team.

Assign occurrence rankings based on how frequently the cause of the failure is likely to occur.

- You need to know the potential cause of the potential to determine the occurrence ranking because, just like the severity ranking is driven by the effect, the occurrence ranking is a function of the cause.
- The occurrence ranking is based on the likelihood or frequency that the cause, or mechanism of failure, will occur.
- If you know the cause, you can better identify how frequently a specific mode of failure will occur.
- The occurrence ranking scale, like the severity ranking, is on a relative scale from 1 to 10.
- An occurrence ranking of "10" means the failure mode occurrence is very high; it happens all the time. Conversely, a "1" means the probability of occurrence is remote.

Assign detection rankings based on the chances the failure will be detected before the operator or detection device can detect it.

- To assign detection rankings, consider the design or asset-related controls already in place for each failure mode and then assign a detection ranking to each control.
- Think of the detection ranking as an evaluation of the ability of the design's controls to prevent or detect the mechanism of failure.

- Prevention controls are always preferred over detection controls.
- Prevention controls prevent the cause or mechanism of failure or the failure mode itself from occurring; they generally impact the frequency of occurrence. Prevention controls come in different forms and levels of effectiveness.
- Detection controls detect the cause, the mechanism of failure, or the failure mode itself after the failure has occurred, BUT before the product is released from the design stage.
- A detection ranking of "1" means the chance of detecting a failure is almost certain. Conversely, a "10" means the detection of a failure or mechanism of failure is absolutely uncertain.

Calculate the RPN, which is equal to Severity x Occurrence x Detection.

- The RPN is the risk priority number. It gives you a relative risk ranking. The higher the RPN, the higher the risk potential.
- The RPN is calculated by multiplying the three rankings together: Severity Ranking X Occurrence Ranking X Detection Ranking. Calculate the RPN for each failure mode and effect.
- Since each of the three relative ranking scales ranges from 1 to 10, the RPN will always be between 1 and 1,000. The higher the RPN, the higher the relative risk. The RPN gives you an excellent tool to prioritize focused improvement efforts.

Develop the action plan for what changes will be made in the design to reduce RPN. Define who will do what by when.

- Taking action means reducing the RPN. The RPN can be reduced by lowering any of the three rankings (severity, occurrence, or detection) individually or in combination with one another.

- A reduction in the severity ranking for a DFMEA is often the most difficult to attain. It usually requires a design change.
- A reduction in the occurrence ranking is accomplished by removing or controlling the potential causes or mechanisms of failure.
- A reduction in the detection ranking is accomplished by adding or improving prevention or detection controls.
- What is considered an acceptable RPN? The answer to that question depends on the organization. For example, an organization may decide any RPN above a maximum target of 200 presents an unacceptable risk and must be reduced. If so, then an action plan identifying who will do what by when is needed.

Take action by implementing the improvements identified by the DFMEA team.

- The action plan outlines what steps are needed to implement the solution, who will do them and when they will be completed.

Recalculate the resulting RPN. Reevaluate each of the potential failures once improvements have been made and determine its impact on the RPNs.

- This step in a DFMEA confirms the action plan had the desired results by calculating the resulting RPN.
- To recalculate the RPN, reassess the severity, occurrence and detection rankings for the failure modes after the action plan has been completed.

There are a number of published guidelines and standards for the requirements and recommended reporting format of DFMEAs. Some of the key published standards for this analysis include:

- SAE J1739;
- AIAG FMEA-3;
- MIL-STD-1629A.

The Automotive Industry Action Group (AIAG) has guidelines and a reference manual very similar to SAE standard J1739.

A sample worksheet/template is shown in Figure 1 (See page 246).

Description of FMEA Worksheet

Potential
Failure Mode and Effects Analysis
(Design FMEA)

System	______	FMEA Number	______
Subsystem	______	Prepared By	______
Component	______	FMEA Date	______
Design Lead	______	Key Date ______	Revision Date ______
Core Team	______	Page ___ of ___	

Item / Function	Potential Failure Mode(s)	Potential Effect(s) of Failure	Sev	Potential Cause(s)/ Mechanism(s) of Failure	Prob	Current Design Controls	Det	RPN	Recommended Action(s)	Responsibility & Target Completion Date	Action Results: Actions Taken	New Sev	New Occ	New Det	New RPN
								0							0
Coolant containment. Hose connection. Coolant fill. M	Crack/break. Burst. Side wall flex. Bad seal. Poor hose rete	Leak	8	Over pressure	8	Burst, validation pressure cycle.	1	64	Test included in prototype and production validation testing.						0
								0							0
								0							0
								0							0
								0							0
															0
															0
								0							0
								0							0
															0
															0
															0
															0
															0
								0							0

Write down each failure mode and potential consequence(s) of that failure.

Severity - On a scale of 1-10, rate the Severity of each failure (10= most severe). See Severity sheet.

Likelihood - Write down the potential cause(s), and on a scale of 1-10, rate the Likelihood of each failure (10= most likely). See Likelihood sheet.

Detectability - Examine the current design, then, on a scale of 1-10, rate the Detectability of each failure (10 = least detectable). See Detectability sheet.

Risk Priority Number - The combined weighting of Severity, Likelihood, and Detectability. RPN = Sev X Occ X Det

Response Plans and Tracking

Figure 1: A sample FMEA worksheet

(Source: https://www.lehigh.edu/~intribos/Resources/FMEA-template.xls)

APPENDIX

C

GUIDELINES FOR DESIGN FOR MANUFACTURABILITY AND ASSEMBLY (DFMA)

The heart of any design for a manufacturing system is a group of design principles or guidelines that are structured to help the designer reduce the cost and difficulty of manufacturing an item. The following is a listing of these guidelines:

1 Minimize the number of components

Reducing the number of parts in an asset is probably the best opportunity to reduce manufacturing and assembly costs. The final asset is more reliable because there are fewer connections. Disassembly for maintenance and repair service is easier. A reduced part count usually means automation is easier to implement. Work in process is reduced and there are fewer inventory control problems. Fewer parts need to be purchased, which reduces ordering costs. In general, it reduces the level of intensity of all activities related to the asset during its entire life.

2 Use standard, commercially available components

Avoiding the design of custom, engineered components by using standard components that are commercially available is encouraged. This practice reduces design time. In addition, standard components are less expensive than custom made items.

The high availability of these components reduces lead times. Also, their reliability factors are well ascertained. Furthermore, the use of standard components addresses production pressures to the supplier, somewhat relieving the manufacturer's concern of meeting production schedules.

3 Use a modular design

The use of modules in asset design simplifies manufacturing activities, such as inspection, testing, assembly, purchasing, redesign, maintenance, service, and so on. A module design adds versatility when updating in the redesign process, helps run tests before the final assembly is put together and allows the use of standard components to minimize product variations.

Each subassembly should be minimized in the use of components, with a limit of five to ten parts. This helps to maintain and repair. Automated and manual assembly is implemented more readily. Inventory requirements are reduced and final assembly time is minimized.

4 Design parts with tolerances that are within process capability

Tolerances tighter than the process capability should be avoided, otherwise, additional processing or sortation will be required. Bilateral tolerances should be specified.

5 Design for ease of part fabrication

Select the optimum combination between the material and fabrication process to minimize the overall manufacturing cost. Simplify part geometry so unnecessary features are avoided. In general, final operations, such as painting, polishing and finish machining, should be minimized or avoided. Excessive tolerance, surface finish requirements, etc., are commonly found problems that result in higher than necessary production costs.

6 Design for ease of assembly

Assembly should be unambiguous. Part features, such as chamfers and tapers, should be designed on mating parts and be assembled only one way. Sometimes, special geometric features must be added to components to achieve foolproof assembly.

Threaded fasteners (e.g., screws, bolts, nuts) should be avoided where possible, especially when automated assembly is used. Instead, fast assembly techniques, such as snap fits and adhesive bonding, should be employed.

The use of fasteners increases the cost of manufacturing a part due to the handling and feeding operations that have to be performed. Besides the high cost of the equipment required for them, these operations are not one hundred percent successful, so they contribute to reducing the overall manufacturing efficiency. In general, fasteners should be avoided and replaced, for example, by using tabs or snap fits.

7 Minimize the use of flexible components

Flexible components include parts made of rubber, belts, gaskets, cables, etc. Flexible components are generally more difficult to handle and assemble.

8 Eliminate or reduce adjustment required

Adjustments during assembly are time-consuming. Designing adjustments into the product mean more opportunities for out of adjustment conditions to arise.

9 Ease of handling and shipping

The asset should be designed so it is easy to handle and transport. Handling consists of positioning, orienting and fixing a part, component and subassemblies.

To facilitate orientation, symmetrical parts should be used whenever possible. If it is not possible, then asymmetry must be exaggerated to avoid failures. Use external guiding features to help the orientation of a part. The subsequent operations should be designed so that the orientation of the part is maintained. Also, tube feeders, magazines, part strips, etc., should be used to keep this orientation between operations.

Try to minimize the flow of material waste, parts, etc., in the manufacturing operation. Also, take packaging into account by selecting appropriate and safe packaging for the asset.

Avoid using flexible parts. If cables have to be used, include a dummy connector to plug the cable (i.e., robotic assembly) so it can be located easily.

Ensure proper lifting devices and hooks are appropriately located to facilitate safe lifting.

APPENDIX D

CONDITION-BASED MAINTENANCE

Condition-based maintenance (CBM), also known as predictive maintenance (PdM) or asset condition management (ACM), attempts to evaluate the condition of an asset by performing periodic or continuous asset health monitoring. Based on asset health condition, maintenance is performed at a point in time when it is most cost-effective, yet before the asset fails in service.

CBM inspections are mostly performed while the asset is operating, thereby minimizing disruption of normal system operations. Adoption of CBM/PdM in the maintenance of an asset can result in substantial cost savings and higher system reliability.

As shown in Figure 1, different technologies, including asset operator support, could be used during the P-F interval to detect failures and correct them before they create catastrophic breakdowns.

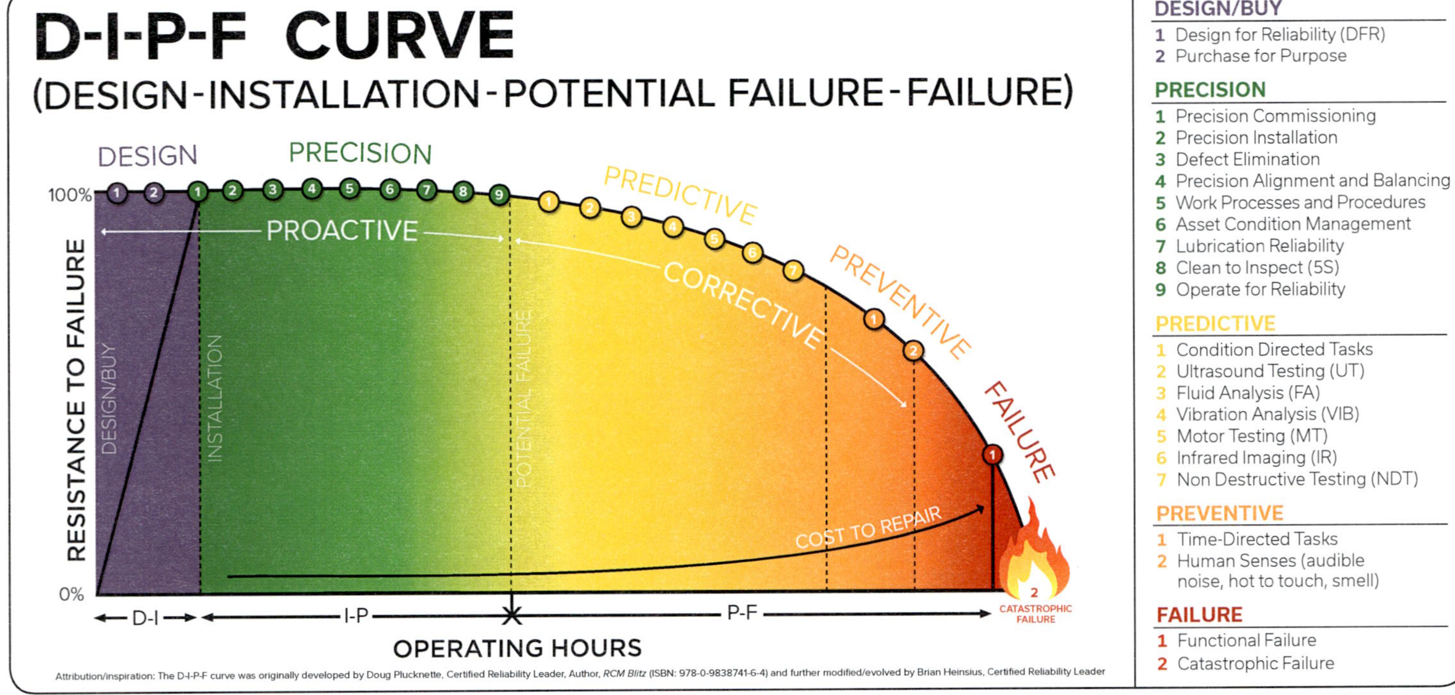

Figure 1: P-F interval chart

A number of different CBM/PdM technologies are used to evaluate the condition of assets. A few of the more common technologies and their corresponding Uptime® Element™ are:

a. Vibration Analysis (Vib);
b. Alignment and Balancing (Ab);
c. Ultrasound Testing (Ut);
d. Infrared Thermal Imaging (Ir);
e. Machinery Lubrication (Lu);
f. Fluid Analysis (Fa);
g. Motor Testing (Mt);
h. Nondestructive Testing (Ndt);
i. Asset Condition Information (Aci).

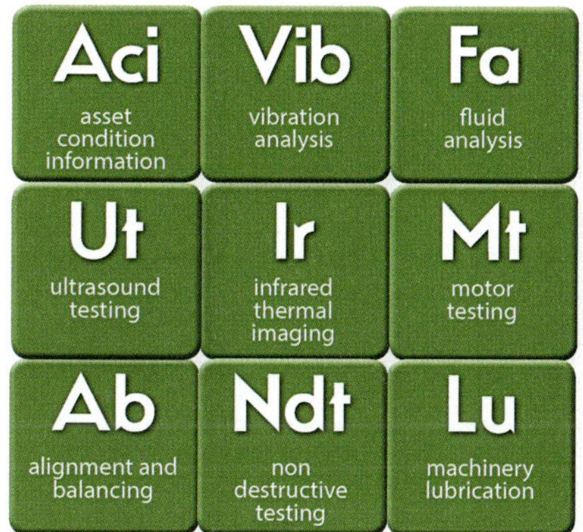

Basically, in the CBM approach, the need for maintenance is based on the actual condition of the machine, rather than on some preset schedule. Activities, such as changing oil, are based on a predetermined schedule or time, such as calendar time or asset run time. For example, most of us change the oil in our cars every 3,000 to 5,000 miles driven. This is effectively basing the oil change on asset run time. No concern is given to the actual condition and performance capability of the oil. It is changed because it's time to change it. This methodology can be compared to a preventive maintenance task.

On the other hand, if we ignore the vehicle run time and have the oil analyzed at some regular period to determine its actual condition and lubrication properties, then we may be able to extend the oil change until the car has been driven 10,000 miles, or maybe even more.

This is the advantage of utilizing condition-based maintenance. CBM is used to define needed maintenance tasks based on quantified asset conditions or performance data. The advantages of CBM are many. A well established CBM program eliminates or reduces asset failures cost-effectively. It also helps with scheduling maintenance activities to minimize overtime costs. In addition, you can minimize inventory and order parts, as required, well ahead of time to support downstream maintenance needs.

a. Vibration Analysis (Vib)

Vibration usually indicates trouble in a machine. Machine and structures vibrate in response to one or more pulsating forces due to imbalance, misalignment, etc. The magnitude of vibration is dependent on the force and properties of the system, both of which may depend on speed.

There are four fundamental characteristics of vibration: frequency, period, amplitude, and phase. *Frequency* is the number of cycles per unit time and is expressed in the number of cycles per minute (CPM) or cycles per second (Hz). *Period* is the time required to complete one cycle of vibration—the reciprocal of frequency. *Amplitude* is the maximum value of vibration at a given location of the machine. *Phase* is the time relationship between vibrations of the same frequency and is measured in degrees.

The three key measures used to evaluate the magnitude of vibrations are:

- Displacement;
- Velocity;
- Acceleration.

The *displacement* measurement is dominant at a low frequency and is caused by stresses in flexible members of the machine. It is typically expressed in mils peak-to-peak.

Velocity is the time rate change of displacement. It is dependent on both displacement and frequency and is related to the fatigue characteristics of the machine. Greater displacement and frequency of vibration relates directly to a greater severity of machine vibration at the measured location.

Acceleration is the dominant measure at higher frequencies that exceed 1,000 Hz. Acceleration is proportional to the force on machine components, such as gears and couplings.

Things to Remember About Vibration Analysis

1. It is the most widely used technology for rotating equipment.
2. The rate of change is equally as important as the actual values.
3. The type and level of alarms are based on specific failure modes.
4. Overall alarms indicate approaching failures, but do not help in detecting specific failure modes.
5. Baseline vibration data is important in detecting any unusual symptoms or problems.

A well-run vibration analysis program will control the quality of asset installations and predict a multitude of failures well in advance. This enables adequate time to ensure asset availability within the desired operating requirements.

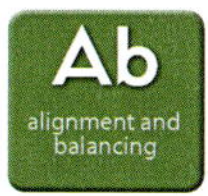

b. Alignment and Balancing (Ab)

With a few exceptions, mechanical troubles in a rotating machine cause vibration. A properly aligned and balanced machine reduces strain on the rotating mass of the machine, thus eliminating or minimizing vibration. This is a proactive approach to extending the life of an asset.

Figure 2: Shaft alignment (Source: Luduca/Pruftechnik Engineer's Guide, 2012)

Common problems that produce vibration are:

- Imbalance of rotating parts;
- Misalignment of couplings and bearings;
- Bent shafts;
- Worn, eccentric, or damaged parts;
- Bad drive belts and chains;
- Damaged or bad bearings;
- Looseness;

- Rubbing;
- Aerodynamics and other forces.

Misalignment of shafted equipment not only causes asset malfunctions or breakdowns, it also may be an indicator of other problems. Checking and adjusting alignment used to be a very slow procedure, but the advent of laser alignment systems has reduced labor time by more than half and increased accuracy significantly.

Laser alignment is a natural complement to vibration analysis. Properly aligning shafts eliminates one of the major causes of vibration in rotating machines and drastically extends bearing life. For the minimal amount of work involved, the payback is great.

Balancing rotating mass is another important practice. An unbalanced component attempts to rotate around its mass center and transmits force to the bearings, creating a high level of vibration. Thus, balancing asset components to an acceptable level reduces the strain and vibration transmitted, resulting in fewer failures, reduced energy requirements and longer asset life.

Soft foot is another issue that can cause misalignment. Just as a wobbly chair or table is an annoyance, a wobbly machine mount causes alignment frustration. When the machine is bolted down, the strain is put on the machine's casing and bearing housings, resulting in vibrations. The machine should be sitting evenly on the foundation before it's properly and accurately aligned and balanced.

Things to Remember About Alignment and Balancing

1. Misalignment and being out of balance are common causes of vibration problems.
2. Alignment and balancing specifications should be part of the procurement document when buying new or modifying rotating type assets.
3. Proper and correct alignment and balancing greatly reduces failures and increases asset life.
4. Baseline alignment and balancing data are important in detecting any unusual symptoms and are a key part of any asset management program.

Accurate alignment and balancing are a key practice to ensure asset reliability and reduce maintenance costs.

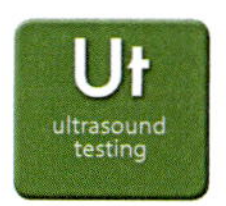

c. Ultrasound Testing (Ut)

Ultrasound testing is extremely useful in the diagnosis of mechanical and electrical problems. Testing instruments are usually portable, handheld devices. Their electronic circuitry converts a narrow band of ultrasound, usually between 20 kHz and 100 kHz, into an audible range so the user can recognize the qualitative sounds of the operating equipment through headphones. The intensity of the signal strength is also displayed on the instrument. Ultrasonic instruments and scanners are most often used to detect gas, liquid, or vacuum leaks.

Ultrasound testing is easy to perform, requires minimal training and the instruments are inexpensive. Airborne ultrasonic devices are highly sensitive listening "guns," similar in size to the radar speed guns used by police at speed traps. They provide a convenient, non-intrusive means of assessing the asset's condition. Airborne ultrasonic monitoring is especially easy and useful in testing remote electrical equipment, as well as shielded electrical equipment, such as connections inside switchgears and panels. In the case of high voltage insulator failures, airborne ultrasonic devices can often detect faults earlier than infrared thermography. Ultrasound devices also can detect noise caused by loose connections as they vibrate inside the panels.

Some of the most common applications of ultrasound detection are:

- Leak detection in pressure and vacuum systems (e.g., boiler, heat exchanger, condensers, chillers, vacuum furnaces, specialty gas systems);
- Bearing inspection;
- Steam trap inspection;
- Pump cavitation;
- Detection of corona in electrical switchgear;

- Valve analysis;
- Integrity of seals and gaskets in tanks and pipe systems;
- Detection in electrical systems:
    - Arcing – Occurs when electricity flows through space, similar to lightning;
    - Corona – When the voltage on an electrical conductor, such as an antenna or high voltage transmission line, exceeds the threshold value, the air around it begins to ionize to form a blue or purple glow;
    - Tracking – Often referred to as baby arcing, it's when electricity follows the path of damaged insulation, using surrounding dirt, debris and moisture as the conductive medium.

Things to Remember About Ultrasound Testing

1. Ultrasound testing can be used to find a variety of problems, including:
    a. Leaks in air systems, steam traps, vacuum leaks, etc.;
    b. Electrical problems, such as corona, arcing and tracking;
    c. Piping inspections to find flows in materials and to measure wall thickness in pipes and pressure vessels;
    d. Fault detection in mechanical systems, such as belts, chains, bearings, etc.

2. Ultrasound testing delivers savings in the areas of energy and equipment uptime and reduces reactive maintenance.

A well-run ultrasound program can be used to find a variety of problems. What's more, an ultrasound testing program reduces failures and improves reliability.

d. Infrared Thermal Imaging (Ir)

As one of the most versatile condition-based maintenance technologies available, infrared thermal imaging, also known as infrared thermography, is used to study everything from individual components of assets to plant systems, roofs and even entire buildings.

Infrared inspections can be qualitative or quantitative. Qualitative inspections look at relative differences, hot and cold spots, and deviations from normal or expected temperatures. Quantitative inspections look at accurate measurement of the temperature of the target. One must be careful not to put too much emphasis on the quantitative side of infrared because temperature-based sensors are better for accurate temperature measurements.

Infrared instruments include an optical system to collect radiant energy from the object and focus it, a detector to convert the focused energy pattern to an electrical signal and an electronic system to amplify the detector's output signal and process it into a form that can be displayed. Most instruments include the ability to produce an image that can be displayed and recorded.

Infrared thermography cameras are non-contact, line of sight thermal measurement and imaging systems. Because infrared thermal imaging is a non-contact technique, it's especially attractive for identifying hot and cold spots in energized electrical equipment, large surface areas, such as boilers and building roofs, and other areas where a standoff temperature measurement is necessary.

Instruments that perform this function detect electromagnetic energy in short wave (between 3 to 5 microns) and long wave (between 8 to 15 microns) bands of the electromagnetic spectrum.

Infrared is used very effectively to identify degrading conditions in a facility's electrical systems, such as transformers, motor control centers, switchgears, substations, switchyards, or power lines. In mechanical systems, infrared thermal imaging identifies blocked flow conditions in heat exchangers, condensers, transformer cooling radiators and pipes. It also is used to verify fluid levels in large containers, such as fuel storage tanks. In addition, infrared thermal imaging identifies insulation system degradation in building walls and roofs, as well as refractory in boilers and furnaces. Temperature monitoring, with infrared thermography in particular, is a reliable technique for finding the moisture induced temperature effects that characterize roof leaks and determining the thermal efficiency of heat exchangers, boilers, building envelopes, etc.

Thermography is limited to line of sight. Errors can be introduced due to the color of the material, material geometry and environmental factors, such as solar heating and wind effects. Emissivity is a key concern, which can introduce a five to twenty percent error in measurements. Shiny or highly polished surfaces are very tricky for thermography to measure, as well as dull, smooth metal surfaces that may not be equally emissive in all directions. Be especially careful where surfaces are highly curved.

Things to Remember About Infrared Thermal Imaging

1. Thermographic images aligned with digital images give a clear indication of fault location.
2. Fault found through infrared thermography may drive the use of other CBM techniques.
3. There is a multitude of applications for infrared thermal imaging to find faults in, including:

    a. Electrical systems – transmission lines, connections, transformers, etc.;
    b. Mechanical systems – overloading, bearing failures, exhaust, cooler blockages, etc.;
    c. Process systems – pipe flow blockages, valve leakages, steam traps, etc.;
    d. Building/facility envelops – heat loss, water leakages, etc.;
    e. Security and policing – security and night surveillance, etc.

An infrared thermal imaging program is used to find failures or provide an early warning of faults for a multitude of applications. The images taken by the infrared camera provides clear, discernible conditions that are easily conveyed to stakeholders.

e. Machinery Lubrication (Lu)

Machinery lubrication is one of the foundational elements of proper maintenance. Numerous studies conclude that improper lubricating practices are the major causes of failures in assets.

Proper lubrication practices include selecting the correct lubricant, storing it properly, distributing it effectively, applying it in the right manner, sampling it correctly, managing its degradation and disposing of it properly. If proper lubrication practices are not implemented correctly, contamination is introduced at every step, creating failure possibility.

Among the failures caused by unmanaged lubrication practices are:

- Selection of the wrong lubricant;
- Dirt and water ingress;
- Under and over lubrication;
- Contamination;
- Excessive leakage.

Things to Remember About Machinery Lubrication

1. The correct selection of lubricant is important for asset health.
2. Too much or too little lubricant, specifically grease, is the biggest cause of failures in most rotating equipment.
3. Correct storage and delivery of the lubricant to the asset are important.
4. You must ensure that contamination does not get introduced when transferring and delivering lubricants.
5. An analysis of the lubricant's condition can provide valuable information about the asset's condition.
6. Developing a proactive relationship with your lubricant supplier is important because this supplier can be very helpful in reducing the cost of your lubrication program.

A well-run lubrication program improves asset reliability and predicts a multitude of failures well in advance.

f. Fluid Analysis (Fa)

The objectives of fluid analysis are to determine:

- An asset's mechanical wear condition;
- Lubricant condition;
- Whether the lubricant has been contaminated.

A wide variety of tests can provide information regarding one or more of these areas. These three areas are not unrelated. Changes in lubricant condition and contamination, if not corrected, will lead to machine wear.

Lubricant Condition

Bad lubricating oil and fluids are either discarded or reconditioned through filtering or by replacing additives. Therefore, analyzing the lubricant to determine its condition is driven by cost. For example, in small machines with small oil reservoirs, the oil is changed on an operating time basis.

In an industrial setup, lubricating fluids can become contaminated from the machine's operating environment, improper filling procedures, or through the mixing of different lubricants in the same machine. For example, if a machine is topped off with oil frequently, you should periodically send the oil out for analysis to check the machine for any serious problems.

The full benefit of fluid analysis can be achieved only by taking frequent samples and trending the data for each asset in the program. The length of the sampling intervals varies based on the different types of equipment and operating conditions. Based on the results of the analyses, lubricants are changed or upgraded to meet the specific operating requirements.

It cannot be overemphasized enough that the sampling technique is critical to a meaningful fluid analysis. Sampling locations must be carefully selected to provide a representative sample and sampling conditions must be uniform so accurate comparisons can be made.

Standard Analytical Test Types

Lubricating oil and hydraulic fluid analysis should proceed from simple, subjective techniques, such as visual and odor examination, to more sophisticated techniques. The more sophisticated tests should be performed when conditions indicate the need for additional information and should be based on asset criticality.

Types of tests include:

- Visual and odor;
- Viscosity;
- Water (moisture);
- Wear particle count;
- Total acid number (TAN);
- Total base number (TBN);
- Spectrometric metals analysis;
- Analytical ferrography;
- Foaming.

Grease is usually not analyzed on a regular basis. Although most of the testing done on oil also can be done on grease, getting a representative sample is usually difficult. The machine may have to be disassembled in order to get a good sample that is a homogeneous mixture of the grease, contaminants and wear.

Oil Sampling and Analysis (Contamination Control Program)

A concern common in all machines with lubricating oil systems is keeping dirt and moisture out of the system. Common components of dirt, such as silica, are abrasive and naturally promote wear of contact surfaces. In hydraulic systems, particles block and abrade the close tolerances of moving parts. Water in oil promotes oxidation and reacts with additives to degrade the performance of the lubrication system. Ideally, there should be *no* dirt or moisture in the lubricant, but this, of course, isn't possible. The lubricant analysis program, therefore, must monitor and control contaminants.

Sampling and frequent oil samples must be collected safely and in a manner that does not introduce dirt and other contaminates into the machine or system, or into the sample. It may be necessary to install permanent sample valves in some lubricating systems.

The oil sample needs to be representative of the oil being circulated in the machine. Therefore, the sample should be collected from a midpoint in reservoirs and upstream of the filter in circulating systems. Clean sample collection bottles and tubing must be used to collect the sample.

Oil analysis is a reliable predictive maintenance tool and is very effective in detecting contaminants in oil that are a result of dirt ingress or internal wear debris generated by the effect of machine degradation and wear. An increase in contaminant levels accelerates the wear out process of all components in industrial machine applications.

Oil cleanliness is measured by the ISO standard, ISO4406 – Cleanliness Codes. For each numerical increase in the ISO contaminant level, a number of contaminants in the oil almost doubles. For example, if the standard is a 16/14/11, then the increase in contaminants in the oil for a 22/21/17 is about 64 times dirtier than the standard.

A basic oil contamination control program can be implemented in three steps:

1. Establish the target fluid cleanliness levels for each machine fluid system.
2. Select and install filtration equipment or upgrade the current filter rating and contaminant exclusion techniques to achieve target cleanliness levels.
3. Monitor fluid cleanliness at regular intervals to achieve target cleanliness levels.

It's good practice to establish a quality control program for incoming oil. Using the ISO standard as guidance, set up a minimum oil cleanliness standard for all oils, new or old, before they are used in the machines.

Things to Remember About Fluid Analysis

1. Fluid analysis allows for the evaluation of the condition of both the lubricant and the asset.
2. Understanding and monitoring the characteristics of the fluid help in reducing the likelihood of lubricant-induced failures.
3. Ensure that samples are taken at the same location and, if possible, in the same operating environment.
4. Create a feedback loop to constantly refine the testing program's alarms and actions.
5. Fluid analysis can be done in-house with the correct training and equipment, or a credible outside laboratory can be used.

Fluid analysis, which is often used in conjunction with other techniques, is a good indicator of asset health. The results of the analysis help point out the source of the problem and the action taken based on these results will improve overall asset reliability.

g. Motor Testing (Mt)

Motor, as well as, electrical condition monitoring encompasses several technologies and techniques to provide a comprehensive system evaluation. Motor or electrical equipment represents a major portion of a facility's capital investment. From the power distribution system to electric motors, the efficient operation of the electrical systems is crucial to maintaining the operational capability of a facility.

Monitoring key electrical parameters provides the information to detect and correct electrical faults, such as high resistance connections, phase imbalance and insulation breakdown. Because faults in electrical systems are seldom visible, these faults are costly due to increased electrical usage and safety concerns. They involve lifecycle cost issues as of result of premature replacement of the expensive assets.

Motor equipment evaluation is divided into two categories: *online monitoring and testing* and *off-line testing.*

Online monitoring is continuous, whereas online testing takes measurements at periodic intervals. Some examples of online monitoring include dissolved gas analysis for transformers, temperature monitoring for motors and transformers, power quality and partial discharge. An example of online testing is current signature analysis, which can detect broken rotor bars and air gap eccentricity in squirrel cage motors. Current signature analysis also detects mechanical imbalances, gear mesh problems, broken fan blades, bearing issues and any other type of problem that results in torque pulsations that cause changes to the current draw.

Much of the off-line testing involves evaluating the equipment's insulation. Other tests, such as low ohm resistance measuring, inspects other aspects of the equipment, such as high resistance connections.

There is a wide array of tests available that use AC signals, DC signals and varying frequency signals. The most common maintenance insulation tests are DC insulation resistance tests, step voltage tests, high potential tests, dissipation/power factor tests and the transformer turns ratio test. Note that insulation tests are sensitive to environmental factors, such as temperature, humidity and contamination or cleanliness of the insulation. Insulation testing is standard industry practice and crucial in determining the condition of the electrical insulation.

Several technologies are also effective when used for acceptance testing and certification for new or modified systems. They are:

- Motor current readings;
- Motor current signature analysis (MCSA);
- AC high potential testing (hipot);
- Surge comparison testing;
- Conductor complex impedance;

- Megohmmeter testing;
- Time-domain reflectometry;
- Radio frequency (RF) monitoring;
- Power factor and harmonic distortion.

Things to Remember About Motor Testing

1. Motor or electrical testing can be classified into two categories: *Online* and *Off-line.*
   a. Online monitoring and/or testing measures any aspect of electrical assets while they are in operation.
   b. Off-line testing takes measurements at periodic intervals when the asset is de-energized.
   c. Both types of testing are important and cannot replace the other.
2. A motor testing program is used to find a variety of problems, including:
   a. Loose connections, ground faults, shorted windings, insulation failures, etc.;
   b. Rotor faults, such as air gaps, phase imbalance, resistive loss, etc.
3. Monitoring of key electrical parameters provides information to detect and correct electrical faults, such as phase imbalance, insulation breakdowns, etc.

A motor and electrical testing program plays a key role in ensuring that motors and electrical systems are operating reliably. It also predicts a multitude of failures well in advance. This enables adequate time to ensure asset availability within the desired operating requirements.

h. Nondestructive Testing (Ndt)

Nondestructive testing plays a critical role in validating the structural integrity of various types of assets. Ndt evaluates material properties and the quality of expensive components or assemblies without damaging the product or its function. It identifies flaws and material characteristics that, if left unaddressed, would result in catastrophic failures.

Typically, Ndt has been associated with the welding of large, high stress components, such as pressure vessels and structural supports. Process plants, such as refineries or chemical plants, use Ndt techniques to ensure the integrity of pressure boundaries for systems processing volatile substances.

The various Ndt techniques are:

- Radiography: Performed to detect subsurface defects, radiography or X-ray is one of the most powerful Ndt techniques available in the industry. Depending on the strength of the radiation source, radiography can provide a clear representation (radiograph) of discontinuities or inclusions in material several inches thick.
- Ultrasound testing or imaging: Provides detection of deep subsurface defects. Ultrasonic inspection of welds and base material is often an alternative or complementary Ndt technique to radiography. Though more dependent on the skill of the operator, ultrasound testing does not produce the harmful radiation experienced with radiography. Ultrasound inspection is based on the difference in the wave reflecting properties of defects and the surrounding material. Due to the time and effort involved in surface preparation and testing, ultrasound inspections are often conducted on representative samples of materials subjected to high stress levels, high corrosion areas and large welds.
- Magnetic particle testing (MPT): Using magnetic particle detection of shallow subsurface defects, it is a very useful technique for localized inspections of weld areas and specific areas of high stress or fatigue loading. MPT provides the ability to locate shallow subsurface defects. Two electrodes are placed several inches apart on the surface of the material to be inspected. An electric current is passed between the electrodes producing magnetic lines. While the current is applied, iron ink or powder is sprinkled on the area of interest. The iron aligns

with the lines of flux. Any defect in the area of interest causes distortions in the lines of magnetic flux, which are visible through the alignment of the powder.

- Dye penetrating testing (DPT): An easily applied and low-cost method to find cracks in nonporous materials. There are two types of dye: one is visual and displays a vivid color contrast and the other is fluorescent and requires an ultraviolet light to brightly display the color contrast.
- Hydrostatic testing: Another Ndt method for detecting defects that completely penetrate pressure boundaries, hydrostatic testing is typically conducted prior to the delivery or operation of completed systems or subsystems that act as pressure boundaries. During the hydrostatic test, the system is filled with water or operating fluid and then sealed. The pressure is increased to approximately 1.5 times the operating pressure. This pressure is held for a defined period. During the test, inspections are conducted to find visible leaks, as well as monitor pressure drops and any make-up water additions. If the pressure drop is out of specification, any leaks must be located and repaired. The principle of hydrostatic testing also can be used with compressed gases. This type of test is typically called an air drop test and is often used to test the integrity of high-pressure air or gas systems.
- Eddy-current testing: Provides a portable, consistent method for detecting surface and shallow subsurface defects. Also known as electromagnetic induction testing, this technique provides the capability of inspecting metal components quickly for defects or homogeneity. By applying rapidly varying AC signals through coils near the surface of the test material, eddy currents are induced into conducting materials. Any discontinuity that affects the material's electrical conductivity or magnetic permeability will influence the results of the test. Component geometry also must be taken into account when analyzing results from this test.

Things to Remember About Nondestructive Testing

1. Ndt involves more than just one methodology and helps in ensuring the asset's structural integrity.
2. In many cases, Ndt helps in the planning of future maintenance or asset replacement decisions.
3. Ndt often supports meeting regulatory requirements

Several methodologies may be required to manage an effective Ndt program. Nevertheless, such a program helps in identifying major issues well in advance that, if not corrected in time, could cause catastrophic failures.

i. Asset Condition Information (Aci)

Asset condition information comprises all the relevant data collected to provide the status of an asset's health. This includes all observations, the CBM/PdM route and continuous monitoring data.

The correct asset condition information helps you make the appropriate decision at the right time to minimize potential failures. The key to Aci management is the correlation of all the information to support the best value-driven solutions.

Data collection is a foundational element of Aci. Asset condition data is collected basically in two ways:

1. Spot readings, which are route-based and performed with portable instruments and checklists;
2. Permanently installed data acquisition equipment for continuous online data collection.

The data collected is used in one of the following ways to determine the condition of the asset and identify precursors of a failure.

- Trend Analysis: This method reviews data to see if an asset is on an obvious and immediate downward slide toward failure. It includes recognizing the changes in data as compared to earlier data or baseline data on similar assets.

- Pattern Recognition: This method reviews data to recognize any causal relationships between certain events and asset failure. For example, you might notice that after asset X is used in a certain production run, component Y fails due to stresses unique to that run. Pattern recognition identifies deviations from established patterns.
- Correlation Analysis: This approach compares data from multiple sources, related technologies, or different analysts.
- Tests Against Limits and Ranges: These tests set alarm limits and check if they are exceeded.
- Statistical Process Analysis: This analysis uses statistical techniques to identify deviations from the norm.

If existing published failure data on a certain asset or component is available, you can compare failure data collected on-site with the published data to verify or disprove the data.

Several CBM technologies are available to assess the condition of an asset or system. In some instances, several technologies are used together to provide a more accurate picture of the asset's condition.

APPENDIX E

LIST OF ASSET MANAGEMENT SUBJECTS FROM THE GLOBAL FORUM ON MAINTENANCE & ASSET MANAGERS (GFMAM)

These are topics in which all employees should have an understanding. The asset management (AM) landscape subjects are provided in the following list.

Landscape Subject Group	Landscape Subject
Strategy & Planning	Asset Management Policy
	Asset Management Strategy & Objectives
	Demand Analysis
	Strategic Planning
	Asset Management Planning
Asset Management Decision-Making	Capital Investment Decision-Making
	Operations & Maintenance Decision-Making
	Lifecycle Value Realization
	Resourcing Strategy
	Shutdowns & Outage Strategy
Lifecycle Delivery	Technical Standards & Legislation
	Asset Creation & Acquisition
	Systems Engineering
	Configuration Management
	Maintenance Delivery
	Reliability Engineering
	Asset Operations
	Resource Management
	Shutdown & Outage Management
	Fault & Incident Response
	Asset Decommissioning and Disposal

Landscape Subject Group	Landscape Subject
Asset Information	Asset Information Strategy
	Asset Information Standards
	Asset Information Systems
	Data & Information Management
Organization & People	Procurement & Supply Chain Management
	Asset Management Leadership
	Organizational Structure
	Organizational Culture
	Competence Management
Risk & Review	Risk Assessment and Management
	Contingency Planning & Resilience Analysis
	Sustainable Development
	Management of Change
	Assets Performance & Health Monitoring
	Asset Management System Monitoring
	Management Review, Audit & Assurance
	Asset Costing & Valuation
	Stakeholder Engagement

Source: *GFMAM Asset Management Landscape Subjects, Second Edition*, http://www.gfmam.org/files/isbn978_0_9871799_2_0_gfmamlandscape_secondedition_english.pdf, (ISBN 978-0-9871799-2-0, www.gfmam.org)

APPENDIX F

AN EXAMPLE OF AN ASSET MANAGEMENT POLICY

Purpose

To provide reliability and stewardship of company assets to deliver the maximum facility availability at the lowest possible cost and to ensure the protection of lives and health of the workforce while keeping the total cost of ownership (TCO) at the optimum level during the entire life of the assets.

1. All assets will be identified and documented in the CMMS utilizing company hierarchical guidelines.
2. All assets will be managed by developing an O&M strategy based on FMEA/RCM principles and incorporating CBM and other industry best practices.
   a. Each asset will have (examples):
      i. a criticality ranking based on company criteria;
      ii. a maintenance and operations strategy/plan;

iii. an optimized PM plan in the CMMS;
iv. a periodic review of asset health;
v. improvement projects developed based on asset health.

3. An annual Integrated O&M Plan or Asset Management Plan will be prepared for operations and maintenance for all assets and to ensure they meet current and future requirements. Technical requirements for production capabilities, as well as reliability and maintainability specifications, will be identified for all asset replacements, upgrades, modifications and other improvements. The asset management plan should be developed by incorporating industry best practices and systems engineering principles. The plan should include:

    a. Current year O&M activities that include operations schedule, PMs, major repair plans, etc.;
    b. Future years (i.e., two to five years) PMs and capital projects;
    c. Anticipated staffing levels;
    d. Budgets requirements;
    e. Training plans, etc.

4. All asset-related work will be planned and scheduled as appropriate to improve cost-effectiveness of available resources.

5. Execution of all asset-related work will be documented appropriately in the CMMS for maintenance/reliability analysis purposes.

6. All new or modified assets or components will be designed or procured with Reliability, Availability, Maintainability, Safety and Sustainability (RAMS[2]) features built in and based on best value principles, not lowest cost.

7. Employees will be trained on the continuing basis for industry best practices and encouraged to participate in professional societies, industry sponsored seminars, etc.

INDEX

C

D

E

F

G

H

I

K

L

M

N

O

P

Q

R

S

T

U

V

W

ABOUT THE AUTHORS

Ramesh Gulati,

PE, CMRP, CMRT,
CRL, CRE, CAMA

Ramesh Gulati is an Asset Management & Reliability Specialist at Jacobs, Asset Management Group, Tullahoma, TN.

He has over 50 years of diversified experience in people, product, process development and improvement as it relates to consumer goods, process/ service and the heavy metal industry. Mr. Gulati has a broad background in operations analysis and process improvements, including kaizen, reengineering, performance measurement/metrics, plant reliability and maintenance process improvement tools/techniques (e.g., CMMS, CBM/PdM, TPM, RCM), implementation of ISO-certified asset management systems, energy management and people development.

An effective leader and change agent with strong analytical, organizational and business management skills, Mr. Gulati has a strong commitment to quality and continuous improvement. He has the ability to motivate and develop a skilled workforce.

He is a world-renowned leader in the maintenance, reliability and asset management field and the author of more than four books, including the award-winning *Maintenance and Reliability Best Practices*. He is also known as a "Reliability Sherpa" in the reliability/asset management arena.

Mr. Gulati has worked at Aerospace Testing Alliance, Jacobs Sverdrup Technology Inc.; Arnold Engineering Development Complex, AFB, TN; Carrier, A/C; True Temper Corp.; Bethlehem Steel; and Heavy Engineering Corp., Foundry Forge plant.

He holds BSME, MSIE and EMBA degrees.

Terrence O'Hanlon,

CMRP

Terrence O'Hanlon, CMRP, is the Publisher of Reliabilityweb.com®, RELIABILITY® Magazine and Uptime® Magazine. He is certified in Asset Management by the Institute of Asset Management and is a Certified Maintenance & Reliability Professional by SMRP.

Mr. O'Hanlon is the acting Executive Director of the Association of Asset Management Professionals (AMP). He is the Executive Editor and Publisher of the 5th Edition of *The (New) Asset Management Handbook.*

Mr. O'Hanlon is a voting member of the U.S. TAG (PC251) for ISO 55000 - ASTM E53 Asset Management Standards Committee. More recently, he was selected as the sole U.S. representation through ANSI for the ISO Working Group 39 to create a standard for competence in assessing and certifying asset management systems known as ISO 17021-5.

Mr. O'Hanlon is also a member of the Institute of Asset Management, American Society of Mechanical Engineers, Association for Facilities Engineering, Society for Maintenance & Reliability Professionals and Society of Tribologists and Lubrication Engineers.

Uptime® Elements

Technical Activities

REM Reliability Engineering for Maintenance

Ca criticality analysis	**Rsd** reliability strategy development
Re reliability engineering	**Rca** root cause analysis
Cp capital project management	**Rcd** reliability centered design

ACM Asset Condition Management

Aci asset condition information	**Vib** vibration analysis	**Fa** fluid analysis
Ut ultrasound testing	**Ir** infrared thermal imaging	**Mt** motor testing
Ab alignment and balancing	**Ndt** non destructive testing	**Lu** machinery lubrication

WEM Work Execution Management

Pm preventive maintenance	**Ps** planning and scheduling
Odr operator driven reliability	**Mro** mro-spares management
De defect elimination	**Cmms** computerized maintenance management system

Leadership

LER Leadership for Reliability

Es executive sponsorship	**Opx** operational excellence
Hcm human capital management	**Cbl** competency based learning
Int integrity	**Rj** reliability journey

Business Processes

AM Asset Management

Sp strategy and plans	**Cr** corporate responsibility	**Samp** strategic asset management plan
Ri risk management	**Ak** asset knowledge	**Alm** asset lifecycle management
Dm decision making	**Pi** performance indicators	**Ci** continuous improvement

A Reliability Framework and Asset Management System™

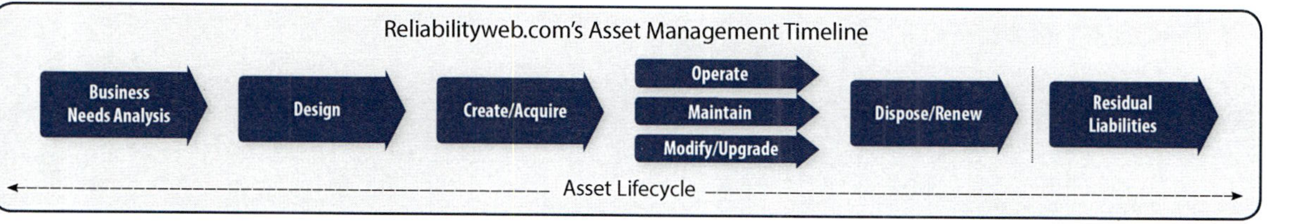

Reprinted with permission from NetexpressUSA Inc. d/b/a Reliabilityweb.com and its affiliates. Copyright 2016-2018. All rights reserved. No part of this graphic may be reproduced or transmitted in any form or by any means without the prior express written consent of NetexpressUSA Inc. Reliabilityweb.com®, Uptime® and A Reliability Framework and Asset Management System™ are trademarks and registered trademarks of NetexpressUSA Inc. in the U.S.A. and several other countries.

reliabilityweb.com • maintenance.org • reliabilityleadership.com

Reliabilityweb.com® and Uptime® Magazine Mission: **To make the people we serve safer and more successful.** One way we support this mission is to suggest a reliability system for asset performance management as pictured above. Our use of the Uptime Elements is designed to assist you in categorizing and organizing your own Body of Knowledge (BoK) whether it be through training, articles, books or webinars. Our hope is to make YOU safer and more successful.

ABOUT RELIABILITYWEB.COM

Created in 1999, Reliabilityweb.com provides educational information and peer-to-peer networking opportunities that enable safe and effective reliability and asset management for organizations around the world.

ACTIVITIES INCLUDE:

Reliabilityweb.com® (www.reliabilityweb.com) includes educational articles, tips, video presentations, an industry event calendar and industry news. Updates are available through free email subscriptions and RSS feeds. **Confiabilidad.net** is a mirror site that is available in Spanish at www.confiabilidad.net

Uptime® Magazine (www.uptimemagazine.com) is a bi-monthly magazine launched in 2005 that is highly prized by the reliability and asset management community. Editions are obtainable in both print and digital, as well as a Spanish digital version.

Reliability Leadership Institute® Conferences and Training Events
(www.reliabilityweb.com) offer events that range from unique, focused-training workshops and seminars to small focused conferences to large industry-wide events, including the International Maintenance Conference, MaximoWorld and The RELIABILITY® Conference.

MRO-Zone Bookstore (www.mro-zone.com) is an online bookstore offering a reliability and asset management focused library of books, DVDs and CDs published by Reliabilityweb.com.

Association of Asset Management Professionals
(www.maintenance.org) is a member organization and online community that encourages professional development and certification and supports information exchange and learning with 50,000+ members worldwide.

A Word About Social Good

Reliabilityweb.com is mission driven to deliver value and social good to the reliability and asset management communities. *Doing good work and making profit is not inconsistent,* and as a result of Reliabilityweb.com's mission-driven focus, financial stability and success has been the outcome. For over a decade, Reliabilityweb.com's positive contributions and commitment to the reliability and asset management communities have been unmatched.

Other Causes

Reliabilityweb.com has financially contributed to include industry associations, such as SMRP, AFE, STLE, ASME and ASTM, and community charities, including the Salvation Army, American Red Cross, Wounded Warrior Project, Paralyzed Veterans of America and the Autism Society of America. In addition, we are proud supporters of our U.S. Troops and first responders who protect our freedoms and way of life. That is only possible by being a for-profit company that pays taxes.

I hope you will get involved with and explore the many resources that are available to you through the Reliabilityweb.com network.

Warmest regards,
Terrence O'Hanlon